15th Conference on Computational Natural Language Learning 2011

(CoNLL 2011 Shared Task)

Co-located with ACL HLT 2011

Portland, Oregon, USA
23-24 June 2011

ISBN: 978-1-61839-236-7

Printed from e-media with permission by:

Curran Associates, Inc.
57 Morehouse Lane
Red Hook, NY 12571

Some format issues inherent in the e-media version may also appear in this print version.

Printed by Curran Associates, Inc. (2011)

For permission requests, please contact the Association for Computational Linguistics at the address below.

Association for Computational Linguistics
209 N. Eighth Street
Stroudsburg, Pennsylvania 18360

Phone: 1-570-476-8006
Fax: 1-570-476-0860

acl@aclweb.org

Additional copies of this publication are available from:

Curran Associates, Inc.
57 Morehouse Lane
Red Hook, NY 12571 USA
Phone: 845-758-0400
Fax: 845-758-2634
Email: curran@proceedings.com
Web: www.proceedings.com

Table of Contents

Introduction

This volume contains a description of the CoNLL-2011 Shared Task and the participating systems. This year, the shared task was based on the English portion of OntoNotes 4.0 corpus. The goal was to identify anaphoric mentions – both entities and events – and perform coreference resolution to create clusters of mentions representing the same entity or event in the text.

The OntoNotes data spans five genres and multiple layers of annotation in addition to coreference, including parses, semantic roles, word sense, and named entities, making it a rich and diverse corpus. One of the challenges for the shared task participants (though they were limited by the time contraints of the task) and also for continuing research going forward is to find effective ways to bring these multiple layers of information to bear on the coreference task to improve upon the current state of the art.

As is traditional with CoNLL, we had two tracks – an *open* and a *closed* track. Since world knowledge is an important factor in coreference resolution, even in the closed task participants were allowed to use some limited, outside sources, including WordNet and a pre-computed table predicting number and gender information for noun phrases. For the open task, as usual, participants were allowed to use any other source of information, such as Wikipedia, gazetteers, etc., that did not violate the evaluation criteria designed to protect the test set.

A total of 23 participants submitted system outputs and 21 of them submitted system description papers. We hope that this data set will provide a useful benchmark and spur further research in this important sub-field of language processing.

Sameer Pradhan, on behalf of the Shared Task organizers
May 22, 2011
Cambridge, MA

Organizers:

Sameer Pradhan (Chair)	BBN Technologies, Cambridge
Mitchell Marcus	University of Pennsylvania, Philadelphia
Martha Palmer	University of Colorado, Boulder
Lance Ramshaw	BBN Technologies, Cambridge
Ralph Weischedel	BBN Technologies, Cambridge
Nianwen Xue	Brandeis University, Waltham

Program Committee:

Jie Cai	Heidelberg Institute for Theoretical Studies, Germany
Claire Cardie	Cornell University
Pascal Denis	INRIA, France
Kadri Hacioglu	Rosetta Stone, Boulder
Alessandro Moschitti	University of Trento, Italy
Vincent Ng	University of Texas, Dallas
Pierre Nugues	Lund University, Sweden
Massimo Poesio	University of Trento, Italy
Vasin Punyakanok	BBN Technologies, Cambridge
Emili Sapena	Universitat Politècnica de Catalunya, Barcelona, Catalunya
Michael Strube	Heidelberg Institute for Theoretical Studies, Germany
Jordi Turmo	Universitat Politècnica de Catalunya, Barcelona, Catalunya

CoNLL-2011 Shared Task:
Modeling Unrestricted Coreference in OntoNotes

Sameer Pradhan
BBN Technologies,
Cambridge, MA 02138
pradhan@bbn.com

Lance Ramshaw
BBN Technologies,
Cambridge, MA 02138
lramshaw@bbn.com

Mitchell Marcus
University of Pennsylvania,
Philadelphia, 19104
mitch@linc.cis.upenn.edu

Martha Palmer
University of Colorado,
Boulder, CO 80309
martha.palmer@colorado.edu

Ralph Weischedel
BBN Technologies,
Cambridge, MA 02138
weischedel@bbn.com

Nianwen Xue
Brandeis University,
Waltham, MA 02453
xuen@cs.brandeis.edu

Abstract

The CoNLL-2011 shared task involved predicting coreference using OntoNotes data. Resources in this field have tended to be limited to noun phrase coreference, often on a restricted set of entities, such as ACE entities. OntoNotes provides a large-scale corpus of general anaphoric coreference not restricted to noun phrases or to a specified set of entity types. OntoNotes also provides additional layers of integrated annotation, capturing additional shallow semantic structure. This paper briefly describes the OntoNotes annotation (coreference and other layers) and then describes the parameters of the shared task including the format, pre-processing information, and evaluation criteria, and presents and discusses the results achieved by the participating systems. Having a standard test set and evaluation parameters, all based on a new resource that provides multiple integrated annotation layers (parses, semantic roles, word senses, named entities and coreference) that could support joint models, should help to energize ongoing research in the task of entity and event coreference.

1 Introduction

The importance of coreference resolution for the entity/event detection task, namely identifying all mentions of entities and events in text and clustering them into equivalence classes, has been well recognized in the natural language processing community. Automatic identification of coreferring entities and events in text has been an uphill battle for several decades, partly because it can require world knowledge which is not well-defined and partly owing to the lack of substantial annotated data. Early work on corpus-based coreference resolution dates back to the mid-90s by McCarthy and Lenhert (1995) where they experimented with using decision trees and hand-written rules. A systematic study was then conducted using decision trees by Soon et al. (2001). Significant improvements have been made in the field of language processing in general, and improved learning techniques have been developed to push the state of the art in coreference resolution forward (Morton, 2000; Harabagiu et al., 2001; McCallum and Wellner, 2004; Culotta et al., 2007; Denis and Baldridge, 2007; Rahman and Ng, 2009; Haghighi and Klein, 2010). Various different knowledge sources from shallow semantics to encyclopedic knowledge are being exploited (Ponzetto and Strube, 2005; Ponzetto and Strube, 2006; Versley, 2007; Ng, 2007). Researchers continued finding novel ways of exploiting ontologies such as WordNet. Given that WordNet is a static ontology and as such has limitation on coverage, more recently, there have been successful attempts to utilize information from much larger, collaboratively built resources such as Wikipedia (Ponzetto and Strube, 2006). In spite of all the progress, current techniques still rely primarily on surface level features such as string match, proximity, and edit distance; syntactic features such as apposition; and shallow semantic features such as number, gender, named entities, semantic class, Hobbs' distance, etc. A better idea of the progress in the field can be obtained by reading recent survey articles (Ng, 2010) and tutorials (Ponzetto and Poesio, 2009) dedicated to this subject.

Corpora to support supervised learning of this task date back to the Message Understanding Conferences (MUC). These corpora were tagged with coreferring entities identified by noun phrases in the text. The de facto standard datasets for current coreference studies are the MUC (Hirschman and Chin-

Proceedings of the 15th Conference on Computational Natural Language Learning: Shared Task, pages 1–27,
Portland, Oregon, 23-24 June 2011.

chor, 1997; Chinchor, 2001; Chinchor and Sundheim, 2003) and the ACE[1] (G. Doddington et al., 2000) corpora. The MUC corpora cover all noun phrases in text, but represent small training and test sets. The ACE corpora, on the other hand, have much more annotation, but are restricted to a small subset of entities. They are also less consistent, in terms of inter-annotator agreement (ITA) (Hirschman et al., 1998). This lessens the reliability of statistical evidence in the form of lexical coverage and semantic relatedness that could be derived from the data and used by a classifier to generate better predictive models. The importance of a well-defined tagging scheme and consistent ITA has been well recognized and studied in the past (Poesio, 2004; Poesio and Artstein, 2005; Passonneau, 2004). There is a growing consensus that in order for these to be most useful for language understanding applications such as question answering or distillation – both of which seek to take information access technology to the next level – we need more consistent annotation of larger amounts of broad coverage data for training better automatic techniques for entity and event identification. Identification and encoding of richer knowledge – possibly linked to knowledge sources – and development of learning algorithms that would effectively incorporate them is a necessary next step towards improving the current state of the art. The computational learning community, in general, is also witnessing a move towards evaluations based on joint inference, with the two previous CoNLL tasks (Surdeanu et al., 2008; Hajič et al., 2009) devoted to joint learning of syntactic and semantic dependencies. A principle ingredient for joint learning is the presence of multiple layers of semantic information.

One fundamental question still remains, and that is – what would it take to improve the state of the art in coreference resolution that has not been attempted so far? Many different algorithms have been tried in the past 15 years, but one thing that is still lacking is a corpus comprehensively tagged on a large scale with consistent, multiple layers of semantic information. One of the many goals of the OntoNotes project[2] (Hovy et al., 2006; Weischedel et al., 2011) is to explore whether it can fill this void and help push the progress further – not only in coreference, but with the various layers of semantics that it tries to capture. As one of its layers, it has created a corpus for general anaphoric coreference that covers entities and events not limited to noun phrases or a limited set of entity types. A small portion of this corpus from the newswire and broadcast news genres (∼120k) was recently used for a SEMEVAL task (Recasens et al., 2010). As mentioned earlier, the coreference layer in OntoNotes constitutes just one part of a multi-layered, integrated annotation of shallow semantic structure in text with high inter-annotator agreement, which also provides a unique opportunity for performing joint inference over a substantial body of data.

The remainder of this paper is organized as follows. Section 2 presents an overview of the OntoNotes corpus. Section 3 describes the coreference annotation in OntoNotes. Section 4 then describes the shared task, including the data provided and the evaluation criteria. Sections 5 and 6 then describe the participating system results and analyze the approaches, and Section 7 concludes.

2 The OntoNotes Corpus

The OntoNotes project has created a corpus of large-scale, accurate, and integrated annotation of multiple levels of the shallow semantic structure in text. The idea is that this rich, integrated annotation covering many layers will allow for richer, cross-layer models enabling significantly better automatic semantic analysis. In addition to coreference, this data is also tagged with syntactic trees, high coverage verb and some noun propositions, partial verb and noun word senses, and 18 named entity types. However, such multi-layer annotations, with complex, cross-layer dependencies, demands a robust, efficient, scalable mechanism for storing them while providing efficient, convenient, integrated access to the the underlying structure. To this effect, it uses a relational database representation that captures both the inter- and intra-layer dependencies and also provides an object-oriented API for efficient, multi-tiered access to this data (Pradhan et al., 2007a). This should facilitate the creation of cross-layer features in integrated predictive models that will make use of these annotations.

Although OntoNotes is a multi-lingual resource with all layers of annotation covering three languages: English, Chinese and Arabic, for the scope of this paper, we will just look at the English portion. Over the years of the development of this corpus, there were various priorities that came into play, and therefore not all the data in the English portion is annotated with all the different layers of annotation. There is a core portion, however, which is roughly

[1] http://projects.ldc.upenn.edu/ace/data/

[2] http://www.bbn.com/nlp/ontonotes

1.3M words which has been annotated with all the layers. It comprises ~450k words from newswire, ~150k from magazine articles, ~200k from broadcast news, ~200k from broadcast conversations and ~200k web data.

OntoNotes comprises the following layers of annotation:

- **Syntax** – A syntactic layer representing a revised Penn Treebank (Marcus et al., 1993; Babko-Malaya et al., 2006).

- **Propositions** – The proposition structure of verbs in the form of a revised PropBank(Palmer et al., 2005; Babko-Malaya et al., 2006).

- **Word Sense** – Coarse grained word senses are tagged for the most frequent polysemous verbs and nouns, in order to maximize coverage. The word sense granularity is tailored to achieve 90% inter-annotator agreement as demonstrated by Palmer et al. (2007). These senses are defined in the sense inventory files and each individual sense has been connected to multiple WordNet senses. This provides a direct access to the WordNet semantic structure for users to make use of. There is also a mapping from the word senses to the PropBank frames and to VerbNet (Kipper et al., 2000) and FrameNet (Fillmore et al., 2003).

- **Named Entities** – The corpus was tagged with a set of 18 proper named entity types that were well-defined and well-tested for inter-annotator agreement by Weischedel and Burnstein (2005).

- **Coreference** – This layer captures general anaphoric coreference that covers entities and events not limited to noun phrases or a limited set of entity types (Pradhan et al., 2007b). We will take a look at this in detail in the next section.

3 Coreference in OntoNotes

General anaphoric coreference that spans a rich set of entities and events – not restricted to a few types, as has been characteristic of most coreference data available until now – has been tagged with a high degree of consistency. Attributive coreference is tagged separately from the more common identity coreference.

Two different types of coreference are distinguished in the OntoNotes data: Identical (IDENT), and Appositive (APPOS). Appositives are treated separately because they function as attributions, as described further below. The IDENT type is used for anaphoric coreference, meaning links between pronominal, nominal, and named mentions of specific referents. It does not include mentions of generic, underspecified, or abstract entities.

Coreference is annotated for all specific entities and events. There is no limit on the semantic types of NP entities that can be considered for coreference, and in particular, coreference is not limited to ACE types.

The mentions over which IDENT coreference applies are typically pronominal, named, or definite nominal. The annotation process begins by automatically extracting all of the NP mentions from the Penn Treebank, though the annotators can also add additional mentions when appropriate. In the following two examples (and later ones), the phrases notated in bold form the links of an IDENT chain.

(1) She had **a good suggestion** and **it** was unanimously accepted by all.

(2) **Elco Industries Inc.** said **it** expects net income in the year ending June 30, 1990, to fall below a recent analyst's estimate of $ 1.65 a share. **The Rockford, Ill. maker of fasteners** also said **it** expects to post sales in the current fiscal year that are "slightly above" fiscal 1989 sales of $ 155 million.

3.1 Verbs

Verbs are added as single-word spans if they can be coreferenced with a noun phrase or with another verb. The intent is to annotate the VP, but we mark the single-word head for convenience. This includes morphologically related nominalizations (3) and noun phrases that refer to the same event, even if they are lexically distinct from the verb (4). In the following two examples, only the chains related to the *growth* event are shown.

(3) Sales of passenger cars **grew** 22%. **The strong growth** followed year-to-year increases.

(4) Japan's domestic sales of cars, trucks and buses in October **rose** 18% from a year earlier to 500,004 units, a record for the month, the Japan Automobile Dealers' Association said. The strong **growth** followed year-to-year increases of 21% in August and 12% in September.

3.2 Pronouns

All pronouns and demonstratives are linked to anything that they refer to, and pronouns in quoted speech are also marked. Expletive or pleonastic pronouns (*it, there*) are not considered for tagging, and generic *you* is not marked. In the following example, the pronoun *you* and *it* would not be marked. (In this and following examples, an asterisk (*) before a boldface phrase identifies entity/event mentions that would *not* be tagged as coreferent.)

(5) Senate majority leader Bill Frist likes to tell a story from his days as a pioneering heart surgeon back in Tennessee. A lot of times, Frist recalls, ***you'd** have a critical patient lying there waiting for a new heart, and ***you'd** want to cut, but ***you** couldn't start unless ***you** knew that the replacement heart would make ***it** to the operating room.

3.3 Generic mentions

Generic nominal mentions can be linked with referring pronouns and other definite mentions, but are not linked to other generic nominal mentions. This would allow linking of the bracketed mentions in (6) and (7), but not (8).

(6) **Officials** said **they** are tired of making the same statements.

(7) **Meetings** are most productive when **they** are held in the morning. **Those meetings**, however, generally have the worst attendance.

(8) Allergan Inc. said it received approval to sell the PhacoFlex intraocular lens, the first foldable silicone lens available for ***cataract surgery**. The lens' foldability enables it to be inserted in smaller incisions than are now possible for ***cataract surgery**.

Bare plurals, as in (6) and (7), are always considered generic. In example (9) below, there are two generic instances of *parents*. These are marked as distinct IDENT chains (with separate chains distinguished by subscripts X, Y and Z), each containing a generic and the related referring pronouns.

(9) **Parents**$_X$ should be involved with **their**$_X$ children's education at home, not in school. **They**$_X$ should see to it that **their**$_X$ kids don't play truant; **they**$_X$ should make certain that the children spend enough time doing homework; **they**$_X$ should scrutinize the report card. **Parents**$_Y$ are too likely to blame schools for the educational limitations of **their**$_Y$ children. If **parents**$_Z$ are dissatisfied with a school, **they**$_Z$ should have the option of switching to another.

In (10) below, the verb "halve" cannot be linked to "a reduction of 50%", since "a reduction" is indefinite.

(10) Argentina said it will ask creditor banks to ***halve** its foreign debt of $64 billion – the third-highest in the developing world . Argentina aspires to reach ***a reduction of 50%** in the value of its external debt.

3.4 Pre-modifiers

Proper pre-modifiers can be coreferenced, but proper nouns that are in a morphologically adjectival form are treated as adjectives, and not coreferenced. For example, adjectival forms of GPEs such as *Chinese* in "the Chinese leader", would not be linked. Thus we could coreference *United States* in "the United States policy" with another referent, but not *American* "the American policy." GPEs and Nationality acronyms (e.g. *U.S.S.R.* or *U.S.*). are also considered adjectival. Pre-modifier acronyms can be coreferenced unless they refer to a nationality. Thus in the examples below, *FBI* can be coreferenced to other mentions, but *U.S.* cannot.

(11) **FBI** spokesman

(12) ***U.S.** spokesman

Dates and monetary amounts can be considered part of a coreference chain even when they occur as pre-modifiers.

(13) The current account deficit on France's balance of payments narrowed to 1.48 billion French francs ($236.8 million) in August from a revised 2.1 billion francs in **July**, the Finance Ministry said. Previously, the **July** figure was estimated at a deficit of 613 million francs.

(14) The company's **$150** offer was unexpected. The firm balked at **the price**.

3.5 Copular verbs

Attributes signaled by copular structures are not marked; these are attributes of the referent they modify, and their relationship to that referent will be captured through word sense and propositional argument tagging.

(15) **John**$_X$ is a linguist. **People**$_Y$ are nervous around **John**$_X$, because **he**$_X$ always corrects **their**$_Y$ grammar.

Copular (or 'linking') verbs are those verbs that function as a copula and are followed by a subject complement. Some common copular verbs are: *be, appear, feel, look, seem, remain, stay, become, end up, get*. Subject complements following such verbs are considered attributes, and not linked. Since *Called* is copular, neither IDENT nor APPOS coreference is marked in the following case.

(16) Called Otto's Original Oat Bran Beer, the brew costs about $12.75 a case.

3.6 Small clauses

Like copulas, small clause constructions are not marked. The following example is treated as if the copula were present ("John considers Fred to be an idiot"):

(17) John considers ***Fred *an idiot**.

3.7 Temporal expressions

Temporal expressions such as the following are linked:

(18) John spent **three years** in jail. In **that time**...

Deictic expressions such as *now, then, today, tomorrow, yesterday,* etc. can be linked, as well as other temporal expressions that are relative to the time of the writing of the article, and which may therefore require knowledge of the time of the writing to resolve the coreference. Annotators were allowed to use knowledge from outside the text in resolving these cases. In the following example, *the end of this period* and *that time* can be coreferenced, as can *this period* and *from three years to seven years*.

(19) The limit could range **from three years to seven years**$_X$, depending on the composition of the management team and the nature of its strategic plan. At **(the end of (this period)**$_X$**)**$_Y$, the poison pill would be eliminated automatically, unless a new poison pill were approved by the then-current shareholders, who would have an opportunity to evaluate the corporation's strategy and management team at **that time**$_Y$.

In multi-date temporal expressions, embedded dates are not separately connected to to other mentions of that date. For example in *Nov. 2, 1999, Nov.* would not be linked to another instance of *November* later in the text.

3.8 Appositives

Because they logically represent attributions, appositives are tagged separately from Identity coreference. They consist of a head, or referent (a noun phrase that points to a specific object/concept in the world), and one or more attributes of that referent. An appositive construction contains a noun phrase that modifies an immediately-adjacent noun phrase (separated only by a comma, colon, dash, or parenthesis). It often serves to rename or further define the first mention. Marking appositive constructions allows us to capture the attributed property even though there is no explicit copula.

(20) **John**$_{\text{head}}$, **a linguist**$_{\text{attribute}}$

The head of each appositive construction is distinguished from the attribute according to the following heuristic specificity scale, in a decreasing order from top to bottom:

Type	Example
Proper noun	John
Pronoun	He
Definite NP	the man
Indefinite specific NP	a man I know
Non-specific NP	man

This leads to the following cases:

(21) **John**$_{\text{head}}$, **a linguist**$_{\text{attribute}}$

(22) **A famous linguist**$_{\text{attribute}}$, **he**$_{\text{head}}$ studied at ...

(23) **a principal of the firm**$_{\text{attribute}}$, **J. Smith**$_{\text{head}}$

In cases where the two members of the appositive are equivalent in specificity, the left-most member of the appositive is marked as the head/referent. Definite NPs include NPs with a definite marker (*the*) as well as NPs with a possessive adjective (his). Thus the first element is the head in all of the following cases:

(24) The chairman, the man who never gives up

(25) The sheriff, his friend

(26) His friend, the sheriff

In the specificity scale, specific names of diseases and technologies are classified as proper names, whether they are capitalized or not.

(27) A dangerous bacteria, bacillium, is found

Type	Description
Annotator Error	An annotator error. This is a catch-all category for cases of errors that do not fit in the other categories.
Genuine Ambiguity	This is just genuinely ambiguous. Often the case with pronouns that have no clear antecedent (especially this & that)
Generics	One person thought this was a generic mention, and the other person didn't
Guidelines	The guidelines need to be clear about this example
Callisto Layout	Something to do with the usage/design of Callisto
Referents	Each annotator thought this was referring to two completely different things
Possessives	One person did not mark this possessive
Verb	One person did not mark this verb
Pre Modifiers	One person did not mark this Pre Modifier
Appositive	One person did not mark this appositive
Extent	Both people marked the same entity, but one person's mention was longer
Copula	Disagreement arose because this mention is part of a copular structure a) Either each annotator marked a different half of the copula b) Or one annotator unnecessarily marked both

Figure 1: Description of various disagreement types

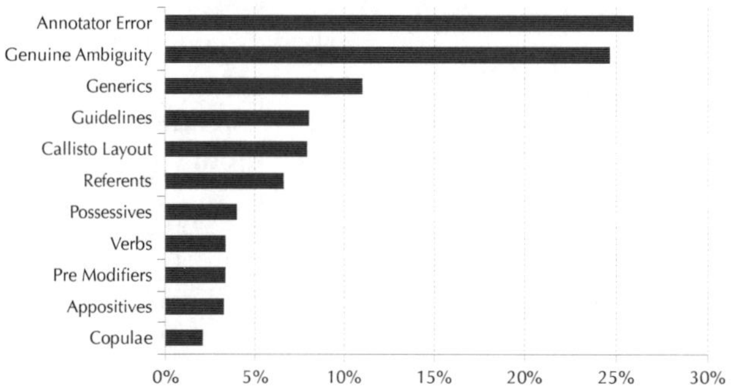

Figure 2: The distribution of disagreements across the various types in Table 1

When the entity to which an appositive refers is also mentioned elsewhere, only the single span containing the entire appositive construction is included in the larger IDENT chain. None of the nested NP spans are linked. In the example below, the entire span can be linked to later mentions to *Richard Godown*. The sub-spans are not included separately in the IDENT chain.

(28) **Richard Godown, president of the Industrial Biotechnology Association**

Ages are tagged as attributes (as if they were ellipses of, for example, *a 42-year-old*):

(29) **Mr.Smith**$_{\text{head}}$, **42**$_{\text{attribute}}$,

3.9 Special Issues

In addition to the ones above, there are some special cases such as:

- No coreference is marked between an organization and its members.

Genre	ANN1-ANN2	ANN1-ADJ	ANN2-ADJ
Newswire	80.9	85.2	88.3
Broadcast News	78.6	83.5	89.4
Broadcast Conversation	86.7	91.6	93.7
Magazine	78.4	83.2	88.8
Web	85.9	92.2	91.2

Table 1: Inter Annotator and Adjudicator agreement for the Coreference Layer in OntoNotes measured in terms of the MUC score.

- GPEs are linked to references to their governments, even when the references are nested NPs, or the modifier and head of a single NP.

3.10 Annotator Agreement and Analysis

Table 1 shows the inter-annotator and annotator-adjudicator agreement on all the genres of OntoNotes. We also analyzed about 15K disagreements in various parts of the data, and grouped them into one of the categories shown in Figure 1. Figure 2 shows the distribution of these different types that were found in that sample. It can be seen that genuine ambiguity and annotator error are the biggest contributors – the latter of which is usually captured during adjudication, thus showing the increased agreement between the adjudicated version and the individual annotator version.

4 CoNLL-2011 Coreference Task

This section describes the CoNLL-2011 Coreference task, including its *closed* and *open* track versions, and characterizes the data used for the task and how it was prepared.

4.1 Why a Coreference Task?

Despite close to a two-decade history of evaluations on coreference tasks, variation in the evaluation criteria and in the training data used have made it difficult for researchers to be clear about the state of the art or to determine which particular areas require further attention. There are many different parameters involved in defining a coreference task. Looking at various numbers reported in literature can greatly affect the perceived difficulty of the task. It can seem to be a very hard problem (Soon et al., 2001) or one that is somewhat easier (Culotta et al., 2007). Given the space constraints, we refer the reader to Stoyanov et al. (2009) for a detailed treatment of the issue.

Limitations in the size and scope of the available datasets have also constrained research progress. The MUC and ACE corpora are the two that have been used most for reporting comparative results, but they differ in the types of entities and coreference annotated. The ACE corpus is also one that evolved over a period of almost five years, with different incarnations of the task definition and different corpus cross-sections on which performance numbers have been reported, making it hard to untangle and interpret the results.

The availability of the OntoNotes data offered an opportunity to define a coreference task based on a larger, more broad-coverage corpus. We have tried to design the task so that it not only can support the current evaluation, but also can provide an ongoing resource for comparing different coreference algorithms and approaches.

4.2 Task Description

The CoNLL-2011 shared task was based on the English portion of the OntoNotes 4.0 data. The task was to automatically identify mentions of entities and events in text and to link the coreferring mentions together to form entity/event chains. The target coreference decisions could be made using automatically predicted information on the other structural layers including the parses, semantic roles, word senses, and named entities.

As is customary for CoNLL tasks, there were two tracks, *closed* and *open*. For the *closed* track, systems were limited to using the distributed resources, in order to allow a fair comparison of algorithm performance, while the *open* track allowed for almost unrestricted use of external resources in addition to the provided data.

4.2.1 Closed Track

In the *closed* track, systems were limited to the provided data, plus the use of *two pre-specified external resources*: i) WordNet and ii) a pre-computed number and gender table by Bergsma and Lin (2006).

For the training and test data, in addition to the underlying text, *predicted* versions of all the supplementary layers of annotation were provided, where those predictions were derived using off-the-shelf tools (parsers, semantic role labelers, named entity taggers, etc.) as described in Section 4.4.2. For the training data, however, in addition to predicted values for the other layers, we also provided manual *gold-standard* annotations for all the layers. Participants were allowed to use either the gold-standard or predicted annotation for training their systems. They were also free to use the gold-standard data to train their own models for the various layers of annotation, if they judged that those would either provide more accurate predictions or alternative predictions for use as multiple views, or wished to use a lattice of predictions.

More so than previous CoNLL tasks, coreference predictions depend on world knowledge, and many state-of-the-art systems use information from external resources such as WordNet, which can add a layer that helps the system to recognize semantic connections between the various lexicalized mentions in the text. Therefore, the use of WordNet was allowed, even for the closed track. Since word senses in OntoNotes are predominantly[3] coarse-grained groupings of WordNet senses, systems could also map from the predicted or gold-standard word senses provided to the sets of underlying WordNet senses. Another significant piece of knowledge that is particularly useful for coreference but that is not available in the layers of OntoNotes is that of *number* and *gender*. There are many different

[3]There are a few instances of novel senses introduced in OntoNotes which were not present in WordNet, and so lack a mapping back to the WordNet senses

ways of predicting these values, with differing accuracies, so in order to ensure that participants in the *closed* track were working from the same data, thus allowing clearer algorithmic comparisons, we specified a particular table of number and gender predictions generated by Bergsma and Lin (2006), for use during both training and testing.

Following the recent CoNLL tradition, participants were allowed to use both the training and the development data for training the final model.

4.2.2 Open Track

In addition to resources available in the *closed* track, the *open* track, systems were allowed to use external resources such as Wikipedia, gazetteers etc. This track is mainly to get an idea of a performance ceiling on the task at the cost of not getting a comparison across all systems. Another advantage of the *open* track is that it might reduce the barriers to participation by allowing participants to field existing research systems that already depend on external resources – especially if there were hard dependencies on these resources. They can participate in the task with minimal or no modification to their existing system.

4.3 Coreference Task Data

Since there are no previously reported numbers on the full version of OntoNotes, we had to create a train/development/test partition. The only portion of OntoNotes that has a previously determined, widely used, standard split is the WSJ portion of the newswire data. For that subcorpus, we maintained the same partition. For all the other portions we created stratified training, development and test partitions over all the sources in OntoNotes using the procedure shown in Algorithm 1. The list of training, development and test document IDs can be found on the task webpage.[4]

4.4 Data Preparation

This section gives details of the different annotation layers including the automatic models that were used to predict them, and describes the formats in which the data were provided to the participants.

4.4.1 Manual Annotation *Gold* Layers

We will take a look at the manually annotated, or *gold* layers of information that were made available for the training data.

[4] http://conll.bbn.com/download/conll-train.id
http://conll.bbn.com/download/conll-dev.id
http://conll.bbn.com/download/conll-test.id

Algorithm 1 Procedure used to create OntoNotes training, development and test partitions.

```
Procedure: GENERATE_PARTITIONS(ONTONOTES) returns TRAIN, DEV, TEST
TRAIN ← ∅
DEV ← ∅
TEST ← ∅
for all SOURCE ∈ ONTONOTES do
    if SOURCE = WALL STREET JOURNAL then
        TRAIN ← TRAIN ∪ SECTIONS 02 – 21
        DEV ← DEV ∪ SECTIONS 00, 01, 22, 24
        TEST ← TEST ∪ SECTION 23
    else
        if Number of files in SOURCE ≥ 10 then
            TRAIN ← TRAIN ∪ FILE IDs ending in 1 – 8
            DEV ← DEV ∪ FILE IDs ending in 0
            TEST ← TEST ∪ FILE IDs ending in 9
        else
            DEV ← DEV ∪ FILE IDs ending in 0
            TEST ← TEST ∪ FILE ID ending in the highest number
            TRAIN ← TRAIN ∪ Remaining FILE IDs for the SOURCE
        end if
    end if
end for
return TRAIN, DEV, TEST
```

Coreference The manual coreference annotation is stored as chains of linked mentions connecting multiple mentions of the same entity. Coreference is the only document-level phenomenon in OntoNotes, and the complexity of annotation increases non-linearly with the length of a document. Unfortunately, some of the documents – especially ones in the broadcast conversation, weblogs, and telephone conversation genre – are very long which prohibited us from efficiently annotating them in entirety. These had to be split into smaller parts. We conducted a few passes to join some adjacent parts, but since some documents had as many as 17 parts, there are still multi-part documents in the corpus. Since the coreference chains are coherent only within each of these document parts, for this task, each such part is treated as a separate document. Another thing to note is that there were some cases of sub-token annotation in the corpus owing to the fact that tokens were not split at hyphens. Cases such as pro-WalMart had the sub-span WalMart linked with another instance of the same. The recent Treebank revision which split tokens at *most* hyphens, made a majority of these sub-token annotations go away. There were still some residual sub-token annotations. Since subtoken annotations cannot be represented in the CoNLL format, and they were a very small quantity – much less than even half a percent – we decided to ignore them.

For various reasons, not all the documents in OntoNotes have been annotated with all the differ-

Corpora	Words				Documents			
	Total	Train	Dev	Test	Total	Train	Dev	Test
MUC-6	25K	12K	13K		60	30	30	
MUC-7	40K	19K	21K		67	30	37	
ACE (2000-2004)	1M	775K	235K		-	-	-	
OntoNotes[5]	1.3M	1M	136K	142K	2,083 (2,999)	1,674 (2,374)	202 (303)	207 (322)

Table 2: Number of documents in the OntoNotes data, and some comparison with the MUC and ACE data sets. The numbers in parenthesis for the OntoNotes corpus indicate the total number of *parts* that correspond to the documents. Each part was considered a separate document for evaluation purposes.

Syntactic category	Train		Development		Test	
	Count	%	Count	%	Count	%
NP	60,345	59.71	8,463	59.31	8,629	53.09
PRP	25,472	25.21	3,535	24.78	5,012	30.84
PRP$	8,889	8.80	1,208	8.47	1,466	9.02
NNP	2,643	2.62	468	3.28	475	2.92
NML	900	0.89	151	1.06	118	0.73
Vx	1,915	1.89	317	2.22	314	1.93
Other	893	0.88	126	0.88	239	1.47
Overall	101,057	100.00	14,268	100.00	16,253	100.00

Table 3: Distribution of mentions in the data by their syntactic category.

	Train	Development	Test
Entities/Chains	26,612	3,752	3,926
Links	74,652	10,539	12,365
Mentions	101,264	14,291	16,291

Table 4: Number of entities, links and mentions in the OntoNotes 4.0 data.

ent layers of annotation, with full coverage.[6] There is a core portion, however, which is roughly 1.3M words which has been annotated with all the layers. This is the portion that we used for the shared task.

The number of documents in the corpus for this task, for each of the different genres, are shown in Table 2. Tables 3 and 4 shows the distribution of mentions by the syntactic categories, and the counts of entities, links and mentions in the corpus respectively. All of this data has been Treebanked and PropBanked either as part of the OntoNotes effort or some preceding effort.

For comparison purposes, Table 2 also lists the number of documents in the MUC-6, MUC-7, and ACE (2000-2004) corpora. The MUC-6 data was taken from the Wall Street Journal, whereas the MUC-7 data was from the New York Times. The ACE data spanned many different genres similar to the ones in OntoNotes.

Parse Trees This represents the syntactic layer that is a revised version of the Penn Treebank. For purposes of this task, traces were removed from the syntactic trees, since the CoNLL-style data format, being indexed by tokens, does not provide any good means of conveying that information. Function tags were also removed, since the parsers that we used for the predicted syntax layer did not provide them. One thing that needs to be dealt with in conversational data is the presence of disfluencies (restarts, etc.). In the original OntoNotes parses, these are marked using a special EDITED[7] phrase tag – as was the case for the Switchboard Treebank. Given the frequency of disfluencies and the performance with which one can identify them automatically,[8] a probable processing pipeline would filter them out before parsing. Since we did not have a readily available tagger for tagging disfluencies, we decided to remove them using oracle information available in the Treebank.

Propositions The propositions in OntoNotes constitute PropBank semantic roles. Most of the verb predicates in the corpus have been annotated with their arguments. Recent enhancements to the PropBank to make it synchronize better with the Treebank (Babko-Malaya et al., 2006) have enhanced the information in the proposition by the addition of two types of LINKs that represent pragmatic coreference (LINK-PCR) and selectional preferences (LINK-SLC). More details can be found in the addendum to the PropBank guidelines[9] in the OntoNotes 4.0 re-

[6]Given the nature of word sense annotation, and changes in project priorities, we could not annotate all the low frequency verbs and nouns in the corpus. Furthermore, PropBank annotation currently only covers verb predicates.

[7]There is another phrase type – EMBED in the telephone conversation genre which is similar to the EDITED phrase type, and sometimes identifies insertions, but sometimes contains logical continuation of phrases, so we decided not to remove that from the data.

[8]A study by Charniak and Johnson (2001) shows that one can identify and remove edits from transcribed conversational speech with an F-score of about 78, with roughly 95 Precision and 67 recall.

[9]doc/propbank/english-propbank.pdf

lease. Since the community is not used to this representation which relies heavily on the trace structure in the Treebank which we are excluding, we decided to *unfold* the LINKs back to their original representation as in the Release 1.0 of the Proposition Bank. This functionality is part of the OntoNotes DB Tool.[10]

Word Sense Gold word sense annotation was supplied using sense numbers as specified in the OntoNotes list of senses for each lemma.[11] The sense inventories that were provided in the OntoNotes 4.0 release were not all mapped to the latest version 3.0 of WordNet, so we provided a revised version of the sense inventories, containing mapping to WordNet 3.0, on the task page for the participants.

Named Entities Named Entities in OntoNotes data are specified using a catalog of 18 Name types.

Other Layers Discourse plays a vital role in coreference resolution. In the case of broadcast conversation, or telephone conversation data, it partially manifests in the form of speakers of a given utterance, whereas in weblogs or newsgroups it does so as the writer, or commenter of a particular article or thread. This information provides an important clue for correctly linking anaphoric pronouns with the right antecedents. This information could be automatically deduced, but since it would add additional complexity to the already complex task, we decided to provide oracle information of this metadata both during training and testing. In other words, speaker and author identification was not treated as an annotation layer that needed to be predicted. This information was provided in the form of another column in the `.conll` table. There were some cases of interruptions and interjections that ideally would associate parts of a sentence to two different speakers, but since the frequency of this was quite small, we decided to make an assumption of one speaker/writer per sentence.

4.4.2 Predicted Annotation Layers

The predicted annotation layers were derived using automatic models trained using cross-validation on other portions of OntoNotes data. As mentioned earlier, there are some portions of the OntoNotes corpus that have not been annotated for coreference but that have been annotated for other layers. For training models for each of the layers, where feasible, we used all the data that we could for that layer from the training portion of the entire OntoNotes release.

Senses	Lemmas
1	1,506
2	1,046
>2	1,016

Table 6: Word sense polysemy over verb and noun lemmas in OntoNotes

Parse Trees Predicted parse trees were produced using the Charniak parser (Charniak and Johnson, 2005).[12] Some additional tag types used in the OntoNotes trees were added to the parser's tagset, including the NML tag that has recently been added to capture internal NP structure, and the rules used to determine head words were appropriately extended. The parser was then re-trained on the training portion of the release 4.0 data using 10-fold cross-validation. Table 5 shows the performance of the re-trained Charniak parser on the CoNLL-2011 test set. We did not get a chance to re-train the re-ranker, and since the stock re-ranker crashes when run on n-best parses containing NMLs, because it has not seen that tag in training, we could not make use of it.

Word Sense We trained a word sense tagger using a SVM classifier and contextual word and part of speech features on all the training portion of the OntoNotes data. The OntoNotes 4.0 corpus comprises a total of 14,662 sense definitions across 4877 verb and noun lemmas[13]. The distribution of senses per lemma is as shown in Table 6. Table 7 shows the performance of this classifier over *both the verbs and nouns* in the CoNLL-2011 test set. Again this performance is not directly comparable to any reported in the literature before, and it seems lower then performances reported on previous versions of OntoNotes because this is over all the genres of OntoNotes, and aggregated over both verbs and nouns in the CoNLL-2011 test set.

Propositions To predict propositional structure, ASSERT[14] (Pradhan et al., 2005) was used, re-trained also on all the training portion of the release

[10] http://cemantix.org/ontonotes.html

[11] It should be noted that word sense annotation in OntoNotes is note complete, so only some of the verbs and nouns have word sense tags specified.

[12] http://bllip.cs.brown.edu/download/reranking-parserAug06.tar.gz

[13] The number of lemmas in Table 6 do not add up to this number because not all of them have examples in the training data, where the total number of instantiated senses amounts to 7933.

[14] http://cemantix.org/assert.html

	All Sentences					Sentence len < 40			
	N	POS	R	P	F	N	R	P	F
Broadcast Conversation (BC)	2,194	95.93	84.30	84.46	84.38	2124	85.83	85.97	85.90
Broadcast News (BN)	1,344	96.50	84.19	84.28	84.24	1278	85.93	86.04	85.98
Magazine (MZ)	780	95.14	87.11	87.46	87.28	736	87.71	88.04	87.87
Newswire (NW)	2,273	96.95	87.05	87.45	87.25	2082	88.95	89.27	89.11
Telephone Conversation (TC)	1,366	93.52	79.73	80.83	80.28	1359	79.88	80.98	80.43
Weblogs and Newsgroups (WB)	1,658	94.67	83.32	83.20	83.26	1566	85.14	85.07	85.11
Overall	9,615	96.03	85.25	85.43	85.34	9145	86.86	87.02	86.94

Table 5: Parser performance on the CoNLL-2011 test set

	Frameset Accuracy	Total Sentences	Total Propositions	% Perfect Propositions	Argument ID + Class		
					P	R	F
Broadcast Conversation (BC)	0.92	2,037	5,021	52.18	82.55	64.84	72.63
Broadcast News (BN)	0.91	1,252	3,310	53.66	81.64	64.46	72.04
Magazine (MZ)	0.89	780	2,373	47.16	79.98	61.66	69.64
Newswire (NW)	0.93	1,898	4,758	39.72	80.53	62.68	70.49
Weblogs and Newsgroups (WB)	0.92	929	2,174	39.19	81.01	60.65	69.37
Overall	0.91	6,896	17,636	46.82	81.28	63.17	71.09

Table 8: Performance on the propositions and framesets in the CoNLL-2011 test set.

	Accuracy
Broadcast Conversation (BC)	0.70
Broadcast News (BN)	0.68
Magazine (MZ)	0.60
Newswire (NW)	0.62
Weblogs and Newsgroups (WB)	0.63
Overall	0.65

Table 7: Word sense performance over both verbs and nouns in the CoNLL-2011 test set

4.0 data. Given time constraints, we had to perform two modifications: i) Instead of a single model that predicts all arguments including NULL arguments, we had to use the two-stage mode where the NULL arguments are first filtered out and the remaining NON-NULL arguments are classified into one of the argument types, and ii) The argument identification module used an ensemble of ten classifiers – each trained on a tenth of the training data and performed an unweighted voting among them. This should still give a close to state of the art performance given that the argument identification performance tends to start to be asymptotic around 10k training instances. At first glance, the performance on the newswire genre is much lower than what has been reported for WSJ Section 23. This could be attributed to two factors: i) the fact that we had to compromise on the training method, but more importantly because ii) the newswire in OntoNotes not only contains WSJ data, but also Xinhua news. One could try to verify using just the WSJ portion of the data, but it would be hard as it is not only a subset of the documents that the performance has been reported on previously, but also the annotation has been significantly revised; it includes propositions for *be* verbs missing from the original PropBank, and the training data is a subset of the original data as well. Table 8 shows the detailed performance numbers.

In addition to automatically predicting the arguments, we also trained a classifier to tag PropBank frameset IDs in the data using the same word sense module as mentioned earlier. OntoNotes 4.0 contains a total of 7337 framesets across 5433 verb lemmas.[15] An overwhelming number of them are monosemous, but the more frequent verbs tend to be polysemous. Table 9 gives the distribution of number of framesets per lemma in the PropBank layer of the OntoNotes 4.0 data.

During automatic processing of the data, we tagged all the tokens that were tagged with a part of speech VBx. This means that there would be cases where the wrong token would be tagged with propositions. The CoNLL-2005 scorer was used to generate the scores.

Named Entities BBN's IdentiFinder™ system was used to predict the named entities. Given the

[15] The number of lemmas in Table 9 do not add up to this number because not all of them have examples in the training data, where the total number of instantiated senses amounts to 4229.

Framesets	Lemmas
1	2,722
2	321
> 2	181

Table 9: Frameset polysemy across lemmas

	Overall	BC	BN	MZ	NW	TC	WB
	F	F	F	F	F	F	F
ALL Named Entities	71.8	64.8	72.2	61.5	84.3	39.5	55.2
Cardinal	68.7	51.8	71.1	66.1	82.8	34.0	68.7
Date	76.1	63.7	77.9	66.7	83.7	60.5	56.0
Event	27.6	00.0	34.8	30.8	47.6	-	13.3
Facility	41.9	55.0	16.7	23.1	66.7	00.0	22.9
GPE	87.9	87.5	90.3	73.7	92.9	65.9	88.7
Language	41.2	-	50.0	50.0	00.0	20.0	75.0
Law	63.0	00.0	85.7	00.0	67.9	00.0	50.0
Location	58.4	59.1	59.6	53.3	68.0	00.0	23.5
Money	74.6	16.7	66.7	73.2	79.4	30.8	61.5
NORP	00.0	00.0	00.0	00.0	00.0	00.0	00.0
Ordinal	73.4	73.8	73.4	78.1	78.4	88.9	37.0
Organization	71.0	57.8	67.1	52.9	86.9	21.2	32.1
Percent	71.2	88.9	76.9	69.6	92.1	01.2	71.6
Person	79.6	78.9	87.7	66.7	91.6	65.1	64.8
Product	46.9	00.0	43.8	00.0	81.8	00.0	00.0
Quantity	47.5	25.3	58.3	61.1	71.9	00.0	22.2
Time	58.6	56.9	64.1	42.9	80.0	23.8	51.7
Work of Art	41.9	26.9	37.1	16.0	77.9	00.0	05.6

Table 10: Named Entity performance on the CoNLL-2011 test set

time constraints, we could not re-train it on the OntoNotes data and so an existing, pre-trained model was used, therefore the results are not a good indicator of the model's best performance. The pre-trained model had also used a somewhat different catalog of name types, which did not include the OntoNotes NORP type (for nationalities, organizations, religions, and political parties), so that category was never predicted. Table 10 shows the overall performance of the tagger on the CoNLL-2011 test set, as well as the performance broken down by individual name types. IdentiFinder performance has been reported to be in the low 90's on WSJ test set.

Other Layers As noted above, systems were allowed to make use of gender and number predictions for NPs using the table from Bergsma and Lin (Bergsma and Lin, 2006).

4.4.3 Data Format

In order to organize the multiple, rich layers of annotation, the OntoNotes project has created a database representation for the raw annotation layers along with a Python API to manipulate them (Pradhan et al., 2007a). In the OntoNotes distribution the data is organized as one file per layer, per document. The API requires a certain hierarchical structure with documents at the leaves inside a hierarchy of language, genre, source and section. It comes with various ways of cleanly querying and manipulating the data and allows convenient access to the sense inventory and propbank frame files instead of having to interpret the raw `.xml` versions. However, maintaining format consistency with earlier CoNLL tasks was deemed convenient for sites that already had tools configured to deal with that format. Therefore, in order to distribute the data so that one could make the best of both worlds, we created a new file type called `.conll` which logically served as another layer in addition to the `.parse`, `.prop`, `.name` and `.coref` layers. Each `.conll` file contained a merged representation of all the OntoNotes layers in the CoNLL-style tabular format with one line per token, and with multiple columns for each token specifying the input annotation layers relevant to that token, with the final column specifying the target coreference layer. Because OntoNotes is not authorized to distribute the underlying text, and many of the layers contain inline annotation, we had to provide a skeletal form (`.skel` of the `.conll` file which was essentially the `.conll` file, but with the word column replaced with a dummy string. We provided an assembly script that participants could use to create a `.conll` file taking as input the `.skel` file and the top-level directory of the OntoNotes distribution that they had separately downloaded from the LDC[16] Once the `.conll` file is created, it can be used to create the individual layers such as `.parse`, `.name`, `.coref` etc. using another set of scripts. Since the propositions and word sense layers are inherently standoff annotation, they were provided as is, and did not require that extra merging step. One thing thing that made this data creation process a bit tricky was the fact that we had dissected some of the trees for the conversation data to remove the EDITED phrases. Table 11 describes the data provided in each of the column of the `.conll` format. Figure 3 shows a sample from a `.conll` file.

4.5 Evaluation

This section describes the evaluation criteria used. Unlike for propositions, word sense and named entities, where it is simply a matter of counting the correct answers, or for parsing, where there are several established metrics, evaluating the accuracy of coreference continues to be contentious. Various al-

[16]OntoNotes is deeply grateful to the Linguistic Data Consortium for making the source data freely available to the task participants.

Column	Type	Description
1	Document ID	This is a variation on the document filename
2	Part number	Some files are divided into multiple parts numbered as 000, 001, 002, ... etc.
3	Word number	This is the word index in the sentence
4	Word	The word itself
5	Part of Speech	Part of Speech of the word
6	Parse bit	This is the bracketed structure broken before the first open parenthesis in the parse, and the word/part-of-speech leaf replaced with a *. The full parse can be created by substituting the asterix with the `([pos] [word])` string (or leaf) and concatenating the items in the rows of that column.
7	Predicate lemma	The predicate lemma is mentioned for the rows for which we have semantic role information. All other rows are marked with a –
8	Predicate Frameset ID	This is the PropBank frameset ID of the predicate in Column 7.
9	Word sense	This is the word sense of the word in Column 3.
10	Speaker/Author	This is the speaker or author name where available. Mostly in Broadcast Conversation and Web Log data.
11	Named Entities	These columns identifies the spans representing various named entities.
12:N	Predicate Arguments	There is one column each of predicate argument structure information for the predicate mentioned in Column 7.
N	Coreference	Coreference chain information encoded in a parenthesis structure.

Table 11: Format of the `.conll` file used on the shared task

```
#begin document (nw/wsj/07/wsj_0771); part 000
...
...
nw/wsj/07/wsj_0771 0  0          ``   ``  (TOP(S(S*           -   -  -  -          *          *          (ARG1*           *           *         -
nw/wsj/07/wsj_0771 0  1  Vandenberg  NNP        (NP*           -   -  -  -   (PERSON)     (ARG1*               *           *           *  (8|(0)
nw/wsj/07/wsj_0771 0  2         and   CC           *           -   -  -  -          *          *               *           *           *         -
nw/wsj/07/wsj_0771 0  3     Rayburn  NNP          *)           -   -  -  -   (PERSON)         *)               *           *           *(23)|8)
nw/wsj/07/wsj_0771 0  4         are  VBP        (VP*          be  01  1  -          *       (V*)               *           *           *         -
nw/wsj/07/wsj_0771 0  5      heroes  NNS   (NP(NP*)           -   -  -  -          *     (ARG2*               *           *           *         -
nw/wsj/07/wsj_0771 0  6          of   IN        (PP*           -   -  -  -          *          *               *           *           *         -
nw/wsj/07/wsj_0771 0  7        mine   NN    (NP*))))           -   -  5  -          *         *)               *           *           *      (15)
nw/wsj/07/wsj_0771 0  8           ,    ,           *           -   -  -  -          *          *               *           *           *         -
nw/wsj/07/wsj_0771 0  9          ''   ''          *)           -   -  -  -          *          *              *)           *           *         -
nw/wsj/07/wsj_0771 0 10         Mr.  NNP        (NP*           -   -  -  -          *          *          (ARG0*      (ARG0*           *       (15
nw/wsj/07/wsj_0771 0 11       Boren  NNP          *)           -   -  -  -   (PERSON)          *              *)          *)           *       15)
nw/wsj/07/wsj_0771 0 12        says  VBZ        (VP*         say  01  1  -          *          *            (V*)           *           *         -
nw/wsj/07/wsj_0771 0 13           ,    ,           *           -   -  -  -          *          *               *           *           *         -
nw/wsj/07/wsj_0771 0 14   referring  VBG     (S(VP*       refer  01  2  -          *          *     (ARGM-ADV*        (V*)           *         -
nw/wsj/07/wsj_0771 0 15          as   RB      (ADVP*           -   -  -  -          *          *               *  (ARGM-DIS*           *         -
nw/wsj/07/wsj_0771 0 16        well   RB          *)           -   -  -  -          *          *               *          *)           *         -
nw/wsj/07/wsj_0771 0 17          to   IN        (PP*           -   -  -  -          *          *               *      (ARG1*           *         -
nw/wsj/07/wsj_0771 0 18         Sam  NNP     (NP(NP*           -   -  -  -   (PERSON*          *               *           *           *       (23
nw/wsj/07/wsj_0771 0 19     Rayburn  NNP          *)           -   -  -  -         *)          *               *           *           *         -
nw/wsj/07/wsj_0771 0 20           ,    ,           *           -   -  -  -          *          *               *           *           *         -
nw/wsj/07/wsj_0771 0 21         the   DT     (NP(NP*           -   -  -  -          *          *               *           *      (ARG0*         -
nw/wsj/07/wsj_0771 0 22  Democratic   JJ           *           -   -  -  -     (NORP)          *               *           *           *         -
nw/wsj/07/wsj_0771 0 23       House  NNP           *           -   -  -  -      (ORG)          *               *           *           *         -
nw/wsj/07/wsj_0771 0 24     speaker   NN          *)           -   -  -  -          *          *               *           *          *)         -
nw/wsj/07/wsj_0771 0 25         who   WP (SBAR(WHNP*)          -   -  -  -          *          *               *           *  (R-ARG0*)         -
nw/wsj/07/wsj_0771 0 26  cooperated  VBD      (S(VP*   cooperate  01  1  -          *          *               *           *        (V*)         -
nw/wsj/07/wsj_0771 0 27        with   IN        (PP*           -   -  -  -          *          *               *           *      (ARG1*         -
nw/wsj/07/wsj_0771 0 28   President  NNP        (NP*           -   -  -  -          *          *               *           *           *         -
nw/wsj/07/wsj_0771 0 29  Eisenhower  NNP *)))))))))))          -   -  -  -   (PERSON)          *              *)          *)          *)       23)
nw/wsj/07/wsj_0771 0 30           .    .         *))           -   -  -  -          *          *               *           *           *         -

nw/wsj/07/wsj_0771 0  0          ``   ``     (TOP(S*           -   -  -  -          *          *               *           -
nw/wsj/07/wsj_0771 0  1        They  PRP       (NP*)           -   -  -  -          *    (ARG0*)               *         (8)
nw/wsj/07/wsj_0771 0  2     allowed  VBD        (VP*       allow  01  1  -          *       (V*)               *           -
nw/wsj/07/wsj_0771 0  3        this   DT     (S(NP*           -   -  -  -          *     (ARG1*          (ARG1*          (6
nw/wsj/07/wsj_0771 0  4     country   NN          *)           -   -  3  -          *          *              *)          6)
nw/wsj/07/wsj_0771 0  5          to   TO        (VP*           -   -  -  -          *          *               *           -
nw/wsj/07/wsj_0771 0  6          be   VB        (VP*          be  01  1  -          *          *            (V*)        (16)
nw/wsj/07/wsj_0771 0  7    credible   JJ (ADJP*))))           -   -  -  -          *         *)         (ARG2*)           -
nw/wsj/07/wsj_0771 0  8           .    .         *))           -   -  -  -          *          *               *           -

#end document
```

Figure 3: Sample portion of the `.conll` file.

ternative metrics have been proposed, as mentioned below, which weight different features of a proposed coreference pattern differently. The choice is not clear in part because the value of a particular set of coreference predictions is integrally tied to the consuming application.

A further issue in defining a coreference metric concerns the granularity of the mentions, and how closely the predicted mentions are required to match those in the gold standard for a coreference prediction to be counted as correct.

Our evaluation criterion was in part driven by the OntoNotes data structures. OntoNotes coreference distinguishes between identity coreference and appositive coreference, treating the latter separately because it is already captured explicitly by other layers of the OntoNotes annotation. Thus we evaluated systems only on the identity coreference task, which links all categories of entities and events together into equivalent classes.

The situation with mentions for OntoNotes is also different than it was for MUC or ACE. OntoNotes data does not explicitly identify the minimum extents of an entity mention, but it does include hand-tagged syntactic parses. Thus for the official evaluation, we decided to use the exact spans of mentions for determining correctness. The NP boundaries for the test data were pre-extracted from the hand-tagged Treebank for annotation, and events triggered by verb phrases were tagged using the verbs themselves. This choice means that scores for the CoNLL-2011 coreference task are likely to be lower than for coref evaluations based on MUC, where the mention spans are specified in the input,[17] or those based on ACE data, where an approximate match is often allowed based on the specified head of the NP mention.

4.5.1 Metrics

As noted above, the choice of an evaluation metric for coreference has been a tricky issue and there does not appear to be any silver bullet approach that addresses all the concerns. Three metrics have been proposed for evaluating coreference performance over an unrestricted set of entity types: i) The **link** based MUC metric (Vilain et al., 1995), ii) The **mention** based B-CUBED metric (Bagga and Baldwin, 1998) and iii) The **entity** based CEAF (Constrained Entity Aligned F-measure) metric (Luo, 2005). Very recently BLANC (BiLateral Assessment of Noun-Phrase Coreference) measure (Recasens and Hovy, 2011) has been proposed as well. Each of the metric tries to address the shortcomings or biases of the earlier metrics. Given a set of key entities $\mathcal{K}$, and a set of response entities $\mathcal{R}$, with each entity comprising one or more mentions, each metric generates its variation of a precision and recall measure. The MUC measure if the oldest and most widely used. It focuses on the **links** (or, pairs of mentions) in the data.[18] The number of common links between entities in $\mathcal{K}$ and $\mathcal{R}$ divided by the number of links in $\mathcal{K}$ represents the recall, whereas, precision is the number of common links between entities in $\mathcal{K}$ and $\mathcal{R}$ divided by the number of links in $\mathcal{R}$. This metric prefers systems that have more mentions per entity – a system that creates a single entity of all the mentions will get a 100% recall without significant degradation in its precision. And, it ignores recall for singleton entities, or entities with only one mention. The B-CUBED metric tries to addresses MUCS's shortcomings, by focusing on the **mentions** and computes recall and precision scores for each mention. If K is the key entity containing mention M, and R is the response entity containing mention M, then recall for the mention M is computed as $\frac{|K \cap R|}{|K|}$ and precision for the same is is computed as $\frac{|K \cap R|}{|R|}$. Overall recall and precision are the average of the individual mention scores. CEAF aligns every response entity with at most *one* key entity by finding the best one-to-one mapping between the entities using an entity similarity metric. This is a maximum bipartite matching problem and can be solved by the Kuhn-Munkres algorithm. This is thus a **entity** based measure. Depending on the similarity, there are two variations – *entity* based CEAF – CEAF_e and a *mention* based CEAF – CEAF_e. Recall is the total similarity divided by the number of mentions in $\mathcal{K}$, and precision is the total similarity divided by the number of mentions in $\mathcal{R}$. Finally, BLANC uses a variation on the Rand index (Rand, 1971) suitable for evaluating coreference. There are a few other measures – one being the ACE value, but since this is specific to a restricted set of entities (ACE types), we did not consider it.

4.5.2 Official Evaluation Metric

In order to determine the best performing system in the shared task, we needed to associate a single number with each system. This could have been one of the metrics above, or some combination of more than one of them. The choice was not simple, and while we consulted various researchers in

[17]as is the case in this evaluation with Gold Mentions

[18]The MUC corpora did not tag single mention entities.

the field, hoping for a strong consensus, their conclusion seemed to be that each metric had its pros and cons. We settled on the MELA metric by Denis and Baldridge (2009), which takes a weighted average of three metrics: MUC, B-CUBED, and CEAF. The rationale for the combination is that each of the three metrics represents a different important dimension, the MUC measure being based on links, the B-CUBED based on mentions, and the CEAF based on entities. For a given task, a weighted average of the three might be optimal, but since we don't have an end task in mind, we decided to use the unweighted mean of the three metrics as the score on which the winning system was judged. We decided to use CEAF_e instead of CEAF_m.

4.5.3 Scoring Metrics Implementation

We used the same core scorer implementation[19] that was used for the SEMEVAL-2010 task, and which implemented all the different metrics. There were a couple of modifications done to this scorer after it was used for the SEMEVAL-2010 task.

1. Only exact matches were considered correct. Previously, for SEMEVAL-2010 non-exact matches were judged partially correct with a 0.5 score if the heads were the same and the mention extent did not exceed the gold mention.

2. The modifications suggested by Cai and Strube (2010) were incorporated in the scorer.

Since there are differences in the version used for CoNLL and the one available on the download site, and it is possible that the latter would be revised in the future, we have archived the version of the scorer on the CoNLL-2011 task webpage.[20]

5 Systems and Results

About 65 different groups demonstrated interest in the shared task by registering on the task webpage. Of these, 23 groups submitted system outputs on the test set during the evaluation week. 18 groups submitted only closed track results, 3 groups only open track results, and 2 groups submitted both closed and open track results. 2 participants in the closed track, did not write system papers, so we don't use their results in the discussion. Their results will be reported on the task webpage.

[19] http://www.lsi.upc.edu/ esapena/downloads/index.php?id=3

[20] http://conll.bbn.com/download/scorer.v4.tar.gz

The official results for the 18 systems that submitted closed track outputs are shown in Table 12, with those for the 5 systems that submitted open track results in Table 13. The official ranking score, the arithmetic mean of the F-scores of MUC, B-CUBED and CEAF_e, is shown in the rightmost column. For convenience, systems will be referred to here using the first portion of the full name, which is unique within each table.

For completeness, the tables include the raw precision and recall scores from which the F-scores were derived. The tables also include two additional scores (BLANC and CEAF_m) that did not factor into the official ranking score. Useful further analysis may be possible based on these results beyond the preliminary results presented here.

As discussed previously in the task description, we will consider three different test input conditions: i) Predicted only (Official), ii) Predicted plus gold mention *boundaries*, and iii) Predicted plus gold *mentions*

5.1 Predicted only (Official)

For the official test, beyond the raw source text, coreference systems were provided only with the predictions from automatic engines as to the other annotation layers (parses, semantic roles, word senses, and named entities).

In this evaluation it is important to note that the mention detection score cannot be considered in isolation of the coreference task as has usually been the case. This is mainly owing to the fact that there are no singleton entities in the OntoNotes data. Most systems removed singletons from the response as a post-processing step, so not only will they not get credit for the singleton entities that they correctly removed from the data, but they will be penalized for the ones that they accidentally linked with another mention. What this number does indicate is the ceiling on recall that a system would have got in absence of being penalized for making mistakes in coreference resolution. A close look at the Table 12 indicates a possible outlier in case of the *sapena* system. The recall for this system is very high, and precision way lower than any other system. Further investigations uncovered that the reason for this aberrant behavior was that fact that this system opted to *keep* singletons in the response. By design, the scorer removes singletons that might be still present in the system, but it does so *after* the mention detection accuracy is computed.

The official scores top out in the high 50's. While this is lower than the figures cited in previous coref-

System	Mention Detection			MUC			B-CUBED			CEAF$_m$			CEAF$_e$			BLANC			Official
	R	P	F	R	P	F^1	R	P	F^2	R	P	F	R	P	F^3	R	P	F	$\frac{F^1+F^2+F^3}{3}$
lee	75.07	66.81	**70.70**	61.76	57.53	59.57	68.40	68.23	68.31	56.37	56.37	**56.37**	43.41	47.75	**45.48**	70.63	76.21	73.02	**57.79**
sapena	92.39	28.19	43.20	56.32	63.16	59.55	62.75	72.08	67.09	53.51	53.51	53.51	44.75	38.38	41.32	69.50	73.07	71.10	55.99
chang	68.08	61.96	64.88	57.15	57.15	57.15	67.14	70.53	**68.79**	54.40	54.40	54.40	41.94	41.94	41.94	71.19	77.09	**73.71**	55.96
nugues	69.87	68.08	68.96	60.20	57.10	58.61	66.74	64.23	65.46	51.45	51.45	51.45	38.09	41.06	39.52	71.99	70.31	71.11	54.53
santos	67.80	63.25	65.45	59.21	54.30	56.65	68.79	62.81	65.66	49.54	49.54	49.54	35.86	40.21	37.91	73.37	66.91	69.46	53.41
song	57.81	80.41	67.26	53.73	67.79	**59.95**	60.65	66.05	63.23	46.29	46.29	46.29	43.37	30.71	35.96	69.49	59.71	61.47	53.05
stoyanov	70.84	64.98	67.78	63.61	54.04	58.43	72.58	53.27	61.44	46.08	46.08	46.08	32.00	40.82	35.88	73.21	58.93	60.88	51.92
sobha	67.82	62.09	64.83	51.08	49.88	50.48	62.63	65.43	64.00	49.48	49.48	49.48	40.65	41.82	41.23	61.40	68.35	63.88	51.90
kobdani	62.06	60.04	61.03	55.64	51.50	53.49	69.66	62.43	65.85	42.70	42.70	42.70	32.33	35.40	33.79	61.86	63.51	62.61	51.04
zhou	61.08	63.59	62.31	45.65	52.79	48.96	57.14	72.91	64.07	47.53	47.53	47.53	43.19	36.79	39.74	61.10	73.94	64.72	50.92
charton	65.90	62.77	64.30	55.09	50.05	52.45	66.26	58.44	62.10	46.82	46.82	46.82	34.33	39.05	36.54	69.94	62.23	64.80	50.36
yang	71.92	57.53	63.93	59.91	46.43	52.31	71.64	55.14	62.32	46.55	46.55	46.55	30.28	42.39	35.33	71.11	61.75	64.63	49.99
hao	64.50	64.11	64.30	57.89	51.42	54.47	67.83	55.43	61.01	45.07	45.07	45.07	30.08	35.76	32.67	72.61	62.37	65.35	49.38
xinxin	65.49	58.71	61.92	48.54	44.85	46.62	61.59	62.28	61.93	44.75	44.75	44.75	35.19	38.62	36.83	63.04	65.83	64.27	48.46
zhang	55.35	68.25	61.13	42.03	55.62	47.88	52.57	73.05	61.14	44.46	44.46	44.46	42.00	30.28	35.19	62.84	69.22	65.21	48.07
kummerfeld	69.77	56.97	62.72	46.39	39.56	42.70	63.60	57.30	60.29	45.35	45.35	45.35	35.05	42.26	38.32	58.74	61.58	59.91	47.10
zhekova	67.49	37.60	48.29	28.87	20.66	24.08	67.14	56.67	61.46	40.43	40.43	40.43	31.57	41.21	35.75	52.77	57.05	53.77	40.43
irwin	17.06	61.09	26.67	12.45	50.60	19.98	35.07	89.90	50.46	31.68	31.68	31.68	45.84	17.38	25.21	51.48	56.83	51.12	31.88

Table 12: Performance of systems in the *official, closed* track using all predicted information

System	Mention Detection			MUC			B-CUBED			CEAF$_m$			CEAF$_e$			BLANC			Official
	R	P	F	R	P	F^1	R	P	F^2	R	P	F	R	P	F^3	R	P	F	$\frac{F^1+F^2+F^3}{3}$
lee	74.31	67.87	**70.94**	62.83	59.34	**61.03**	68.85	69.01	**68.93**	56.70	56.70	**56.70**	43.29	46.80	**44.98**	71.90	76.55	73.96	**58.31**
cai	67.15	67.64	67.40	56.73	58.90	57.80	64.60	71.03	67.66	53.37	53.37	53.37	42.71	40.68	41.67	69.77	73.96	71.62	55.71
uryupina	70.60	66.31	68.39	59.70	55.70	57.63	66.29	64.12	65.18	51.42	51.42	51.42	38.34	42.17	40.16	69.23	68.54	68.88	54.32
klenner	64.41	60.28	62.28	49.04	50.71	49.86	61.70	68.61	64.97	50.03	50.03	50.03	41.28	39.70	40.48	66.05	73.90	69.05	51.77
irwin	24.60	62.27	35.27	18.56	51.01	27.21	38.97	85.57	53.55	33.86	33.86	33.86	43.33	19.36	26.76	51.62	52.91	51.76	35.84

Table 13: Performance of systems in the *official, open* track using all predicted information

System	Mention Detection			MUC			B-CUBED			CEAF$_m$			CEAF$_e$			BLANC			Official
	R	P	F	R	P	F^1	R	P	F^2	R	P	F	R	P	F^3	R	P	F	$\frac{F^1+F^2+F^3}{3}$
lee	79.52	71.25	**75.16**	65.87	62.05	**63.90**	69.52	70.55	**70.03**	59.26	59.26	**59.26**	46.29	50.48	**48.30**	72.00	78.55	**74.77**	**60.74**
nugues	74.18	70.74	72.42	64.33	60.05	62.12	68.26	65.17	66.68	53.84	53.84	53.84	39.86	44.23	41.93	72.53	71.04	71.75	56.91
chang	63.37	73.18	67.92	55.00	65.50	59.79	62.16	76.65	68.65	54.95	54.95	54.95	46.77	37.17	41.42	70.97	79.30	74.29	56.62
santos	65.82	69.90	67.80	57.76	61.39	59.52	64.49	70.27	67.26	51.87	51.87	51.87	41.42	38.16	39.72	72.72	71.97	72.34	55.50
kobdani	67.11	65.09	66.08	62.63	56.80	59.57	73.20	62.22	67.27	44.49	44.49	44.49	32.87	37.25	34.92	64.07	64.13	64.10	53.92
stoyanov	76.90	64.73	70.29	69.81	55.01	61.54	77.07	52.54	62.48	48.08	48.08	48.08	30.97	44.84	36.64	76.57	60.33	62.96	53.55
zhang	59.62	71.19	64.89	46.06	58.75	51.64	53.89	73.41	62.16	46.62	46.62	46.62	43.49	32.11	36.95	64.11	70.47	66.54	50.25
song	58.43	77.64	66.68	46.66	68.40	55.48	54.40	70.19	61.29	43.62	43.62	43.62	43.77	25.88	32.53	66.29	58.76	60.22	49.77
zhekova	69.19	57.27	62.67	33.48	37.15	35.22	55.47	68.23	61.20	41.31	41.31	41.31	38.29	34.65	36.38	53.45	63.33	54.79	44.27

Table 14: Performance of systems in the supplementary *closed* track using predicted information plus *gold boundaries*

System	Mention Detection			MUC			B-CUBED			CEAF$_m$			CEAF$_e$			BLANC			Official
	R	P	F	R	P	F^1	R	P	F^2	R	P	F	R	P	F^3	R	P	F	$\frac{F^1+F^2+F^3}{3}$
lee	78.71	72.33	75.39	66.93	63.91	65.39	70.09	71.49	70.78	59.78	59.78	59.78	46.34	49.62	47.92	73.38	79.00	75.83	61.36

Table 15: Performance of systems in the supplementary *open* track using predicted information plus *gold boundaries*

System	Mention Detection			MUC			B-CUBED			CEAF$_m$			CEAF$_e$			BLANC			Official
	R	P	F	R	P	F^1	R	P	F^2	R	P	F	R	P	F^3	R	P	F	$\frac{F^1+F^2+F^3}{3}$
chang	100	100	100	80.46	84.75	82.55	72.84	74.57	73.70	69.71	69.71	69.71	70.45	60.75	65.24	78.01	76.57	77.26	73.83

Table 16: Performance of systems in the *supplementary, closed* track using predicted information plus *gold mentions*

System	Mention Detection			MUC			B-CUBED			CEAF$_m$			CEAF$_e$			BLANC			Official
	R	P	F	R	P	F^1	R	P	F^2	R	P	F	R	P	F^3	R	P	F	$\frac{F^1+F^2+F^3}{3}$
lee	83.37	100	90.93	74.79	89.68	81.56	67.46	86.88	75.95	70.73	70.73	70.73	77.75	51.05	61.64	76.65	85.85	80.35	73.05

Table 17: Performance of systems in the *supplementary, open* track using predicted information plus *gold mentions*

System	Mention Detection			MUC			B-CUBED			CEAF$_m$			CEAF$_e$			BLANC			Official
	R	P	F	R	P	F^1	R	P	F^2	R	P	F	R	P	F^3	R	P	F	$\frac{F^1+F^2+F^3}{3}$
lee	76.79	68.34	**72.32**	63.29	58.96	61.05	68.84	68.72	68.78	57.28	57.28	**57.28**	44.19	48.75	**46.36**	70.93	76.58	73.36	**58.73**
sapena	95.27	29.07	44.55	56.99	63.91	60.25	62.83	72.31	67.27	53.90	53.90	53.90	45.22	38.70	41.71	69.71	73.32	71.32	56.41
chang	69.88	63.61	66.60	58.48	58.48	58.48	67.42	70.91	**69.12**	55.21	55.21	55.21	42.66	42.66	42.66	71.42	77.36	**73.96**	56.75
nugues	72.96	71.08	72.01	62.68	59.46	61.03	67.24	64.89	66.04	52.82	52.82	52.82	39.25	42.50	40.81	72.57	70.86	71.68	55.96
santos	70.39	65.67	67.95	61.28	56.20	58.63	69.25	63.16	66.07	50.47	50.47	50.47	36.51	41.15	38.69	73.92	67.32	69.93	54.46
song	59.24	82.39	68.92	54.92	69.29	61.27	60.83	66.27	63.46	46.97	46.97	46.97	44.49	31.15	36.65	69.73	59.87	61.61	53.79
stoyanov	74.43	68.28	71.22	67.18	57.08	**61.72**	74.05	53.45	62.09	47.40	47.40	47.40	32.78	42.52	37.02	74.10	59.34	61.31	53.61
sobha	71.06	65.06	67.93	53.91	52.64	53.27	63.17	66.14	64.62	50.80	50.80	50.80	41.77	43.03	42.39	61.91	69.15	64.49	53.43
kobdani	65.98	63.83	64.89	59.22	54.81	56.93	70.49	63.12	66.60	44.17	44.14	44.15	33.19	36.50	34.77	62.52	64.25	63.32	52.77
zhou	64.11	66.74	65.40	48.00	55.51	51.48	57.13	73.71	64.40	48.40	48.40	48.40	44.18	37.35	40.48	61.54	74.86	65.30	52.12
charton	71.01	67.64	69.28	59.24	53.82	56.40	67.10	59.02	62.80	48.91	48.91	48.91	35.96	41.39	38.48	70.65	62.71	65.34	52.56
yang	73.73	58.97	65.53	61.23	47.45	53.47	71.83	55.13	62.40	47.05	47.05	47.05	30.54	43.16	35.77	71.39	61.92	64.83	50.55
hao	66.79	66.38	66.59	59.55	52.89	56.02	68.27	55.46	61.20	45.95	45.95	45.95	30.76	36.81	33.51	73.22	62.73	65.78	50.24
xinxin	69.05	61.91	65.28	50.99	47.11	48.97	61.59	62.70	62.14	45.64	45.64	45.64	35.86	39.57	37.62	63.42	66.29	64.68	49.58
zhang	57.41	70.78	63.40	43.48	57.53	49.53	52.44	73.60	61.24	44.97	44.97	44.97	42.71	30.44	35.55	63.12	69.63	65.53	48.77
kummerfeld	71.05	58.01	63.87	47.42	40.44	43.65	63.73	57.39	60.39	45.76	45.76	45.76	35.30	42.72	38.66	58.89	61.77	60.07	47.57
zhekova	72.65	40.48	51.99	31.73	22.70	26.46	66.92	56.68	61.37	41.04	41.04	41.04	31.93	42.17	36.34	53.09	57.86	54.22	41.39
irwin	17.58	62.96	27.49	12.69	51.59	20.37	34.83	89.98	50.27	31.71	31.71	31.71	46.13	17.33	25.20	51.51	56.93	51.14	31.95

Table 18: *Head word based* performance of systems in the *official, closed* track using all predicted information

System	Mention Detection			MUC			B-CUBED			CEAF$_m$			CEAF$_e$			BLANC			Official
	R	P	F	R	P	F^1	R	P	F^2	R	P	F	R	P	F^3	R	P	F	$\frac{F^1+F^2+F^3}{3}$
lee	76.01	69.43	**72.57**	64.40	60.83	**62.57**	69.34	69.57	**69.45**	57.68	57.68	**57.68**	44.15	47.85	**45.92**	72.23	76.94	**74.32**	**59.31**
cai	69.32	69.82	69.57	58.39	60.63	59.49	64.83	71.53	68.04	54.36	54.36	54.36	43.74	41.58	42.64	70.13	74.39	72.01	56.72
uryupina	72.10	67.72	69.84	60.74	56.68	58.64	66.43	64.25	65.32	52.00	52.00	52.00	38.87	42.85	40.76	69.43	68.73	69.07	54.91
klenner	71.73	67.14	69.36	55.17	57.04	56.09	62.67	70.69	66.44	53.25	53.25	53.25	44.27	42.39	43.31	67.45	75.92	70.68	55.28
irwin	25.24	63.87	36.18	18.90	51.94	27.71	38.79	85.64	53.40	33.89	33.89	33.89	43.59	19.31	26.76	51.66	52.98	51.80	35.96

Table 19: *Head word based* performance of systems in the *official, open* track using all predicted information

erence evaluations, that is as expected, given that the task here includes predicting the underlying mentions and mention boundaries, the insistence on exact match, and given that the relatively easier appositive coreference cases are not included in this measure. The top-performing system (*lee*) had a score of 57.79 which is about 1.8 points higher than that of the second (*sapena*) and third (*chang*) ranking systems, which scored 55.99 and 55.96 respectively. Another 1.5 points separates them from the fourth best score of 54.53 (*nugues*). Thus the performance differences between the better-scoring systems were not large, with only about three points separating the top four systems.

This becomes even clearer if we merge in the results of systems that participated only in the open track but that made relatively limited use of outside resources.[21] Comparing that way, the *cai* system scores in the same ball park as the second rank systems (*sapena* and *chang*). The *uryupina* system similarly scores very close to *nugues*'s 54.53

Given that our choice of the official metric was somewhat arbitrary, if is also useful to look at the individual metrics, including the mention-based CEAF$_m$ and BLANC metrics that were not part of the official metric. The *lee* system which scored the best using the official metric does slightly worse than *song* on the MUC metric, and also does slightly worse than *chang* on the B-CUBED and BLANC metrics. However, it does much better than every other group on the entity-based CEAF$_e$, and this is the primary reason for its 1.8 point advantage in the official score. If the CEAF$_e$ measure does indicate the accuracy of entities in the response, this suggests that the *lee* system is doing better on getting coherent entities than any other system. This could be partly due to the fact that that system is primarily a precision-based system that would tend to create purer entities. The CEAF$_e$ measure also seems to penalize other systems more harshly than do the other measures.

We cannot compare these results to the ones obtained in the SEMEVAL-2010 coreference task using a small portion of OntoNotes data because it was only using nominal entities, and had heuristically added singleton mentions to the OntoNotes data[22]

5.2 Predicted plus gold mention *boundaries*

We also explored performance when the systems were provided with the gold mention boundaries, that is, with the exact spans (expressed in terms of token offsets) for all of the NP constituents in the human-annotated parse trees for the test data. Systems could use this additional data to ensure that the output mention spans in their entity chains would not clash with those in the answer set. Since this was a secondary evaluation, it was an *optional* element, and not all participants ran their systems on this task variation. The results for those systems that did participate in this optional task are shown in Tables 14 (closed track) and 15 (open track).

Most of the better scoring systems did supply these results. While all systems did slightly better here in terms of raw scores, the performance was not much different from the official task, indicating that mention boundary errors resulting from problems in parsing do not contribute significantly to the final output.[23]

One side benefit of performing this supplemental evaluation was that it revealed a subtle bug in the automatic scoring routine that we were using that could double-count duplicate correct mentions in a given entity chain. These can occur, for example, if the system considers a unit-production NP-PRP combination as two mentions that identify the exact same token in the text, and reports them as separate mentions. Most systems had a filter in their processing that selected only one of these duplicate mentions, but the *kobdani* system considered both as potential mentions, and its developers tuned their algorithm using that flawed version of the scorer.

When we fixed the scorer and re-evaluated all of the systems, the *kobdani* system was the only one whose score was affected significantly, dropping by about 8 points, which lowered that system's rank from second to ninth. It is not clear how much of this was owing to the fact that the system's param-

[21]The *cai* system specifically mentions that, and the only resource that the *uryupina* system used outside of the closed track setting was the Stanford named entity tagger.

[22]The documentation that comes with the SEMEVAL data package from LDC (LDC2011T01) states: "Only nominal mentions and identical (IDENT) types were taken from the OntoNotes coreference annotation, thus excluding coreference relations with verbs and appositives. Since OntoNotes is only annotated with multi-mention entities, singleton referential elements were identified heuristically: all NPs and possessive determiners were annotated as singletons excluding those functioning as appositives or as pre-modifiers but for NPs in the possessive case. In coordinated NPs, single constituents as well as the entire NPs were considered to be mentions. There is no reliable heuristic to automatically detect English expletive pronouns, thus they were (although inaccurately) also annotated as singletons."

[23]It would be interesting to measure the overlap between the entity clusters for these two cases, to see whether there was any substantial difference in the mention chains, besides the expected differences in boundaries for individual mentions.

eters had been tuned using the scorer with the bug, which double-credited duplicate mentions. To find out for sure, one would have to re-tune the system using the modified scorer.

One difficulty with this supplementary evaluation using gold mention boundaries is that those boundaries alone provide only very partial information. For the roughly 10% of mentions that the automatic parser did not correctly identify, while the systems knew the correct boundaries, they had no hierarchical parser or semantic role label information, and they also had to further approximate the already heuristic head word identification. This incomplete data complicated the systems' task and also complicates interpretation of the results.

5.3 Predicted plus gold *mentions*

The final supplementary condition that we explored was if the systems were supplied with the manually-annotated spans for exactly those mentions that did participate in the gold standard coreference chains. This supplies significantly more information than the previous case, where exact spans were supplied for all NPs, since the gold mentions list here will also include verb headwords that are linked to event NPs, but will not include singleton mentions, which do not end up as part of any chain. The latter constraint makes this test seem somewhat artificial, since it directly reveals part of what the systems are designed to determine, but it still has some value in quantifying the impact that mention detection has on the overall task and what the results are if the mention detection is perfect.

Since this was a logical extension of the task and since the data was available to the participants for the development set, a few of the sites did run experiments of this type. Therefore we decided to provide the gold *mentions* data to a few sites who had reported these scores, so that we could compute the performance on the test set. The results of these experiments are shown in Tables 16 and 17. The results show that performance does go up significantly, indicating that it is markedly easier for the systems to generate better entities given gold *mentions*. Although, ideally, one would expect a perfect mention detection score, it is the case that one of the two systems – *lee* – did not get a 100% Recall. This could possibly be owing to unlinked singletons that were removed in post-processing.

The *lee* system developers also ran a further experiment where both gold mentions for the elements of the coreference chains and also gold *annotations* for all the other layers were available to the system. Surprisingly, the improvement in coreference performance from having gold annotation of the other layers was almost negligible. This suggests that either: i) the automatic models are predicting those layers well enough that switching to gold doesn't make much difference; ii) information from the other layers does not provide much leverage for coreference resolution; or iii) current coreference models are not capable of utilizing the information from these other layers effectively. Given the performance numbers on the individual layers cited earlier, (i) seems unlikely, and we hope that further research in how best to leverage these layers will result in models that can benefit from them more definitively.

5.4 Head word based scoring

In order to check how stringent the *official*, exact match scoring is, we also performed a relaxed scoring. Unlike ACE and MUC, the OntoNotes data does not have manually annotated minimum spans that a mention must contain to be considered correct. However, OntoNotes does have manual syntactic analysis in the form of the Treebank. Therefore, we decided to approximate the minimum spans by using the head words of the mentions using the gold standard syntax tree. If the response mention contained the head word and did not exceed the true mention boundary, then it was considered correct – both from the point of view of mention detection, and coreference resolution. The scores using this relaxed strategy for the *open* and *closed* track submissions using predicted data are shown in Tables 18 and 19. It can be observed that the relaxed, head word based, scoring does not improve performance very much. The only exception was the *klenner* system whose performance increased from 51.77 to 55.28. Overall, the ranking remained quite stable, though it did change for some adjacent systems which had very close *exact match* scores.

5.5 Genre variation

In order to check how the systems did on various genres, we scored their performance per genre as well. Tables 20 and 21 summarize genre based performance for the *closed* and *open* track participants respectively. System performance does not seem to vary as much across the different genres as is normally the case with language processing tasks, which could suggest that coreference is relatively genre insensitive, or it is possible that scores are two low for the difference to be apparent. Comparisons are difficult, however, because the spoken gen-

		MD F	MUC F	BCUB F	C_m F	C_e F	BLANC F	O F
lee	GENRE							
	BC	72.2	60.0	66.2	53.9	43.7	71.7	56.7
	BN	72.0	59.0	68.7	57.6	48.7	68.8	58.8
	MZ	70.1	58.0	72.2	61.6	50.9	75.0	60.4
	NW	65.4	54.3	69.4	56.5	45.5	70.4	56.4
	TC	75.9	66.8	69.5	59.3	41.3	81.6	59.2
	WB	73.0	63.9	65.7	54.2	42.7	73.4	57.5
sapena								
	BC	48.7	58.8	64.6	50.8	39.4	70.4	54.3
	BN	47.1	60.0	69.1	57.4	45.0	74.3	58.0
	MZ	35.3	59.2	72.3	60.4	48.2	75.0	59.9
	NW	35.2	57.9	69.7	55.3	41.9	73.8	56.5
	TC	60.4	64.3	63.3	48.3	35.1	68.8	54.2
	WB	46.3	60.1	62.5	49.1	37.4	67.4	53.3
chang								
	BC	65.5	56.4	67.1	51.5	39.8	71.6	54.4
	BN	66.6	57.4	69.1	56.0	45.6	70.5	57.4
	MZ	61.6	52.7	71.3	57.6	46.4	72.9	56.8
	NW	61.0	53.3	69.1	54.1	42.1	71.9	54.8
	TC	72.2	68.5	71.4	59.6	37.7	81.7	59.2
	WB	66.4	59.7	66.7	52.7	39.4	74.7	55.3
nugues								
	BC	71.4	59.2	62.4	48.2	37.2	68.4	52.9
	BN	70.0	58.5	67.4	54.5	43.1	73.1	56.3
	MZ	65.4	53.6	68.6	54.2	42.2	70.1	54.8
	NW	61.8	51.9	67.0	51.3	39.2	69.4	52.7
	TC	77.2	69.2	63.9	53.0	37.9	72.2	57.0
	WB	72.9	64.2	63.4	51.1	38.5	74.3	55.4
santos								
	BC	66.6	57.2	64.8	48.5	37.2	68.6	53.0
	BN	66.9	57.3	66.9	52.3	41.0	71.8	55.1
	MZ	62.7	51.0	65.9	48.9	37.8	64.5	51.6
	NW	58.4	49.5	66.2	48.1	37.4	66.9	51.0
	TC	74.2	66.9	65.9	52.5	35.5	72.5	56.1
	WB	70.4	63.2	63.4	49.5	38.2	70.3	55.0
song								
	BC	68.9	61.4	61.0	44.1	34.3	59.5	52.2
	BN	66.2	58.4	64.8	49.0	38.2	65.2	53.8
	MZ	63.7	53.4	65.5	49.9	39.0	63.4	52.6
	NW	62.4	53.6	64.3	48.0	37.2	62.7	51.7
	TC	76.9	74.4	62.0	43.3	33.2	58.1	56.5
	WB	70.0	63.0	60.1	43.3	31.8	60.8	51.6
stoyanov								
	BC	69.5	59.1	57.6	43.5	34.0	58.7	50.2
	BN	69.2	59.1	65.4	50.4	40.0	65.5	54.8
	MZ	66.7	55.1	65.5	51.0	39.9	63.7	53.5
	NW	61.8	52.0	63.3	46.2	36.1	62.0	50.5
	TC	72.6	66.6	57.6	42.3	31.0	57.6	51.7
	WB	71.5	63.9	58.3	44.8	33.1	61.1	51.8
sobha								
	BC	68.3	51.7	61.4	47.8	40.4	62.9	51.2
	BN	66.5	51.9	66.5	53.7	45.5	66.3	54.6
	MZ	68.8	54.9	70.3	58.9	49.3	69.8	58.1
	NW	55.1	43.1	65.8	48.6	39.0	64.9	49.3
	TC	71.5	55.1	57.5	44.2	36.7	60.5	49.7
	WB	70.5	55.7	59.2	46.6	39.8	62.6	51.6
kobdani								
	BC	63.2	56.3	65.8	40.6	32.4	61.9	51.5
	BN	63.5	55.7	68.5	46.9	37.5	64.6	53.9
	MZ	57.5	52.2	69.8	45.7	36.4	61.7	52.8
	NW	52.2	41.7	64.4	43.2	33.7	62.6	46.6
	TC	67.7	60.2	65.3	36.6	28.5	57.6	51.3
	WB	68.7	62.8	62.4	42.5	32.9	64.0	52.7

		MD F	MUC F	BCUB F	C_m F	C_e F	BLANC F	O F
zhou	GENRE							
	BC	64.1	49.5	62.1	45.3	38.8	61.8	50.1
	BN	60.8	45.9	64.4	49.5	41.2	66.8	50.5
	MZ	58.8	44.4	66.9	50.1	41.8	64.6	51.0
	NW	57.7	44.8	65.7	48.7	40.3	63.1	50.2
	TC	69.2	58.1	60.8	43.1	35.7	62.6	51.5
	WB	67.4	55.4	62.8	47.9	39.2	69.1	52.5
charton								
	BC	65.8	53.1	59.1	44.6	35.2	64.4	49.1
	BN	65.5	52.0	64.0	50.0	39.6	65.9	51.9
	MZ	61.7	46.3	64.6	49.7	39.9	64.1	50.3
	NW	57.6	44.6	64.5	48.2	37.7	67.0	48.9
	TC	73.1	66.8	56.2	42.8	29.9	58.1	51.0
	WB	67.6	57.6	59.3	45.1	33.3	66.6	50.0
yang								
	BC	65.7	53.8	62.3	46.8	35.0	67.5	50.3
	BN	66.0	53.1	63.8	49.1	40.0	63.1	52.3
	MZ	58.8	43.9	59.7	42.6	32.8	55.5	45.5
	NW	57.2	44.7	62.9	45.3	35.0	62.7	47.6
	TC	74.2	66.8	66.3	55.3	36.0	76.1	56.4
	WB	67.6	57.6	57.0	42.6	32.1	60.1	48.9
hao								
	BC	68.9	58.7	58.9	44.8	31.7	64.9	49.8
	BN	62.0	51.1	63.0	46.2	35.5	64.1	49.9
	MZ	60.3	46.7	61.5	46.3	34.3	61.9	47.5
	NW	57.2	47.7	63.3	45.5	32.9	66.0	48.0
	TC	67.9	60.4	58.8	44.7	30.3	68.3	49.8
	WB	71.4	61.8	55.7	42.6	30.0	64.4	49.2
xinxin								
	BC	64.8	47.8	60.2	43.9	35.5	65.1	47.9
	BN	61.5	44.7	63.2	47.0	38.9	65.8	48.9
	MZ	54.6	35.5	64.5	45.7	37.7	61.0	45.9
	NW	54.3	39.5	64.0	45.0	37.5	61.1	47.0
	TC	74.2	62.0	57.9	45.4	33.4	66.5	51.1
	WB	66.9	52.6	58.5	42.2	35.9	63.4	49.0
zhang								
	BC	65.8	50.6	61.1	45.3	35.5	67.3	49.1
	BN	56.3	43.9	61.0	45.8	35.8	66.8	46.9
	MZ	57.1	35.1	62.2	44.4	36.1	59.4	44.5
	NW	49.9	37.8	61.8	43.2	35.2	59.8	44.9
	TC	75.4	65.9	60.2	46.0	32.1	67.1	52.7
	WB	69.2	55.4	57.4	42.5	34.6	64.7	49.1
kummerfield								
	BC	66.4	41.5	55.6	41.7	36.2	57.9	44.4
	BN	68.3	48.2	63.4	51.7	44.7	61.6	52.1
	MZ	58.0	39.9	65.8	51.0	43.4	64.1	49.7
	NW	55.2	41.3	64.7	46.8	37.0	63.5	47.6
	TC	61.8	34.5	51.5	34.7	30.0	54.1	38.7
	WB	68.2	48.1	56.0	44.4	38.6	59.6	47.6
zhekova								
	BC	50.5	23.8	60.6	39.4	35.1	53.4	39.8
	BN	51.2	26.0	62.4	42.5	37.5	54.3	42.0
	MZ	44.0	22.6	63.4	43.3	37.3	56.0	41.1
	NW	39.7	19.4	62.8	41.0	35.8	53.7	39.3
	TC	59.4	31.6	58.2	37.7	33.6	54.1	41.1
	WB	54.1	27.8	58.7	38.5	34.7	53.0	40.4
irwin								
	BC	23.5	16.1	46.0	29.4	23.6	49.8	28.6
	BN	24.9	20.0	49.7	34.2	27.1	52.9	32.3
	MZ	23.2	17.9	55.9	36.2	28.5	53.0	34.1
	NW	27.5	21.6	56.4	33.9	27.3	52.6	35.1
	TC	28.0	19.3	38.2	24.5	18.7	49.0	25.4
	WB	33.6	24.8	47.6	29.7	23.0	50.2	31.8

Table 20: Detailed look at the performance per *genre* for the *official, closed* track using automatic performance. MD represents MENTION DETECTION; BCUB represents B-CUBED; C_m represents CEAF$_m$; C_e represents CEAF$_e$ and O represents the OFFICIAL score.

res were treated here with perfect speech recognition accuracy and perfect speaker turn information. Under more realistic application conditions, the spread in performance between genres might be greater.

		MD F	MUC F	BCUB F	C_m F	C_e F	BLANC F	O F
lee	GENRE							
	BC	72.7	61.7	67.0	54.5	43.6	72.7	57.4
	BN	72.0	60.6	69.4	57.9	48.1	70.3	59.3
	MZ	69.9	58.4	72.1	61.2	50.1	75.2	60.2
	NW	65.3	55.8	70.0	56.7	44.9	71.7	56.9
	TC	76.6	68.4	70.4	59.6	40.8	82.1	59.9
	WB	73.8	65.5	66.2	54.5	42.1	74.2	57.9
cai								
	BC	69.7	59.1	66.0	50.5	39.9	69.2	55.0
	BN	68.6	57.6	67.8	55.4	45.5	68.2	56.9
	MZ	64.0	51.1	69.5	55.9	45.6	71.2	55.4
	NW	60.3	49.9	67.8	52.7	41.2	69.1	53.0
	TC	75.6	70.5	72.2	59.6	38.0	80.3	60.2
	WB	71.7	63.9	65.0	51.8	39.8	72.8	56.2
uryupina								
	BC	70.2	58.3	62.7	48.7	38.0	68.7	53.0
	BN	69.0	57.6	66.8	53.6	43.1	69.2	55.8
	MZ	65.7	52.4	68.3	54.3	43.6	68.8	54.8
	NW	62.6	52.1	68.3	53.2	41.2	71.3	53.9
	TC	75.7	67.1	61.0	50.7	34.6	67.1	54.2
	WB	72.0	61.7	60.9	48.8	38.3	67.6	53.6
klenner								
	BC	63.2	50.3	63.4	48.2	38.9	66.8	50.8
	BN	63.1	48.6	65.0	51.0	42.6	66.0	52.1
	MZ	59.1	43.7	67.1	52.9	45.3	65.0	52.0
	NW	55.3	41.3	65.0	48.0	39.6	64.5	48.7
	TC	73.9	64.9	67.9	56.4	39.0	78.0	57.3
	WB	66.8	58.1	64.0	50.1	39.6	72.7	53.9
irwin								
	BC	36.6	27.6	50.9	32.0	25.5	50.2	34.7
	BN	30.8	24.6	51.9	36.4	28.6	54.8	35.0
	MZ	26.1	20.0	57.3	37.6	29.4	54.3	35.6
	NW	32.3	24.7	58.4	34.7	27.9	51.1	37.0
	TC	46.4	34.3	44.6	29.4	21.9	51.7	33.6
	WB	41.7	32.9	50.5	32.9	25.1	53.2	36.2

Table 21: Detailed look at the performance per *genre* for the *official, open* track using predicted information. MD represents MENTION DETECTION; BCUB represents B-CUBED; C_m represents CEAF$_m$; C_e represents CEAF$_e$ and O represents the OFFICIAL score.

6 Approaches

Tables 22 and 23 summarize the approaches of the participating systems along with some of the important dimensions.

Most of the systems broke the problem into two phases, first identifying the potential mentions in the text and then linking the mentions to form coreference chains. Most participants also used rule-based approaches for mention detection, though two did use trained models. While trained morels seem able to better balance precision and recall, and thus to achieve a higher F-score on the mention task itself, their recall tends to be quite a bit lower than that achievable by rule-based systems designed to favor recall. This impacts coreference scores because the full coreference system has no way to recover if the mention detection stage misses a potentially anaphoric mention.

Only one of the participating systems *cai* attempted to do joint mention detection and coreference resolution. While it did not happen to be among the top-performing systems, the difference in performance could be due to the richer features used by other systems rather than to the use of a joint model.

Most systems represented the markable mentions internally in terms of the parse tree NP constituent span, but some systems used shared attribute models, where the attributes of the merged entity are determined collectively by heuristically merging the attribute types and values of the different constituent mentions.

Various types of trained models were used for predicting coreference. It is interesting to note that some of the systems, including the best-performing one, used a completely rule-based approach even for this component.

Most participants appear not to have focused much on eventive coreference, those coreference chains that build off verbs in the data. This usually meant that mentions that should have linked to the eventive verb were instead linked in with some other entity. Participants may have chosen not to focus on events because they pose unique challenges while making up only a small portion of the data. Roughly 91% of mentions in the data are NPs and pronouns.

In the systems that used trained models, many systems used the approach described in Soon et al. (2001) for selecting the positive and negative training examples, while others used some of the alternative approaches that have been introduced in the research literature more recently. Many of the trained systems also were able to improve their performance by using feature selection, though things varied some depending on the example selection strategy and the classifier used. Almost half of the trained systems used the feature selection strategy from Soon et al. (2001) and found it beneficial. It is not clear whether the other systems did not explore this path, or whether it just did not prove as useful in their case.

7 Conclusions

In this paper we described the anaphoric coreference information and other layers of annotation in the

	Task	Syntax	Learning Framework	Markable Identification	Markable	Verb	Feature Selection	# Features	Training
lee	C+O	P	Rule-based	Rules to exclude Copular construction, Appositives, Pleonastic *it*, etc.	Feature dependent with shared attributes	×	×		—
sapena	C	P	Decision Tree + Relaxation Labeling	NP (maximal span) + PRP + NE + Capitalized noun heuristic	Full phrase	×	×		Train + Dev
chang	C	P	Learning Based Java	NP, NE, PRP, PRP$	Full phrase	×	×		Train + Dev
cai	O	P	Compute hyperedge weights on 30% of training data	NP, PRP, PRP$, Base phrase chunks, Pleonastic *it* filter	Full phrase	×	×		—
nugues	C	D	Logistic Regression (LIBLINEAR)	NP, PRP$ and sequence of NNP(s) in post processing using ALIAS and STRINGMATCH	Head word	×	Forward + Backward starting from Soon feature set	24	Train + Dev
uryupina	O	P	Decision Tree. Different classifiers for Pronominal and non-Pronominal mentions	NP, NE, PRP, PRP$, and rules to exclude some specific cases	Full phrase	×	Multi-Objective Optimization on three splits. NSGA-II	46	Train + Dev
santos	C	P	ETL (Entropy guided Transformational Learning) committee and Random Forest (WEKA)	All NP and all pronouns and PER, ORG, GPE in NP	Full phrase	×	Inherent to the classifiers		Train + Dev
song	C	P	MaxEnt (OpenNLP)	Mention detection classifier	Full phrase	×	Same feature set, but per classifier	40	Train
stoyanov	C	P	Averaged perceptron	NE and possessives in addition to ACE based system	Full phrase	×	×	76	—
sobha	C	P	CRF for non-pronominal and salience factor for pronominal resolution	Machine learned pleonastic *it*, plus NP, PRP, PRP$ and NE	Minimal (Chunk/NE) and Maximum span	×	×		Train
klenner	O	D	Rule-based. Salience measure using dependencies generated from training data	NP, NE, PRP, PRP$	Shared attributed/transitivity by using a virtual prototype	×	×		—
kobdani	C	P	Decision Tree	NP (no mention of PRP$)	Start word, End word and Head of NP	×	Information gain ratio		Train
zhou	C	P	SVM tree kernel using BC portion of the data	Rule-based; Five rules: PRP$, PRP, NE, smallest NP subsuming NE and DET+NP	Full phrase	×	×	17	Train + Dev
charton	C	P	Multi-layer perceptron	Rules based on POS, NE and filter out pleonastic *it* using rule-based filter	Full phrase	×	×	22	Train
yang	C	P	MaxEnt (MALLET)	NP, PRP, PRP$, pre-modifiers and verbs	Full phrase	√	×	40	Train + Dev
hao	C	P	MaxEnt	NP, PRP, PRP$, VBD	full phrase	√	×		Train + Dev
xinxin	C	P	ILP/Information gain	NP, PRP, PRP$	Full phrase	×	Information gain ratio	65	—
zhang	C	P	SVM	IOB classification	Full phrase	×	×		—
kummerfield	C	P	Unsupervised generative model	NP, PRP, PRP$ with maximal span	Full phrase	×	×		—
zhekova	C	P	TIMBL memory based learner	NP, Proper nouns, PRP, PRP$, plus verb with predicate lemma	Head word	√	×		Train + Dev
irwin	C+O	P	Classification-based ranker	NP, PRP, PRP$	Shared attributes	×	×		—

Table 22: Participating system profiles – Part I. In the Task column, C/O represents whether the system participated in the *closed*, *open* or both tracks. In the Syntax column, a P represents that the systems used a phrase structure grammar representation of syntax, whereas a D represents that they used a dependency representation.

	Positive Training Examples	Negative Training Examples	Decoding	Parse Configuration
lee	—	—	Multi-pass Sieves	
sapena	All mention pairs and longer of nested mentions with common head kept	Mention pairs with less than threshold (5) number of different attribute values are considered (22% out of 99% original are discarded)	Iterative	1-best
chang	Closest antecedent	All preceding mentions in a union of of *gold* and *predicted* mentions. Mentions where the first is pronoun and other not are not considered	Best link and All links strategy; with and without constraints – Best link without constraints was selected for the official run	
cai	Weights are trained on part of the training data		Recursive 2-way Spectral clustering (Agarwal, 2005)	
nugues	Closest Antecedent (Soon, 2001)	Negative examples in between anaphor and closest antecedent (Soon, 2001)	Closest-first clustering for pronouns and Best-first clustering for non-pronouns	1-best
uryupina	Closest antecedent (Soon, 2001)	Negative examples in between anaphor and closest antecedent (Soon, 2001)	mention pair model without ranking as in Soon 2001	
santos	Extended version of Soon (2001) where in addition to their strategy, positive and negative examples from mentions in the sentence of the closest preceding antecedent are considered		Limited number of preceding mentions 60 for automatic and 40 given gold boundaries; Aggressive-merge clustering (Mccarthy and Lenhert, 1995)	
song	Pre-cluster pair models separate for each pair NP-NP, NP-PRP and PRP-PRP		Pre-clusters, with singleton pronoun pre-clusters, and use closest-first clustering. Different link models based on the type of linking mentions – NP-PRP, PRP-PRP and NP-NP	
stoyanov	Smart Pair Generation (SmartPG) where the type of antecedent is determined by the type of anaphor using a set of rules		Single-link clustering by computing transitive closure between pairwise positives.	
sobha	Closest antecedent (Soon, 2001)	Negative examples in between anaphor and closest antecedent (Soon, 2001)	Pronominal: all preceding NPs in the sentence and preceding 4 sentences	
klenner	—	—	Incremental entity creation	
kobdani	Closest antecedent (Soon, 2001)	Negative examples in between anaphor and closest antecedent (Soon, 2001)	Best-first clustering. Threshold of 100 words used for long documents	1-best
zhou	Closest antecedent (Soon, 2001)	Negative examples in between anaphor and closest antecedent (Soon, 2001)	—	
charton	From the end of the document, until an antecedent is found, or 10 mentions	Negative examples in between anaphor and closest antecedent	MLP with score of 0.5 used for linking and 10 mentions	
yang	Closest antecedent (Soon, 2001)	Negative examples in between anaphor and closest antecedent (Soon, 2001)	Maximum 23 sentences to the left; Constrained clustering	
hao	Closest antecedent (Soon, 2001)	Negative examples in between anaphor and closest antecedent (Soon, 2001)	Beam search (Luo, 2004)	Packed forest
xinxin	Closest antecedent (Soon, 2001)	Negative examples in between anaphor and closest antecedent (Soon, 2001)	Best-first clustering followed by ILP optimization	
zhang	Closest antecedent (Soon, 2001)	Negative examples in between anaphor and closest antecedent (Soon, 2001)	Window of 100 markables	
kummerfield	—	—	Pre- and post- resolution filters	Given + Berkeley parser parses; parses without NMLs improved performance slightly; re-trained Berkeley parser
zhekova	Examples in the past three sentences		From last possible mention in document	
irwin	Cluster query with NULL cluster for discourse new mentions		Cluster-ranking approach (rahman, 2009)	

Table 23: Participating system profiles – Part II. This focuses on the way positive and negative examples were generated and the decoding strategy used.

OntoNotes corpus, and presented the results from an evaluation on learning such unrestricted entities and events in text. The following represent our conclusions on reviewing the results:

- Perhaps the most surprising finding was that the best-performing system (*lee*) was completely rule-based, rather than trained. This suggests that their rule-based approach was able to do a more effective job of combining the multiple sources of evidence than the trained systems. The features for coreference prediction are certainly more complex than for many other language processing tasks, which makes it more challenging to generate effective feature combinations. The rule-based approach used by the best-performing system seemed to benefit from a heuristic that captured the most confident links before considering less confident ones, and also made use of the information in the guidelines in a slightly more refined manner than other systems. They also included appositives and copular constructions in their calculations. Although OntoNotes does not count those as instances of IDENT coreference, using that information may have helped their system discover additional useful links.

- It is interesting to note that the developers of the *lee* system also did the experiment of running their system using gold standard information on the individual layers, rather than automatic model predictions. The somewhat surprising result was that using perfect information for the other layers did not end up improving coreference performance much, if at all. It is not clear whether this means that: i) Automatic predictors for the individual layers are accurate enough already; ii) Information captured by those supplementary layers actually does not provide much leverage for resolving coreference; or iii) researchers have yet have found an effective way of capturing and utilizing the extra information provided by these layers.

- It does seem that collecting information about an entity by merging information across the various attributes of the mentions that comprise it can be useful, though not all systems that attempted this achieved a benefit.

- System performance did not seem to vary as much across the different genres as is normally the case with language processing tasks, which could suggest that coreference is relatively genre insensitive, or it is possible that scores are two low for the difference to be apparent. Comparisons are difficult, however, because the spoken genres were treated here with perfect speech recognition accuracy and perfect speaker turn information. Under more realistic application conditions, the spread in performance between genres might be greater.

- It is noteworthy that systems did not seem to attempt the kind of joint inference that could make use of the full potential of various layers available in OntoNotes, but this could well have been owing to the limited time available for the shared task.

- We had expected to see more attention paid to event coreference, which is a novel feature in this data, but again, given the time constraints and given that events represent only a small portion of the total, it is not surprising that most systems chose not to focus on it.

- Scoring coreference seems to remain a significant challenge. There does not seem to be an objective way to establish one metric in preference to another in the absence of a specific application. On the other hand, the system rankings do not seem terribly sensitive to the particular metric chosen. It is interesting that both versions of the CEAF metric – which tries to capture the goodness of the entities in the output – seem much lower than the other metric, though it is not clear whether that means that our systems are doing a poor job of creating coherent entities or whether that metric is just especially harsh.

Finally, it is interesting to note that the problem of coreference does not seem to be following the same kind of learning curve that we are used to with other problems of this sort. While performance has improved somewhat, it is not clear how far we will be able to go given the strategies at hand, or whether new techniques will be needed to capture additional information from the texts or from world knowledge. We hope that this corpus and task will provide a useful resource for continued experimentation to help resolve this issue.

Acknowledgments

We gratefully acknowledge the support of the Defense Advanced Research Projects Agency

(DARPA/IPTO) under the GALE program, DARPA/CMO Contract No. HR0011-06-C-0022. We would like to thank all the participants. Without their hard work, patience and perseverance this evaluation would not have been a success. We would also like to thank the Linguistic Data Consortium for making the OntoNotes 4.0 corpus freely and timely available to the participants. Emili Sapena, who graciously allowed the use of his scorer implementation, and made available enhancements and immediately fixed issues that were uncovered during the evaluation. Finally, we offer our special thanks to Lluís Màrquez and Joakim Nivre for their wonderful support and guidance without which this task would not have been successful.

References

Olga Babko-Malaya, Ann Bies, Ann Taylor, Szuting Yi, Martha Palmer, Mitch Marcus, Seth Kulick, and Libin Shen. 2006. Issues in synchronizing the English treebank and propbank. In *Workshop on Frontiers in Linguistically Annotated Corpora 2006*, July.

Amit Bagga and Breck Baldwin. 1998. Algorithms for Scoring Coreference Chains. In *The First International Conference on Language Resources and Evaluation Workshop on Linguistics Coreference*, pages 563–566.

Shane Bergsma and Dekang Lin. 2006. Bootstrapping path-based pronoun resolution. In *Proceedings of the 21st International Conference on Computational Linguistics and 44th Annual Meeting of the Association for Computational Linguistics*, pages 33–40, Sydney, Australia, July.

Jie Cai and Michael Strube. 2010. Evaluation metrics for end-to-end coreference resolution systems. In *Proceedings of the 11th Annual Meeting of the Special Interest Group on Discourse and Dialogue*, SIGDIAL '10, pages 28–36.

Eugene Charniak and Mark Johnson. 2001. Edit detection and parsing for transcribed speech. In *Proceedings of the Second Meeting of North American Chapter of the Association of Computational Linguistics*, June.

Eugene Charniak and Mark Johnson. 2005. Coarse-to-fine n-best parsing and maxent discriminative reranking. In *Proceedings of the 43rd Annual Meeting of the Association for Computational Linguistics (ACL)*, Ann Arbor, MI, June.

Nancy Chinchor and Beth Sundheim. 2003. Message understanding conference (MUC) 6. In *LDC2003T13*.

Nancy Chinchor. 2001. Message understanding conference (MUC) 7. In *LDC2001T02*.

Aron Culotta, Michael Wick, Robert Hall, and Andrew McCallum. 2007. First-order probabilistic models for coreference resolution. In *HLT/NAACL*, pages 81–88.

Pascal Denis and Jason Baldridge. 2007. Joint determination of anaphoricity and coreference resolution using integer programming. In *Proceedings of HLT/NAACL*.

Pascal Denis and Jason Baldridge. 2009. Global joint models for coreference resolution and named entity classification. *Procesamiento del Lenguaje Natural*, (42):87–96.

Charles Fillmore, Christopher Johnson, and Miriam R. L. Petruck. 2003. Background to framenet. *International Journal of Lexicography*, 16(3).

G. G. Doddington, A. Mitchell, M. Przybocki, L. Ramshaw, S. Strassell, and R. Weischedel. 2000. The automatic content extraction (ACE) program-tasks, data, and evaluation. In *Proceedings of LREC*.

Aria Haghighi and Dan Klein. 2010. Coreference resolution in a modular, entity-centered model. In *Human Language Technologies: The 2010 Annual Conference of the North American Chapter of the Association for Computational Linguistics*, pages 385–393, Los Angeles, California, June.

Jan Hajič, Massimiliano Ciaramita, Richard Johansson, Daisuke Kawahara, Maria Antònia Martí, Lluís Màrquez, Adam Meyers, Joakim Nivre, Sebastian Padó, Jan Štěpánek, Pavel Straňák, Mihai Surdeanu, Nianwen Xue, and Yi Zhang. 2009. The CoNLL-2009 shared task: Syntactic and semantic dependencies in multiple languages. In *Proceedings of the Thirteenth Conference on Computational Natural Language Learning (CoNLL 2009): Shared Task*, pages 1–18, Boulder, Colorado, June.

Sanda M. Harabagiu, Razvan C. Bunescu, and Steven J. Maiorano. 2001. Text and knowledge mining for coreference resolution. In *NAACL*.

L. Hirschman and N. Chinchor. 1997. Coreference task definition (v3.0, 13 jul 97). In *Proceedings of the Seventh Message Understanding Conference*.

Eduard Hovy, Mitchell Marcus, Martha Palmer, Lance Ramshaw, and Ralph Weischedel. 2006. OntoNotes: The 90% solution. In *Proceedings of HLT/NAACL*, pages 57–60, New York City, USA, June. Association for Computational Linguistics.

Karin Kipper, Anna Korhonen, Neville Ryant, and Martha Palmer. 2000. A large-scale classification of english verbs. *Language Resources and Evaluation*, 42(1):21 – 40.

Xiaoqiang Luo. 2005. On coreference resolution performance metrics. In *Proceedings of Human Language Technology Conference and Conference on Empirical*

Methods in Natural Language Processing, pages 25–32, Vancouver, British Columbia, Canada, October.

Mitchell P. Marcus, Beatrice Santorini, and Mary Ann Marcinkiewicz. 1993. Building a large annotated corpus of English: The Penn treebank. *Computational Linguistics*, 19(2):313–330, June.

Andrew McCallum and Ben Wellner. 2004. Conditional models of identity uncertainty with application to noun coreference. In *Advances in Neural Information Processing Systems (NIPS)*.

Joseph McCarthy and Wendy Lehnert. 1995. Using decision trees for coreference resolution. In *Proceedings of the Fourteenth International Conference on Artificial Intelligence*, pages 1050–1055.

Thomas S. Morton. 2000. Coreference for nlp applications. In *Proceedings of the 38th Annual Meeting of the Association for Computational Linguistics*, October.

Vincent Ng. 2007. Shallow semantics for coreference resolution. In *Proceedings of the IJCAI*.

Vincent Ng. 2010. Supervised noun phrase coreference research: The first fifteen years. In *Proceedings of the 48th Annual Meeting of the Association for Computational Linguistics*, pages 1396–1411, Uppsala, Sweden, July.

Martha Palmer, Daniel Gildea, and Paul Kingsbury. 2005. The Proposition Bank: An annotated corpus of semantic roles. *Computational Linguistics*, 31(1):71–106.

Martha Palmer, Hoa Trang Dang, and Christiane Fellbaum. 2007. Making fine-grained and coarse-grained sense distinctions, both manually and automatically.

R. Passonneau. 2004. Computing reliability for coreference annotation. In *Proceedings of LREC*.

Massimo Poesio and Ron Artstein. 2005. The reliability of anaphoric annotation, reconsidered: Taking ambiguity into account. In *Proceedings of the Workshop on Frontiers in Corpus Annotations II: Pie in the Sky*.

Massimo Poesio. 2004. The mate/gnome scheme for anaphoric annotation, revisited. In *Proceedings of SIGDIAL*.

Simone Paolo Ponzetto and Massimo Poesio. 2009. State-of-the-art nlp approaches to coreference resolution: Theory and practical recipes. In *Tutorial Abstracts of ACL-IJCNLP 2009*, page 6, Suntec, Singapore, August.

Simone Paolo Ponzetto and Michael Strube. 2005. Semantic role labeling for coreference resolution. In *Companion Volume of the Proceedings of the 11th Meeting of the European Chapter of the Association for Computational Linguistics*, pages 143–146, Trento, Italy, April.

Simone Paolo Ponzetto and Michael Strube. 2006. Exploiting semantic role labeling, WordNet and Wikipedia for coreference resolution. In *Proceedings of the HLT/NAACL*, pages 192–199, New York City, N.Y., June.

Sameer Pradhan, Kadri Hacioglu, Valerie Krugler, Wayne Ward, James Martin, and Dan Jurafsky. 2005. Support vector learning for semantic argument classification. *Machine Learning Journal*, 60(1):11–39.

Sameer Pradhan, Eduard Hovy, Mitchell Marcus, Martha Palmer, Lance Ramshaw, and Ralph Weischedel. 2007a. OntoNotes: A Unified Relational Semantic Representation. *International Journal of Semantic Computing*, 1(4):405–419.

Sameer Pradhan, Lance Ramshaw, Ralph Weischedel, Jessica MacBride, and Linnea Micciulla. 2007b. Unrestricted Coreference: Indentifying Entities and Events in OntoNotes. In *in Proceedings of the IEEE International Conference on Semantic Computing (ICSC)*, September 17-19.

Altaf Rahman and Vincent Ng. 2009. Supervised models for coreference resolution. In *Proceedings of the 2009 Conference on Empirical Methods in Natural Language Processing*, pages 968–977, Singapore, August. Association for Computational Linguistics.

W. M. Rand. 1971. Objective criteria for the evaluation of clustering methods. *Journal of the American Statistical Association*, 66(336).

Marta Recasens and Eduard Hovy. 2011. Blanc: Implementing the rand index for coreference evaluation. *Natural Language Engineering*.

Marta Recasens, Lluís Màrquez, Emili Sapena, M. Antònia Martí, Mariona Taulé, Véronique Hoste, Massimo Poesio, and Yannick Versley. 2010. Semeval-2010 task 1: Coreference resolution in multiple languages. In *Proceedings of the 5th International Workshop on Semantic Evaluation*, pages 1–8, Uppsala, Sweden, July.

W. Soon, H. Ng, and D. Lim. 2001. A machine learning approach to coreference resolution of noun phrase. *Computational Linguistics*, 27(4):521–544.

Veselin Stoyanov, Nathan Gilbert, Claire Cardie, and Ellen Riloff. 2009. Conundrums in noun phrase coreference resolution: Making sense of the state-of-the-art. In *Proceedings of the Joint Conference of the 47th Annual Meeting of the ACL and the 4th International Joint Conference on Natural Language Processing of the AFNLP*, pages 656–664, Suntec, Singapore, August. Association for Computational Linguistics.

Mihai Surdeanu, Richard Johansson, Adam Meyers, Lluís Màrquez, and Joakim Nivre. 2008. The CoNLL 2008 shared task on joint parsing of syntactic and semantic dependencies. In *CoNLL 2008: Proceedings of the Twelfth Conference on Computational Natural Language Learning*, pages 159–177, Manchester, England, August.

Yannick Versley. 2007. Antecedent selection techniques for high-recall coreference resolution. In *Proceedings of the 2007 Joint Conference on Empirical Methods in Natural Language Processing and Computational Natural Language Learning (EMNLP-CoNLL).*

M. Vilain, J. Burger, J. Aberdeen, D. Connolly, and L. Hirschman. 1995. A model theoretic coreference scoring scheme. In *Proceedings of the Sixth Message Undersatnding Conference (MUC-6)*, pages 45–52.

Ralph Weischedel and Ada Brunstein. 2005. BBN pronoun coreference and entity type corpus LDC catalog no.: LDC2005T33. BBN Technologies.

Ralph Weischedel, Eduard Hovy, Martha Palmer, Mitch Marcus, Robert Belvin, Sameer Pradhan, Lance Ramshaw, and Nianwen Xue. 2011. OntoNotes: A Large Training Corpus for Enhanced Processing. In Joseph Olive, Caitlin Christianson, and John McCary, editors, *Handbook of Natural Language Processing and Machine Translation*. Springer.

Stanford's Multi-Pass Sieve Coreference Resolution System at the CoNLL-2011 Shared Task

Heeyoung Lee, Yves Peirsman, Angel Chang, Nathanael Chambers,
Mihai Surdeanu, Dan Jurafsky
Stanford NLP Group
Stanford University, Stanford, CA 94305
{heeyoung,peirsman,angelx,natec,mihais,jurafsky}@stanford.edu

Abstract

This paper details the coreference resolution system submitted by Stanford at the CoNLL-2011 shared task. Our system is a collection of deterministic coreference resolution models that incorporate lexical, syntactic, semantic, and discourse information. All these models use global document-level information by sharing mention attributes, such as gender and number, across mentions in the same cluster. We participated in both the open and closed tracks and submitted results using both predicted and gold mentions. Our system was ranked first in both tracks, with a score of 57.8 in the closed track and 58.3 in the open track.

1 Introduction

This paper describes the coreference resolution system used by Stanford at the CoNLL-2011 shared task (Pradhan et al., 2011). Our system extends the multi-pass sieve system of Raghunathan et al. (2010), which applies tiers of deterministic coreference models one at a time from highest to lowest precision. Each tier builds on the entity clusters constructed by previous models in the sieve, guaranteeing that stronger features are given precedence over weaker ones. Furthermore, this model propagates global information by sharing attributes (e.g., gender and number) across mentions in the same cluster.

We made three considerable extensions to the Raghunathan et al. (2010) model. First, we added five additional sieves, the majority of which address the semantic similarity between mentions, e.g., using WordNet distance, and shallow discourse understanding, e.g., linking speakers to compatible pronouns. Second, we incorporated a mention detection sieve at the beginning of the processing flow. This sieve filters our syntactic constituents unlikely to be mentions using a simple set of rules on top of the syntactic analysis of text. And lastly, we added a post-processing step, which guarantees that the output of our system is compatible with the shared task and OntoNotes specifications (Hovy et al., 2006; Pradhan et al., 2007).

Using this system, we participated in both the closed[1] and open[2] tracks, using both predicted and gold mentions. Using predicted mentions, our system had an overall score of 57.8 in the closed track and 58.3 in the open track. These were the top scores in both tracks. Using gold mentions, our system scored 60.7 in the closed track in 61.4 in the open track.

We describe the architecture of our entire system in Section 2. In Section 3 we show the results of several experiments, which compare the impact of the various features in our system, and analyze the performance drop as we switch from gold mentions and annotations (named entity mentions and parse trees) to predicted information. We also report in this section our official results in the testing partition.

[1]Only the provided data can be used, i.e., WordNet and gender gazetteer.

[2]Any external knowledge source can be used. We used additional animacy, gender, demonym, and country and states gazetteers.

Proceedings of the 15th Conference on Computational Natural Language Learning: Shared Task, pages 28–34,
Portland, Oregon, 23-24 June 2011.

2 System Architecture

Our system consists of three main stages: mention detection, followed by coreference resolution, and finally, post-processing. In the first stage, mentions are extracted and relevant information about mentions, e.g., gender and number, is prepared for the next step. The second stage implements the actual coreference resolution of the identified mentions. Sieves in this stage are sorted from highest to lowest precision. For example, the first sieve (i.e., highest precision) requires an exact string match between a mention and its antecedent, whereas the last one (i.e., lowest precision) implements pronominal coreference resolution. Post-processing is performed to adjust our output to the task specific constraints, e.g., removing singletons.

It is important to note that the first system stage, i.e., the mention detection sieve, favors recall heavily, whereas the second stage, which includes the actual coreference resolution sieves, is precision oriented. Our results show that this design lead to state-of-the-art performance despite the simplicity of the individual components. This strategy has been successfully used before for information extraction, e.g., in the BioNLP 2009 event extraction shared task (Kim et al., 2009), several of the top systems had a first high-recall component to identify event anchors, followed by high-precision classifiers, which identified event arguments and removed unlikely event candidates (Björne et al., 2009). In the coreference resolution space, several works have shown that applying a list of rules from highest to lowest precision is beneficial for coreference resolution (Baldwin, 1997; Raghunathan el al., 2010). However, we believe we are the first to show that this high-recall/high-precision strategy yields competitive results for the complete task of coreference resolution, i.e., including mention detection and both nominal and pronominal coreference.

2.1 Mention Detection Sieve

In our particular setup, the recall of the mention detection component is more important than its precision, because any missed mentions are guaranteed to affect the final score, but spurious mentions may not impact the overall score if they are left as singletons, which are discarded by our post-processing step. Therefore, our mention detection algorithm focuses on attaining high recall rather than high precision. We achieve our goal based on the list of sieves sorted by recall (from highest to lowest). Each sieve uses syntactic parse trees, identified named entity mentions, and a few manually written patterns based on heuristics and OntoNotes specifications (Hovy et al., 2006; Pradhan et al., 2007). In the first and highest recall sieve, we mark all noun phrase (NP), possessive pronoun, and named entity mentions in each sentence as candidate mentions. In the following sieves, we remove from this set all mentions that match any of the exclusion rules below:

1. We remove a mention if a larger mention with the same head word exists, e.g., we remove *The five insurance companies* in *The five insurance companies approved to be established this time.*

2. We discard numeric entities such as percents, money, cardinals, and quantities, e.g., 9%, $10,000, *Tens of thousands, 100 miles.*

3. We remove mentions with partitive or quantifier expressions, e.g., *a total of 177 projects.*

4. We remove pleonastic *it* pronouns, detected using a set of known expressions, e.g., *It is possible that.*

5. We discard adjectival forms of nations, e.g., *American.*

6. We remove stop words in a predetermined list of 8 words, e.g., *there, ltd., hmm.*

Note that the above rules extract both mentions in appositive and copulative relations, e.g., *[[Yongkang Zhou] , the general manager]* or *[Mr. Savoca] had been [a consultant. . .].* These relations are not annotated in the OntoNotes corpus, e.g., in the text *[[Yongkang Zhou] , the general manager]*, only the larger mention is annotated. However, appositive and copulative relations provide useful (and highly precise) information to our coreference sieves. For this reason, we keep these mentions as candidates, and remove them later during post-processing.

2.2 Mention Processing

Once mentions are extracted, we sort them by sentence number, and left-to-right breadth-first traversal order in syntactic trees in the same sentence (Hobbs, 1977). We select for resolution only the first mentions in each cluster,[3] for two reasons: (a) the first mention tends to be better defined (Fox, 1993), which provides a richer environment for feature extraction; and (b) it has fewer antecedent candidates, which means fewer opportunities to make a mistake. For example, given the following ordered list of mentions, $\{m_1^1, m_2^2, m_3^2, m_4^3, m_5^1, m_6^2\}$, where the subscript indicates textual order and the superscript indicates cluster id, our model will attempt to resolve only m_2^2 and m_4^3. Furthermore, we discard first mentions that start with indefinite pronouns (e.g., *some, other*) or indefinite articles (e.g., *a, an*) if they have no antecedents that have the exact same string extents.

For each selected mention m_i, all previous mentions $m_{i-1}, \ldots, m_1$ become antecedent candidates. All sieves traverse the candidate list until they find a coreferent antecedent according to their criteria or reach the end of the list. Crucially, when comparing two mentions, our approach uses information from the entire clusters that contain these mentions instead of using just information local to the corresponding mentions. Specifically, mentions in a cluster share their attributes (e.g., number, gender, animacy) between them so coreference decision are better informed. For example, if a cluster contains two mentions: *a group of students*, which is `singular`, and *five students*, which is `plural`, the `number` attribute of the entire cluster becomes `singular or plural`, which allows it to match other mentions that are both singular and plural. Please see (Raghunathan et al., 2010) for more details.

2.3 Coreference Resolution Sieves

2.3.1 Core System

The core of our coreference resolution system is an incremental extension of the system described in Raghunathan et al. (2010). Our core model includes two new sieves that address nominal mentions and are inserted based on their precision in a held-out corpus (see Table 1 for the complete list of sieves deployed in our system). Since these two sieves use simple lexical constraints without semantic information, we consider them part of the baseline model.

[3]We initialize the clusters as singletons and grow them progressively in each sieve.

Ordered sieves
1. **Mention Detection Sieve**
2. **Discourse Processing Sieve**
3. Exact String Match Sieve
4. **Relaxed String Match Sieve**
5. Precise Constructs Sieve (e.g., appositives)
6-8. Strict Head Matching Sieves A-C
9. **Proper Head Word Match Sieve**
10. **Alias Sieve**
11. Relaxed Head Matching Sieve
12. **Lexical Chain Sieve**
13. Pronouns Sieve

Table 1: The sieves in our system; sieves new to this paper are in bold.

Relaxed String Match: This sieve considers two nominal mentions as coreferent if the strings obtained by dropping the text following their head words are identical, e.g., *[Clinton]* and *[Clinton, whose term ends in January]*.

Proper Head Word Match: This sieve marks two mentions headed by proper nouns as coreferent if they have the same head word and satisfy the following constraints:

Not i-within-i - same as Raghunathan et al. (2010).

No location mismatches - the modifiers of two mentions cannot contain different location named entities, other proper nouns, or spatial modifiers. For example, *[Lebanon]* and *[southern Lebanon]* are not coreferent.

No numeric mismatches - the second mention cannot have a number that does not appear in the antecedent, e.g., *[people]* and *[around 200 people]* are not coreferent.

In addition to the above, a few more rules are added to get better performance for predicted mentions.

Pronoun distance - sentence distance between a pronoun and its antecedent cannot be larger than 3.

Bare plurals - bare plurals are generic and cannot have a coreferent antecedent.

2.3.2 Semantic-Similarity Sieves

We first extend the above system with two new sieves that exploit semantics from WordNet, Wikipedia infoboxes, and Freebase records, drawing on previous coreference work using these databases (Ng & Cardie, 2002; Daumé & Marcu, 2005; Ponzetto & Strube, 2006; Ng, 2007; Yang & Su,

2007; Bengston & Roth, 2008; Huang et al., 2009; inter alia). Since the input to a sieve is a collection of mention clusters built by the previous (more precise) sieves, we need to link mention clusters (rather than individual mentions) to records in these three knowledge bases. The following steps generate a query for these resources from a mention cluster.

First, we select the most representative mention in a cluster by preferring mentions headed by proper nouns to mentions headed by common nouns, and nominal mentions to pronominal ones. In case of ties, we select the longer string. For example, the mention selected from the cluster {*President George W. Bush, president, he*} is *President George W. Bush*. Second, if this mention returns nothing from the knowledge bases, we implement the following query relaxation algorithm: (a) remove the text following the mention head word; (b) select the lowest noun phrase (NP) in the parse tree that includes the mention head word; (c) use the longest proper noun (NNP*) sequence that ends with the head word; (d) select the head word. For example, the query *president Bill Clinton, whose term ends in January* is successively changed to *president Bill Clinton*, then *Bill Clinton*, and finally *Clinton*. If multiple records are returned, we keep the top two for Wikipedia and Freebase, and all synsets for WordNet.

Alias Sieve

This sieve addresses name aliases, which are detected as follows. Two mentions headed by proper nouns are marked as aliases (and stored in the same entity cluster) if they appear in the same Wikipedia infobox or Freebase record in either the 'name' or 'alias' field, or they appear in the same synset in WordNet. As an example, this sieve correctly detects *America Online* and *AOL* as aliases. We also tested the utility of Wikipedia categories, but found little gain over morpho-syntactic features.

Lexical Chain Sieve

This sieve marks two nominal mentions as coreferent if they are linked by a WordNet lexical chain that traverses hypernymy or synonymy relations. We use all synsets for each mention, but restrict it to mentions that are at most three sentences apart, and lexical chains of length at most four. This sieve correctly links *Britain* with *country*, and *plane* with *aircraft*.

To increase the precision of the above two sieves, we use additional constraints before two mentions can match: attribute agreement (number, gender, animacy, named entity labels), no i-within-i, no location or numeric mismatches (as in Section 2.3.1), and we do not use the abstract entity synset in WordNet, except in chains that include 'organization'.

2.3.3 Discourse Processing Sieve

This sieve matches speakers to compatible pronouns, using shallow discourse understanding to handle quotations and conversation transcripts. Although more complex discourse constraints have been proposed, it has been difficult to show improvements (Tetreault & Allen, 2003; 2004).

We begin by identifying *speakers* within text. In non-conversational text, we use a simple heuristic that searches for the subjects of reporting verbs (e.g., *say*) in the same sentence or neighboring sentences to a quotation. In conversational text, speaker information is provided in the dataset.

The extracted speakers then allow us to implement the following sieve heuristics:

- ⟨I⟩s[4] assigned to the same speaker are coreferent.
- ⟨you⟩s with the same speaker are coreferent.
- The speaker and ⟨I⟩s in her text are coreferent.

For example, *I*, *my*, and *she* in the following sentence are coreferent: *"[I] voted for [Nader] because [he] was most aligned with [my] values," [she] said.*

In addition to the above sieve, we impose speaker constraints on decisions made by subsequent sieves:

- The speaker and a mention which is not ⟨I⟩ in the speaker's utterance cannot be coreferent.
- Two ⟨I⟩s (or two ⟨you⟩s, or two ⟨we⟩s) assigned to different speakers cannot be coreferent.
- Two different person pronouns by the same speaker cannot be coreferent.
- Nominal mentions cannot be coreferent with ⟨I⟩, ⟨you⟩, or ⟨we⟩ in the same turn or quotation.
- In conversations, ⟨you⟩ can corefer only with the previous speaker.

For example, *[my]* and *[he]* are not coreferent in the above example (third constraint).

[4] We define ⟨I⟩ as *'I', 'my', 'me'*, or *'mine'*, ⟨we⟩ as first person plural pronouns, and ⟨you⟩ as second person pronouns.

Annotations	Coref	R	P	F1
Gold	Before	92.8	37.7	53.6
Gold	After	75.1	70.1	72.6
Not gold	Before	87.9	35.6	50.7
Not gold	After	71.7	68.4	70.0

Table 2: Performance of the mention detection component, before and after coreference resolution, with both gold and actual linguistic annotations.

2.4 Post Processing

To guarantee that the output of our system matches the shared task requirements and the OntoNotes annotation specification, we implement two post-processing steps:

- We discard singleton clusters.
- We discard the mention that appears later in text in appositive and copulative relations. For example, in the text *[[Yongkang Zhou] , the general manager]* or *[Mr. Savoca] had been [a consultant...]*, the mentions *Yongkang Zhou* and *a consultant...* are removed in this stage.

3 Results and Discussion

Table 2 shows the performance of our mention detection algorithm. We show results before and after coreference resolution and post-processing (when singleton mentions are removed). We also list results with gold and predicted linguistic annotations (i.e., syntactic parses and named entity recognition). The table shows that the recall of our approach is 92.8% (if gold annotations are used) or 87.9% (with predicted annotations). In both cases, precision is low because our algorithm generates many spurious mentions due to its local nature. However, as the table indicates, many of these mentions are removed during post-processing, because they are assigned to singleton clusters during coreference resolution. The two main causes for our recall errors are lack of recognition of event mentions (e.g., verbal mentions such as *growing*) and parsing errors. Parsing errors often introduce incorrect mention boundaries, which yield both recall and precision errors. For example, our system generates the predicted mention, *the working meeting of the "863 Program" today*, for the gold mention *the working meeting of the "863 Program"*. Due to this boundary mismatch, all mentions found to be coreferent with this predicted mention are counted as precision errors, and all mentions in the same coreference cluster with the gold mention are counted as recall errors.

Table 3 lists the results of our end-to-end system on the development partition. "External Resources", which were used only in the open track, includes: (a) a hand-built list of genders of first names that we created, incorporating frequent names from census lists and other sources, (b) an animacy list (Ji and Lin, 2009), (c) a country and state gazetteer, and (d) a demonym list. "Discourse" stands for the sieve introduced in Section 2.3.3. "Semantics" stands for the sieves presented in Section 2.3.2. The table shows that the discourse sieve yields an improvement of almost 2 points to the overall score (row 1 versus 3), and external resources contribute 0.5 points. On the other hand, the semantic sieves do not help (row 3 versus 4). The latter result contradicts our initial experiments, where we measured a minor improvement when these sieves were enabled and gold mentions were used. Our hypothesis is that, when predicted mentions are used, the semantic sieves are more likely to link spurious mentions to existing clusters, thus introducing precision errors. This suggests that a different tuning of the sieve parameters is required for the predicted mention scenario. For this reason, we did not use the semantic sieves for our submission. Hence, rows 2 and 3 in the table show the performance of our official submission in the development set, in the closed and open tracks respectively.

The last three rows in Table 3 give insight on the impact of gold information. This analysis indicates that using gold linguistic annotation yields an improvement of only 2 points. This implies that the quality of current linguistic processors is sufficient for the task of coreference resolution. On the other hand, using gold mentions raises the overall score by 15 points. This clearly indicates that pipeline architectures where mentions are identified first are inadequate for this task, and that coreference resolution might benefit from the joint modeling of mentions and coreference chains.

Finally, Table 4 lists our results on the held-out testing partition. Note that in this dataset, the gold mentions included singletons and generic mentions

Components					MUC			B^3			CEAFE			BLANC			
ER	D	S	GA	GM	R	P	F1	R	P	F1	R	P	F1	R	P	F1	avg F1
√					58.8	56.5	57.6	68.0	68.7	68.4	44.8	47.1	45.9	68.8	73.5	70.9	57.3
	√				59.1	57.5	58.3	69.2	71.0	70.1	46.5	48.1	47.3	72.2	78.1	74.8	58.6
√	√				60.1	59.5	59.8	69.5	71.9	70.7	46.5	47.1	46.8	73.8	78.6	76.0	59.1
√	√	√			60.3	58.5	59.4	69.9	71.1	70.5	45.6	47.3	46.4	73.9	78.2	75.8	58.8
√	√		√		63.8	61.5	62.7	71.4	72.3	71.9	47.1	49.5	48.3	75.6	79.6	77.5	61.0
√	√			√	73.6	90.0	81.0	69.8	89.2	78.3	79.4	52.5	63.2	79.1	89.2	83.2	74.2
√	√		√	√	74.0	90.1	81.3	70.2	89.3	78.6	79.7	53.1	63.7	79.5	89.6	83.6	74.5

Table 3: Comparison between various configurations of our system. ER, D, S stand for External Resources, Discourse, and Semantics sieves. GA and GM stand for Gold Annotations, and Gold Mentions. The top part of the table shows results using only predicted annotations and mentions, whereas the bottom part shows results of experiments with gold information. Avg F1 is the arithmetic mean of MUC, B^3, and CEAFE. We used the development partition for these experiments.

		MUC			B^3			CEAFE			BLANC			
Track	Gold Mention Boundaries	R	P	F1	R	P	F1	R	P	F1	R	P	F1	avg F1
Close	Not Gold	61.8	57.5	59.6	68.4	68.2	68.3	43.4	47.8	45.5	70.6	76.2	73.0	57.8
Open	Not Gold	62.8	59.3	61.0	68.9	69.0	68.9	43.3	46.8	45.0	71.9	76.6	74.0	58.3
Close	Gold	65.9	62.1	63.9	69.5	70.6	70.0	46.3	50.5	48.3	72.0	78.6	74.8	60.7
Open	Gold	66.9	63.9	65.4	70.1	71.5	70.8	46.3	49.6	47.9	73.4	79.0	75.8	61.4

Table 4: Results on the official test set.

as well, whereas in development (lines 6 and 7 in Table 3), gold mentions included only mentions part of an actual coreference chain. This explains the large difference between, say, line 6 in Table 3 and line 4 in Table 4.

Our scores are comparable to previously reported state-of-the-art results for coreference resolution with predicted mentions. For example, Haghighi and Klein (2010) compare four state-of-the-art systems on three different corpora and report B^3 scores between 63 and 77 points. While the corpora used in (Haghighi and Klein, 2010) are different from the one in this shared task, our result of 68 B^3 suggests that our system's performance is competitive. In this task, our submissions in both the open and the closed track obtained the highest scores.

4 Conclusion

In this work we showed how a competitive end-to-end coreference resolution system can be built using only deterministic models (or sieves). Our approach starts with a high-recall mention detection component, which identifies mentions using only syntactic information and named entity boundaries, followed by a battery of high-precision deterministic coreference sieves, applied one at a time from highest to lowest precision. These models incorporate lexical, syntactic, semantic, and discourse information, and have access to document-level information (i.e., we share mention attributes across clusters as they are built). For this shared task, we extended our existing system with new sieves that model shallow discourse (i.e., speaker identification) and semantics (lexical chains and alias detection). Our results demonstrate that, despite their simplicity, deterministic models for coreference resolution obtain competitive results, e.g., we obtained the highest scores in both the closed and open tracks (57.8 and 58.3 respectively). The code used for this shared task is publicly released.[5]

Acknowledgments

We thank the shared task organizers for their effort.

This material is based upon work supported by the Air Force Research Laboratory (AFRL) under prime contract no. FA8750-09-C-0181. Any opinions, findings, and conclusion or recommendations expressed in this material are those of the authors and do not necessarily reflect the view of the Air Force Research Laboratory (AFRL).

[5]See `http://nlp.stanford.edu/software/dcoref.shtml` for the standalone coreference resolution system and `http://nlp.stanford.edu/software/corenlp.shtml` for Stanford's suite of natural language processing tools, which includes this coreference resolution system.

References

B. Baldwin. 1997. CogNIAC: high precision coreference with limited knowledge and linguistic resources. In *Proceedings of a Workshop on Operational Factors in Practical, Robust Anaphora Resolution for Unrestricted Texts*.

E. Bengston & D. Roth. 2008. Understanding the value of features for coreference resolution. In *EMNLP*.

Jari Björne, Juho Heimonen, Filip Ginter, Antti Airola, Tapio Pahikkala, and Tapio Salakoski. 2009. *Extracting Complex Biological Events with Rich Graph-Based Feature Sets*. Proceedings of the Workshop on BioNLP: Shared Task.

H. Daumé III and D. Marcu. 2005. A large-scale exploration of effective global features for a joint entity detection and tracking model. In *EMNLP-HLT*.

B. A. Fox 1993. *Discourse structure and anaphora: written and conversational English*. Cambridge University Press.

A. Haghighi and D. Klein. 2010. Coreference resolution in a modular, entity-centered model. In Proc. of *HLT-NAACL*.

E. Hovy, M. Marcus, M. Palmer, L. Ramshaw, and R. Weischedel 2006. OntoNotes: The 90% Solution. In *HLT/NAACL*.

Z. Huang, G. Zeng, W. Xu, and A. Celikyilmaz 2009. Accurate semantic class classifier for coreference resolution. In *EMNLP*.

J.R. Hobbs. 1977. Resolving pronoun references. *Lingua*.

H. Ji and D. Lin. 2009. Gender and animacy knowledge discovery from web-scale n-grams for unsupervised person mention detection. In *PACLIC*.

Jin-Dong Kim, Tomoko Ohta, Sampo Pyysalo, Yoshinobu Kano, and Jun'ichi Tsujii. 2009. *Overview of the BioNLP'09 Shared Task on Event Extraction*. Proceedings of the NAACL-HLT 2009 Workshop on Natural Language Processing in Biomedicine (BioNLP'09).

V. Ng 2007. Semantic Class Induction and Coreference Resolution. In *ACL*.

V. Ng and C. Cardie. 2002. Improving Machine Learning Approaches to Coreference Resolution. in *ACL 2002*

S. Ponzetto and M. Strube. 2006. Exploiting semantic role labeling, Wordnet and Wikipedia for coreference resolution. *Proceedings of NAACL*.

Sameer Pradhan, Lance Ramshaw, Ralph Weischedel, Jessica MacBride, and Linnea Micciulla. 2007. Unrestricted Coreference: Indentifying Entities and Events in OntoNotes. In *Proceedings of the IEEE International Conference on Semantic Computing (ICSC)*.

Sameer Pradhan, Lance Ramshaw, Mitchell Marcus, Martha Palmer, Ralph Weischedel, and Nianwen Xue. 2011. CoNLL-2011 Shared Task: Modeling Unrestricted Coreference in OntoNotes. In *Proceedings of the Fifteenth Conference on Computational Natural Language Learning (CoNLL 2011)*.

K. Raghunathan, H. Lee, S. Rangarajan, N. Chambers, M. Surdeanu, D. Jurafsky, and C. Manning 2010. A Multi-Pass Sieve for Coreference Resolution. In *EMNLP*.

J. Tetreault and J. Allen. 2003. An Empirical Evaluation of Pronoun Resolution and Clausal Structure. In *Proceedings of the 2003 International Symposium on Reference Resolution*.

J. Tetreault and J. Allen. 2004. Dialogue Structure and Pronoun Resolution. In *DAARC*.

X. Yang and J. Su. 2007. Coreference Resolution Using Semantic Relatedness Information from Automatically Discovered Patterns. In *ACL*.

RelaxCor Participation in CoNLL Shared Task on Coreference Resolution

Emili Sapena, Lluís Padró and Jordi Turmo*
TALP Research Center
Universitat Politècnica de Catalunya
Barcelona, Spain
{esapena, padro, turmo}@lsi.upc.edu

Abstract

This paper describes the participation of RELAXCOR in the CoNLL-2011 shared task: "Modeling Unrestricted Coreference in Ontonotes". RELAXCOR is a constraint-based graph partitioning approach to coreference resolution solved by relaxation labeling. The approach combines the strengths of groupwise classifiers and chain formation methods in one global method.

1 Introduction

The CoNLL-2011 shared task (Pradhan et al., 2011) is concerned with intra-document coreference resolution in English, using Ontonotes corpora. The core of the task is to identify which expressions (usually NPs) in a text refer to the same discourse entity.

This paper describes the participation of RELAXCOR and is organized as follows. Section 2 describes RELAXCOR, the system used in the task. Next, Section 3 describes the tuning needed by the system to adapt it to the task issues. The same section also analyzes the obtained results. Finally, Section 4 concludes the paper.

2 System description

RELAXCOR (Sapena et al., 2010a) is a coreference resolution system based on constraint satisfaction. It represents the problem as a graph connecting any pair of candidate coreferent mentions and applies relaxation labeling, over a set of constraints, to decide the set of most compatible coreference relations. This approach combines classification and clustering in one step. Thus, decisions are taken considering the entire set of mentions, which ensures consistency and avoids local classification decisions. The RELAXCOR implementation used in this task is an improved version of the system that participated in the SemEval-2010 Task 1 (Recasens et al., 2010).

The knowledge of the system is represented as a set of weighted constraints. Each constraint has an associated weight reflecting its confidence. The sign of the weight indicates that a pair or a group of mentions corefer (positive) or not (negative). Only constraints over pairs of mentions were used in the current version of RELAXCOR. However, RELAXCOR can handle higher-order constraints. Constraints can be obtained from any source, including a training data set from which they can be manually or automatically acquired.

The coreference resolution problem is represented as a graph with mentions in the vertices. Mentions are connected to each other by edges. Edges are assigned a weight that indicates the confidence that the mention pair corefers or not. More specifically, an edge weight is the sum of the weights of the constraints that apply to that mention pair. The larger the edge weight in absolute terms, the more reliable.

RELAXCOR uses relaxation labeling for the resolution process. Relaxation labeling is an iterative algorithm that performs function optimization based on local information. It has been widely used to solve NLP problems. An array of probability values

*Research supported by the Spanish Science and Innovation Ministry, via the KNOW2 project (TIN2009-14715-C04-04) and from the European Community's Seventh Framework Programme (FP7/2007-2013) under Grant Agreement number 247762 (FAUST)

Proceedings of the 15th Conference on Computational Natural Language Learning: Shared Task, pages 35–39,
Portland, Oregon, 23-24 June 2011.

is maintained for each vertex/mention. Each value corresponds to the probability that the mention belongs to a specific entity given all the possible entities in the document. During the resolution process, the probability arrays are updated according to the edge weights and probability arrays of the neighboring vertices. The larger the edge weight, the stronger the influence exerted by the neighboring probability array. The process stops when there are no more changes in the probability arrays or the maximum change does not exceed an *epsilon* parameter.

2.1 Attributes and Constraints

For the present study, all constraints were learned automatically using more than a hundred attributes over the mention pairs in the training sets. Usual attributes were used for each pair of mentions (m_i,m_j) –where $i < j$ following the order of the document–, like those in (Sapena et al., 2010b), but binarized for each possible value. In addition, a set of new mention attributes were included such as SAME_SPEAKER when both mentions have the same speaker[1] (Figures 1 and 2).

A decision tree was generated from the training data set, and a set of constraints was extracted with the C4.5 rule-learning algorithm (Quinlan, 1993). The so-learned constraints are conjunctions of attribute-value pairs. The weight associated with each constraint is the constraint precision minus a balance value, which is determined using the development set. Figure 3 is an example of a constraint.

2.2 Training data selection

Generating an example for each possible pair of mentions produces an unbalanced dataset where more than 99% of the examples are negative (not coreferent), even more considering that the mention detection system has a low precision (see Section 3.1). So, it generates large amounts of not coreferent mentions. In order to reduce the amount of negative pair examples, a clustering process is run using the positive examples as the centroids. For each positive example, only the negative examples with distance equal or less than a threshold d are included in the final training data. The distance is computed as the number of different attribute values

Distance and position:
Distance between m_i and m_j in sentences:
DIST_SEN_0: same sentence
DIST_SEN_1: consecutive sentences
DIST_SEN_L3: less than 3 sentences
Distance between m_i and m_j in phrases:
DIST_PHR_0, DIST_PHR_1, DIST_PHR_L3
Distance between m_i and m_j in mentions:
DIST_MEN_0, DIST_MEN_L3, DIST_MEN_L10
APPOSITIVE: One mention is in apposition with the other.
I/J_IN_QUOTES: $m_{i/j}$ is in quotes or inside a NP or a sentence in quotes.
I/J_FIRST: $m_{i/j}$ is the first mention in the sentence.
Lexical:
STR_MATCH: String matching of m_i and m_j
PRO_STR: Both are pronouns and their strings match
PN_STR: Both are proper names and their strings match
NONPRO_STR: String matching like in Soon et al. (2001) and mentions are not pronouns.
HEAD_MATCH: String matching of NP heads
TERM_MATCH: String matching of NP terms
I/J_HEAD_TERM: $m_{i/j}$ head matches with the term
Morphological:
The number of both mentions match:
NUMBER_YES, NUMBER_NO, NUMBER_UN
The gender of both mentions match:
GENDER_YES, GENDER_NO, GENDER_UN
Agreement: Gender and number of both mentions match:
AGREEMENT_YES, AGREEMENT_NO, AGREEMENT_UN
Closest Agreement: m_i is the first agreement found looking backward from m_j: C_AGREEMENT_YES, C_AGREEMENT_NO, C_AGREEMENT_UN
I/J_THIRD_PERSON: $m_{i/j}$ is 3rd person
I/J_PROPER_NAME: $m_{i/j}$ is a proper name
I/J_NOUN: $m_{i/j}$ is a common noun
ANIMACY: Animacy of both mentions match (person, object)
I/J_REFLEXIVE: $m_{i/j}$ is a reflexive pronoun
I/J_POSSESSIVE: $m_{i/j}$ is a possessive pronoun
I/J_TYPE_P/E/N: $m_{i/j}$ is a pronoun (p), NE (e) or nominal (n)

Figure 1: Mention-pair attributes (1/2).

inside the feature vector. After some experiments over development data, the value of d was assigned to 5. Thus, the negative examples were discarded when they have more than five attribute values different than any positive example. So, in the end, 22.8% of the negative examples are discarded. Also, both positive and negative examples with distance zero (contradictions) are discarded.

2.3 Development process

The current version of RELAXCOR includes a parameter optimization process using the development data sets. The optimized parameters are *balance* and *pruning*. The former adjusts the constraint weights to improve the balance between precision and recall as shown in Figure 4; the latter limits the number of neighbors that a vertex can have. Limiting

[1]This information is available in the column "speaker" of the corpora.

Syntactic:

I/J_DEF_NP: $m_{i/j}$ is a definite NP.
I/J_DEM_NP: $m_{i/j}$ is a demonstrative NP.
I/J_INDEF_NP: $m_{i/j}$ is an indefinite NP.
NESTED: One mention is included in the other.
MAXIMALNP: Both mentions have the same NP parent or they are nested.
I/J_MAXIMALNP: $m_{i/j}$ is not included in any other NP.
I/J_EMBEDDED: $m_{i/j}$ is a noun and is not a maximal NP.
C_COMMANDS_IJ/JI: $m_{i/j}$ C-Commands $m_{j/i}$.
BINDING_POS: Condition A of binding theory.
BINDING_NEG: Conditions B and C of binding theory.
I/J_SRL_ARG_N/0/1/2/X/M/L/Z: Syntactic argument of $m_{i/j}$.
SAME_SRL_ARG: Both mentions are the same argument.
I/J_COORDINATE: $m_{i/j}$ is a coordinate NP

Semantic:

Semantic class of both mentions match (the same as (Soon et al., 2001))
SEMCLASS_YES, SEMCLASS_NO, SEMCLASS_UN
One mention is an alias of the other:
ALIAS_YES, ALIAS_NO, ALIAS_UN
I/J_PERSON: $m_{i/j}$ is a person.
I/J_ORGANIZATION: $m_{i/j}$ is an organization.
I/J_LOCATION: $m_{i/j}$ is a location.
SRL_SAMEVERB: Both mentions have a semantic role for the same verb.
SRL_SAME_ROLE: The same semantic role.
SAME_SPEAKER: The same speaker for both mentions.

Figure 2: Mention-pair attributes (2/2).

DIST_SEN_1 & **GENDER_YES** & $\overline{I\_FIRST}$ & **I_MAXIMALNP** & **J_MAXIMALNP** & **I_SRL_ARG_0** & **J_SRL_ARG_0** & **I_TYPE_P** & **J_TYPE_P**

Precision: 0.9581
Training examples: 501

Figure 3: Example of a constraint. It applies when the distance between m_i and m_j is exactly 1 sentence, their gender match, both are maximal NPs, both are argument 0 (subject) of their respective sentences, both are pronouns, and m_i is not the first mention of its sentence. The final weight will be $weight = precision - balance$.

the number of neighbors reduces the computational cost significantly and improves overall performance too. Optimizing this parameter depends on properties like document size and the quality of the information given by the constraints.

The development process calculates a grid given the possible values of both parameters: from 0 to 1 for balance with a step of 0.05, and from 2 to 14 for pruning with a step of 2. Both parameters were empirically adjusted on the development set for the evaluation measure used in this shared task: the unweighted average of MUC (Vilain et al., 1995), B^3 (Bagga and Baldwin, 1998) and entity-based CEAF (Luo, 2005).

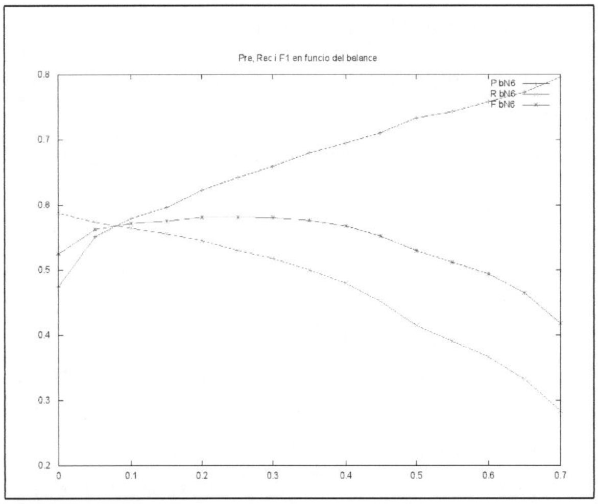

Figure 4: Development process. The figure shows MUC's precision (red), recall (green), and F_1 (blue) for each balance value with pruning adjusted to 6.

3 CoNLL shared task participation

RELAXCOR has participated in the CoNLL task in the Closed mode. All the knowledge required by the feature functions is obtained from the annotations of the corpora and no external resources have been used with the exception of WordNet (Miller, 1995), gender and number information (Bergsma and Lin, 2006) and sense inventories. All of them are allowed by the task organization and available in their website.

There are many remarkable features that make this task different and more difficult but realistic than previous ones. About mention annotation, it is important to emphasize that singletons are not annotated, mentions must be detected by the system and the mapping between system and true mentions is limited to exact matching of boundaries. Moreover, some verbs have been annotated as corefering mentions. Regarding the evaluation, the scorer uses the modification of (Cai and Strube, 2010), unprecedented so far, and the corpora was published very recently and there are no published results yet to use as reference. Finally, all the preprocessed information is automatic for the test dataset, carring out some noisy errors which is a handicap from the point of view of machine learning.

Following there is a description of the mention detection system developed for the task and an analysis of the obtained results in the development dataset.

3.1 Mention detection system

The mention detection system extracts one mention for every NP found in the syntactic tree, one for every pronoun and one for every named entity. Then, the head of every NP is determined using part-of-speech tags and a set of rules from (Collins, 1999). In case that some NPs share the same head, the larger NP is selected and the rest discarded. Also the mention repetitions with exactly the same boundaries are discarded. In addition, nouns with capital letters and proper names not included yet, that appear two or more times in the document, are also included. For instance, the NP "*an Internet business*" is added as a mention, but also "*Internet*" itself is added in the case that the word is found once again in the document.

As a result, taking into account that just exact boundary matching is accepted, the mention detection achieves an acceptable recall, higher than 90%, but a low precision (see Table 1). The most typical error made by the system is to include extracted NPs that are not referential (e.g., predicative and appositive phrases) and mentions with incorrect boundaries. The incorrect boundaries are mainly due to errors in the predicted syntactic column and some mention annotation discrepancies. Furthermore, verbs are not detected by this algorithm, so most of the missing mentions are verbs.

3.2 Results analysis

The results obtained by RELAXCOR can be found in Tables 1 and 2. Due to the lack of annotated singletons, mention-based metrics B^3 and CEAF produce lower scores –near 60% and 50% respectively– than the ones typically achieved with different annotations and mapping policies –usually near 80% and 70%. Moreover, the requirement that systems use automatic preprocessing and do their own mention detection increase the difficulty of the task which obviously decreases the scores in general.

The measure which remains more stable on its scores is MUC given that it is link-based and not takes singletons into account anyway. Thus, it is the only one comparable with the state of the art right now. The results obtained with MUC scorer show an improvement of RELAXCOR's recall, a feature that needed improvement given the previous published results with a MUCs recall remarkably low (Sapena et al., 2010b).

Measure	Recall	Precision	F_1
Mention detection	92.45	27.34	42.20
mention-based CEAF	55.27	55.27	55.27
entity-based CEAF	47.20	40.01	43.31
MUC	54.53	62.25	58.13
B^3	63.72	73.83	68.40
(CEAFe+MUC+B^3)/3	-	-	56.61

Table 1: Results on the development data set

Measure	Recall	Precision	F_1
mention-based CEAF	53.51	53.51	53.51
entity-based CEAF	44.75	38.38	41.32
MUC	56.32	63.16	59.55
B^3	62.16	72.08	67.09
BLANC	69.50	73.07	71.10
(CEAFe+MUC+B^3)/3	-	-	**55.99**

Table 2: Official test results

4 Conclusion

The participation of RELAXCOR to the CoNLL shared task has been useful to evaluate the system using data never seen before in a totally automatic context: predicted preprocessing and system mentions. Many published systems typically use the same data sets (ACE and MUC) and it is easy to unintentionally adapt the system to the corpora and not just to the problem. This kind of tasks favor comparisons between systems with the same framework and initial conditions.

The obtained performances confirm the robustness of RELAXCOR and a recall improvement. And the overall performance seems considerably good taking into account the unprecedented scenario. However, a deeper error analysis is needed, specially in the mention detection system with a low precision and the training data selection process which may be discarding positive examples that could help improving recall.

Acknowledgments

The research leading to these results has received funding from the European Community's Seventh Framework Programme (FP7/2007-2013) under Grant Agreement number 247762 (FAUST), and from the Spanish Science and Innovation Ministry, via the KNOW2 project (TIN2009-14715-C04-04).

References

Amit Bagga and Breck Baldwin. 1998. Algorithms for scoring coreference chains. In *Proceedings of the Linguistic Coreference Workshop at LREC 98*, pages 563–566, Granada, Spain.

S. Bergsma and D. Lin. 2006. Bootstrapping path-based pronoun resolution. In *Proceedings of the 21st International Conference on Computational Linguistics and the 44th annual meeting of the Association for Computational Linguistics*, pages 33–40. Association for Computational Linguistics.

Jie Cai and Michael Strube. 2010. Evaluation metrics for end-to-end coreference resolution systems. In *Proceedings of SIGDIAL*, pages 28–36, University of Tokyo, Japan.

M. Collins. 1999. *Head-driven statistical models for natural language parsing*. Ph.D. thesis, University of Pennsylvania.

Xiaoqiang Luo. 2005. On coreference resolution performance metrics. In *Proceedings of the Joint Conference on Human Language Technology and Empirical Methods in Natural Language Processing (HLT-EMNLP 2005*, pages 25–32, Vancouver, B.C., Canada.

G.A. Miller. 1995. WordNet: a lexical database for English.

Sameer Pradhan, Lance Ramshaw, Mitchell Marcus, Martha Palmer, Ralph Weischedel, and Nianwen Xue. 2011. Conll-2011 shared task: Modeling unrestricted coreference in ontonotes. In *Proceedings of the Fifteenth Conference on Computational Natural Language Learning (CoNLL 2011)*, Portland, Oregon, June.

J.R. Quinlan. 1993. *C4.5: Programs for Machine Learning*. Morgan Kaufmann.

Marta Recasens, Lluís Màrquez, Emili Sapena, M. Antònia Martí, Mariona Taulé, Véronique Hoste, Massimo Poesio, and Yannick Versley. 2010. Semeval-2010 task 1: Coreference resolution in multiple languages. In *Proceedings of the 5th International Workshop on Semantic Evaluation*, pages 1–8, Uppsala, Sweden, July. Association for Computational Linguistics.

Emili Sapena, Lluís Padró, and Jordi Turmo. 2010a. A Global Relaxation Labeling Approach to Coreference Resolution. In *Proceedings of 23rd International Conference on Computational Linguistics, COLING*, Beijing, China, August.

Emili Sapena, Lluís Padró, and Jordi Turmo. 2010b. RelaxCor: A Global Relaxation Labeling Approach to Coreference Resolution. In *Proceedings of the ACL Workshop on Semantic Evaluations (SemEval-2010)*, Uppsala, Sweden, July.

W.M. Soon, H.T. Ng, and D.C.Y. Lim. 2001. A Machine Learning Approach to Coreference Resolution of Noun Phrases. *Computational Linguistics*, 27(4):521–544.

Marc Vilain, John Burger, John Aberdeen, Dennis Connolly, and Lynette Hirschman. 1995. A model-theoretic coreference scoring scheme. In *Proceedings of the Sixth Message Understanding Conference (MUC-6)*, pages 45–52.

Inference Protocols for Coreference Resolution

Kai-Wei Chang Rajhans Samdani
Alla Rozovskaya Nick Rizzolo
Mark Sammons Dan Roth
University of Illinois at Urbana-Champaign
{kchang10|rsamdan2|rozovska|rizzolo|mssammon|danr}@illinois.edu

Abstract

This paper presents *Illinois-Coref*, a system for coreference resolution that participated in the CoNLL-2011 shared task. We investigate two inference methods, *Best-Link* and *All-Link*, along with their corresponding, pairwise and structured, learning protocols. Within these, we provide a flexible architecture for incorporating linguistically-motivated constraints, several of which we developed and integrated. We compare and evaluate the inference approaches and the contribution of constraints, analyze the mistakes of the system, and discuss the challenges of resolving coreference for the OntoNotes-4.0 data set.

1 Introduction

The coreference resolution task is challenging, requiring a human or automated reader to identify denotative phrases ("mentions") and link them to an underlying set of referents. Human readers use syntactic and semantic cues to identify and disambiguate the referring phrases; a successful automated system must replicate this behavior by linking mentions that refer to the same underlying entity.

This paper describes *Illinois-Coref*, a coreference resolution system built on Learning Based Java (Rizzolo and Roth, 2010), that participated in the "closed" track of the CoNLL-2011 shared task (Pradhan et al., 2011). Building on elements of the coreference system described in Bengtson and Roth (2008), we design an end-to-end system (Sec. 2) that identifies candidate mentions and then applies one of two inference protocols, *Best-Link* and *All-Link* (Sec. 2.3), to disambiguate and cluster them. These protocols were designed to easily incorporate domain knowledge in the form of constraints. In Sec. 2.4, we describe the constraints that we develop and incorporate into the system. The different strategies for mention detection and inference, and the integration of constraints are evaluated in Sections 3 and 4.

2 Architecture

Illinois-Coref follows the architecture used in Bengtson and Roth (2008). First, candidate mentions are detected (Sec. 2.1). Next, a pairwise classifier is applied to each pair of mentions, generating a score that indicates their compatibility (Sec. 2.2). Next, at inference stage, a coreference decoder (Sec. 2.3) aggregates these scores into mention clusters. The original system uses the *Best-Link* approach; we also experiment with *All-Link* decoding. This flexible decoder architecture allows linguistic or knowledge-based constraints to be easily added to the system: constraints may force mentions to be coreferent or non-coreferent and can be optionally used in either of the inference protocols. We designed and implemented several such constraints (Sec. 2.4). Finally, since mentions that are in singleton clusters are not annotated in the OntoNotes-4.0 data set, we remove those as a post-processing step.

2.1 Mention Detection

Given a document, a mention detector generates a set of mention candidates that are used by the subsequent components of the system. A robust mention detector is crucial, as detection errors will propagate to the coreference stage. As we show in Sec. 3, the system that uses gold mentions outperforms the system that uses predicted mentions by a large margin, from 15% to 18% absolute difference.

Proceedings of the 15th Conference on Computational Natural Language Learning: Shared Task, pages 40–44,
Portland, Oregon, 23-24 June 2011.

For the ACE 2004 coreference task, a good performance in mention detection is typically achieved by training a classifier e.g., (Bengtson and Roth, 2008). However, this model is not appropriate for the OntoNotes-4.0 data set, in which (in contrast to the ACE 2004 corpus) singleton mentions are not annotated: a specific noun phrase (NP) may correspond to a mention in one document but will not be a mention in another document. Therefore, we designed a high recall ($\sim 90\%$) and low precision ($\sim 35\%$) rule-based mention detection system that includes all phrases recognized as Named Entities (NE's) and all phrases tagged as NPs in the syntactic parse of the text. As a post-processing step, we remove all predicted mentions that remain in singleton clusters after the inference stage.

The best mention detection result on the DEV set[1] is 64.93% in F1 score (after coreference resolution) and is achieved by our best inference protocol, *Best-Link* with constraints.

2.2 Pairwise Mention Scoring

The basic input to our inference algorithm is a pairwise mention score, which indicates the compatibility score of a pair of mentions. For any two mentions u and v, the compatibility score w_{uv} is produced by a pairwise scoring component that uses extracted features $\phi(u, v)$ and linguistic constraints c:

$$w_{uv} = \mathbf{w} \cdot \phi(u, v) + c(u, v) + t, \tag{1}$$

where $\mathbf{w}$ is a weight vector learned from training data, $c(u, v)$ is a compatibility score given by the constraints, and t is a threshold parameter (to be tuned). We use the same features as Bengtson and Roth (2008), with the knowledge extracted from the OntoNotes-4.0 annotation. The exact use of the scores and the procedure for learning weights $\mathbf{w}$ are specific to the inference algorithm and are described next.

2.3 Inference

In this section, we present our inference techniques for coreference resolution. These clustering techniques take as input a set of pairwise mention scores over a document and aggregate them into globally consistent cliques representing entities. We investigate the traditional *Best-Link* approach and a more intuitively appealing *All-Link* algorithm.

[1]In the shared task, the data set is split into three sets: TRAIN, DEV, and TEST.

2.3.1 Best-Link

Best-Link is a popular approach to coreference resolution. For each mention, it considers the best mention on its left to connect to (best according the pairwise score w_{uv}) and creates a link between them if the pairwise score is above some threshold. Although its strategy is simple, Bengtson and Roth (2008) show that with a careful design, it can achieve highly competitive performance.

Inference: We give an integer linear programming (ILP) formulation of *Best-Link* inference in order to present both of our inference algorithms within the same framework. Given a pairwise scorer $\mathbf{w}$, we can compute the compatibility scores — w_{uv} from Eq. (1) — for all mention pairs u and v. Let y_{uv} be a binary variable, such that $y_{uv} = 1$ *only if* u and v are in the same cluster. For a document d, *Best-Link* solves the following ILP formulation:

$$\begin{aligned} \arg\max_y \quad & \sum\nolimits_{u,v} w_{uv} y_{uv} \\ \text{s.t} \quad & \sum\nolimits_{u<v} y_{uv} \leq 1 \; \forall v, \\ & y_{uw} \in \{0, 1\}. \end{aligned} \tag{2}$$

Eq. (2) generates a set of connected components and all the mentions in each connected component constitute an entity.

Learning: We follow the strategy in (Bengtson and Roth, 2008, Section 2.2) to learn the pairwise scoring function $\mathbf{w}$. The scoring function is trained on:

- Positive examples: for each mention u, we construct a positive example (u, v), where v is the closest preceding mention in u's equivalence class.
- Negative examples: all mention pairs (u, v), where v is a preceding mention of u and u, v are not in the same class.

As a result of the singleton mentions not being annotated, there is an inconsistency in the sample distributions in the training and inference phases. Therefore, we apply the mention detector to the training set, and train the classifier using the union set of gold and predicted mentions.

2.3.2 All-Link

The *All-Link* inference approach scores a clustering of mentions by including all possible pairwise links in the score. It is also known as correlational clustering (Bansal et al., 2002) and has been applied to coreference resolution in the form of supervised clustering (Mccallum and Wellner, 2003; Finley and Joachims, 2005).

Inference: Similar to *Best-Link*, for a document d, *All-Link* inference finds a clustering All-Link$(d; w)$ by solving the following ILP problem:

$$\begin{aligned} \arg\max_y \quad & \sum\nolimits_{u,v} w_{uv} y_{uv} \\ \text{s.t} \quad & y_{uw} \geq y_{uv} + y_{vw} - 1 \; \forall u, w, v, \\ & y_{uw} \in \{0, 1\}. \end{aligned} \tag{3}$$

The inequality constraints in Eq. (3) enforce the transitive closure of the clustering. The solution of Eq. (3) is a set of cliques, and the mentions in the same cliques corefer.

Learning: We present a structured perceptron algorithm, which is similar to supervised clustering algorithm (Finley and Joachims, 2005) to learn w. Note that as an approximation, it is certainly possible to use the weight parameter learned by using, say, averaged perceptron over positive and negative links. The pseudocode is presented in Algorithm 1.

Algorithm 1 Structured Perceptron like learning algorithm for All-Link inference

Given: Annotated documents D and initial weight w_{init}
Initialize $w \leftarrow w_{init}$
for Document d in D **do**
  Clustering $y \leftarrow$ All-Link$(d; w)$
  for all pairs of mentions u and v **do**
    $\mathcal{I}^1(u, v) = [u, v \text{ coreferent in } D]$
    $\mathcal{I}^2(u, v) = [y(u) = y(v)]$
    $w \leftarrow w + \left(\mathcal{I}^1(u, v) - \mathcal{I}^2(u, v)\right) \phi(u, v)$
  end for
end for
return w

For the *All-Link* clustering, we drop one of the three transitivity constraints for each triple of mention variables. Similar to Pascal and Baldridge (2009), we observe that this improves accuracy — the reader is referred to Pascal and Baldridge (2009) for more details.

2.4 Constraints

The constraints in our inference algorithm are based on the analysis of mistakes on the DEV set[2]. Since the majority of errors are mistakes in recall, where the system fails to link mentions that refer to the same entity, we define three high precision constraints that improve recall on NPs with definite determiners and mentions whose heads are NE's.

The patterns used by constraints to match mention pairs have some overlap with those used by the pairwise mention scorer, but their formulation as constraints allow us to focus on a subset of mentions to which a certain pattern applies with high precision. For example, the constraints use a rule-based string similarity measure that accounts for the inferred semantic type of the mentions compared. Examples of mention pairs that are correctly linked by the constraints are: *Governor Bush* ⇒ *Bush*; *a crucial swing state , Florida* ⇒ *Florida*; *Sony itself* ⇒ *Sony*; *Farmers* ⇒ *Los Angeles - based Farmers*.

3 Experiments and Results

In this section, we present the performance of the system on the OntoNotes-4.0 data set. A previous experiment using an earlier version of this data can be found in (Pradhan et al., 2007). Table 1 shows the performance for the two inference protocols, with and without constraints. *Best-Link* outperforms *All-Link* for both predicted and gold mentions. Adding constraints improves the performance slightly for *Best-Link* on predicted mentions. In the other configurations, the constraints either do not affect the performance or slightly degrade it.

Table 2 shows the results obtained on TEST, using the best system configurations found on DEV. We report results on predicted mentions with predicted boundaries, predicted mentions with gold boundaries, and when using gold mentions[3].

[2] We provide a more detailed analysis of the errors in Sec. 4.

[3] Note that the *gold boundaries* results are different from the *gold mention* results. Specifying gold mentions requires coreference resolution to exclude singleton mentions. Gold boundaries are provided by the task organizers and also include singleton mentions.

Method	Pred. Mentions w/Pred. Boundaries					Gold Mentions			
	MD	MUC	BCUB	CEAF	AVG	MUC	BCUB	CEAF	AVG
Best-Link	64.70	55.67	69.21	43.78	56.22	80.58	75.68	64.69	**73.65**
Best-Link W/ Const.	64.69	55.8	69.29	43.96	**56.35**	80.56	75.02	64.24	73.27
All-Link	63.30	54.56	68.50	42.15	55.07	77.72	73.65	59.17	70.18
All-Link W/ Const.	63.39	54.56	68.46	42.20	55.07	77.94	73.43	59.47	70.28

Table 1: The performance of the two inference protocols on both gold and predicted mentions. The systems are trained on the TRAIN set and evaluated on the DEV set. We report the F1 scores (%) on mention detection (MD) and coreference metrics (MUC, BCUB, CEAF). The column AVG shows the averaged scores of the three coreference metrics.

Task	MD	MUC	BCUB	CEAF	AVG
Pred. Mentions w/ Pred. Boundaries	64.88	57.15	67.14	41.94	55.96
Pred. Mentions w/ Gold Boundaries	67.92	59.79	68.65	41.42	56.62
Gold Mentions	-	82.55	73.70	65.24	73.83

Table 2: The results of our submitted system on the TEST set. The system uses *Best-Link* decoding with constraints on predicted mentions and *Best-Link* decoding without constraints on gold mentions. The systems are trained on a collection of TRAIN and DEV sets.

4 Discussion

Most of the mistakes made by the system are due to not linking co-referring mentions. The constraints improve slightly the recall on a subset of mentions, and here we show other common errors for the system. For instance, the system fails to link the two mentions, *the Emory University hospital in Atlanta* and *the hospital behind me*, since each of the mentions has a modifier that is not part of the other mention. Another common error is related to pronoun resolution, especially when a pronoun has several antecedents in the immediate context, appropriate in gender, number, and animacy, as in " *E. Robert Wallach* was sentenced by *a U.S. judge* in New York to six years in prison and fined $ 250,000 for *his* racketeering conviction in the Wedtech scandal .": both *E. Robert Wallach* and *a U.S. judge* are appropriate antecedents for the pronoun *his*. Pronoun errors are especially important to address since 35% of the mentions are pronouns.

The system also incorrectly links some mentions, such as: "*The suspect* said *it* took months to repackage..." ("it" cannot refer to a human); "*They* see *them*." (subject and object in the same sentence are linked); and "Many freeway accidents occur simply because people stay inside *the car* and sort out..." (the NP *the car* should not be linked to any other mention, since it does not refer to a specific entity).

5 Conclusions

We have investigated a coreference resolution system that uses a rich set of features and two popular types of clustering algorithm.

While the *All-Link* clustering seems to be capable of taking more information into account for making clustering decisions, as it requires each mention in a cluster to be compatible with all other mentions in that cluster, the *Best-Link* approach still outperforms it. This raises a natural algorithmic question regarding the inherent nature of clustering style most suitable for coreference and regarding possible ways of infusing more knowledge into different coreference clustering styles. Our approach accommodates infusion of knowledge via constraints, and we have demonstrated its utility in an end-to-end coreference system.

Acknowledgments This research is supported by the Defense Advanced Research Projects Agency (DARPA) Machine Reading Program under Air Force Research Laboratory (AFRL) prime contract no. FA8750-09-C-0181 and the Army Research Laboratory (ARL) under agreement W911NF-09-2-0053. Any opinions, findings, and conclusion or recommendations expressed in this material are those of the author(s) and do not necessarily reflect the view of the DARPA, AFRL, ARL or the US government.

References

N. Bansal, A. Blum, and S. Chawla. 2002. Correlation clustering. In *Proceedings of the 43rd Symposium on Foundations of Computer Science*.

E. Bengtson and D. Roth. 2008. Understanding the value of features for coreference resolution. In *EMNLP*, 10.

T. Finley and T. Joachims. 2005. Supervised clustering with support vector machines. In *Proceedings of the International Conference on Machine Learning (ICML)*.

A. Mccallum and B. Wellner. 2003. Toward conditional models of identity uncertainty with application to proper noun coreference. In *The Conference on Advances in Neural Information Processing Systems (NIPS)*.

D. Pascal and J. Baldridge. 2009. Global joint models for coreference resolution and named entity classification. In *Procesamiento del Lenguaje Natural*.

S. Pradhan, L. Ramshaw, R. Weischedel, J. MacBride, and L. Micciulla. 2007. Unrestricted Coreference: Identifying Entities and Events in OntoNotes. In *in Proceedings of the IEEE International Conference on Semantic Computing (ICSC)*, September 17-19.

S. Pradhan, L. Ramshaw, M. Marcus, M. Palmer, R. Weischedel, and N. Xue. 2011. Conll-2011 shared task: Modeling unrestricted coreference in ontonotes. In *Proceedings of the Annual Conference on Computational Natural Language Learning (CoNLL)*.

N. Rizzolo and D. Roth. 2010. Learning Based Java for Rapid Development of NLP Systems. In *Proceedings of the International Conference on Language Resources and Evaluation (LREC)*, Valletta, Malta, 5.

Exploring Lexicalized Features for Coreference Resolution

Anders Björkelund
Lund University / LTH
Lund / Sweden
Anders.Bjorkelund@cs.lth.se

Pierre Nugues
Lund University / LTH
Lund / Sweden
Pierre.Nugues@cs.lth.se

Abstract

In this paper, we describe a coreference solver based on the extensive use of lexical features and features extracted from dependency graphs of the sentences. The solver uses Soon et al. (2001)'s classical resolution algorithm based on a pairwise classification of the mentions.

We applied this solver to the closed track of the CoNLL 2011 shared task (Pradhan et al., 2011). We carried out a systematic optimization of the feature set using cross-validation that led us to retain 24 features. Using this set, we reached a MUC score of 58.61 on the test set of the shared task. We analyzed the impact of the features on the development set and we show the importance of lexicalization as well as of properties related to dependency links in coreference resolution.

1 Introduction

In this paper, we present our contribution to the closed track of the 2011 CoNLL shared task (Pradhan et al., 2011). We started from a baseline system that uses Soon et al. (2001)'s architecture and features. Mentions are identified by selecting all noun phrases and possessive pronouns. Then, the resolution algorithm relies on a pairwise classifier that determines whether two mentions corefer or not.

Lexicalization has proved effective in numerous tasks of natural language processing such as part-of-speech tagging or parsing. However, lexicalized models require a good deal of annotated data to avoid overfit. The data set used in the CoNLL 2011 shared task has a considerable size compared to corpora traditionally used in coreference resolution – the training set comprises 2,374 documents. See Pradhan et al. (2007) for a previous work using an earlier version of this dataset. Leveraging this size, we investigated the potential of lexicalized features.

Besides lexical features, we created features that use part-of-speech tags and semantic roles. We also constructed features using dependency tree paths and labels by converting the constituent trees provided in the shared task into dependency graphs. The final feature set was selected through an automated feature selection procedure using cross-validation.

2 System Architecture

During both training and decoding, we employed the same mention detection and preprocessing steps. We considered all the noun phrases (NP) and possessive pronouns (PRP$) as mentions. In order to extract head words from the NP constituents, we converted the constituent trees provided in the data sets to dependency graphs using the Penn treebank converter of Johansson and Nugues (2007). Using the dependency tree, we extracted the head word of all the NPs by taking the word that dominates the subtree constructed from the NP.

The dependency tree is also used later to extract features of mentions based on dependency tree paths, which is further described in Sec. 3.

In the preprocessing step, we assigned a number and a gender to each mention. For the pronominal mentions, we used a manually compiled lists of pronouns, where we marked the number and gender.

Proceedings of the 15th Conference on Computational Natural Language Learning: Shared Task, pages 45–50,
Portland, Oregon, 23-24 June 2011.

For nonpronominal mentions, we used the number and gender data (Bergsma and Lin, 2006) provided by the task organizers and queried it for the head word of the mention. In cases of ambiguity (e.g. the pronoun *you*), or missing entries in the data for nonpronominals, we assigned an *unknown* value.

2.1 Generation of training examples

To create a set of training examples, we used pairs of mentions following the method outlined by Soon et al. (2001). For each anaphoric mention m_j and its closest preceding antecedent m_i, we built a positive example: $P = \{(m_i, m_j)\}$. We constructed the negative examples with noncoreferring pairs of mentions, where the first term is a mention occurring between m_i and m_j and the second one is m_j: $N = \{(m_k, m_j) | i < k < j)\}$.

The training examples collected from the CoNLL 2011 training set consist of about 5.5% of positive examples and 94.5% of negative ones.

2.2 Learning method

We evaluated two types of classifiers: decision trees and logistic regression. We used the decision trees and the C4.5 algorithm from the Weka distribution (Hall et al., 2009) for our baseline system. We then opted for linear logistic regression as it scaled better with the number of features and feature values.

Logistic regression is faster to train and allowed us to carry out an automated feature selection, which is further described in Sec. 3.4. In addition, the logistic classifiers enabled us to interpret their results in terms of probabilities, which we used for the decoding step. We trained the logistic regression classifiers using the LIBLINEAR package (Fan et al., 2008).

2.3 Decoding

The decoding algorithm devised by Soon et al. (2001) selects the closest preceding mention deemed to be coreferent by the classifier. This clustering algorithm is commonly referred to as *closest-first clustering*. Ng and Cardie (2002) suggested a different clustering procedure, commonly referred to as *best-first clustering*. This algorithm selects the most likely antecedent classified as coreferent with the anaphoric mention. During early experiments, we found that while the best-first method increases the performance on nonpronominal anaphoric expressions, it has the opposite effect on pronominal anaphoric expressions. Consequently, we settled on using the closest-first clustering method for pronominal mentions, and the best-first clustering method otherwise. For the best-first clustering, we used the probability output from our logistic classifiers and a threshold of 0.5.

After clustering mentions in a document, we discard all remaining singleton mentions, as they were excluded from the annotation in the CoNLL 2011 shared task.

2.4 Postprocessing

The initial detection of mentions is a direct mapping from two categories of constituents: NP and PRP$. In the postprocessing step, we reclaim some of the mentions that we missed in the initial step.

The automatically generated constituent trees provided in the data set contain errors and this causes the loss of many mentions. Another source of loss is the bracketing of complex NPs, where the internal structure uses the tag NML. In a few cases, these nested nodes participate in coreference chains. However, when we tried to include this tag in the mention detection, we got worse results overall. This is possibly due to an even more skewed distribution of positive and negative training examples.

In the postprocessing step, we therefore search each document for sequences of one or more proper noun tokens, i.e. tokens with the part-of-speech tags NNP or NNPS. If their common ancestor, i.e. the parse tree node that encloses all the tokens, is not already in a mention, we try to match this sequence to any existing chain using the binary features: STRINGMATCH and ALIAS (cf. Sec. 3). If either of them evaluates to true, we add this span of proper nouns to the matched chain.

3 Features

For our baseline system, we started with the feature set described in Soon et al. (2001). Due to space limitations, we omit the description of these features and refer the reader to their paper.

We also defined a large number of feature templates based on the syntactic dependency tree, as well as features based on semantic roles. In the following sections, we describe these features as well as the naming conventions we use. The final feature set we used is given in Sec. 4.

3.1 Mention-based features

On the mention level, we considered the head word (HD) of the mention, and following the edges in the dependency tree, we considered the left-most and right-most children of the head word (HDLMC and HDRMC), the left and right siblings of the head word (HDLS and HDRS), as well as the governor[1] of the head word (HDGOV).

For each of the above mentioned tokens, we extracted the surface form (FORM), the part-of-speech tag (POS), and the grammatical function of the token (FUN), i.e. the label of the dependency edge of the token to its parent. For head words that do not have any leftmost or rightmost children, or left or right siblings, we used a null-value placeholder.

In each training pair, we extracted these values from both mentions in the pair, i.e. both the anaphor and the tentative antecedent. Table 3 shows the features we used in our system. We used a naming nomenclature consisting of the role in the anaphora, where I stands for antecedent and J for anaphor; the token we selected from the dependency graph, e.g. HD or HDLMC; and the value extracted from the token, e.g. POS or FUN. For instance, the part-of-speech tag of the governor of the head word of the anaphor is denoted: J-HDGOVPOS.

The baseline features taken from Soon et al. (2001) include features such as I-PRONOUN and J-DEMONSTRATIVE that are computed using a word list and by looking at the first word in the mention, respectively. Our assumption is that these traits can be captured by our new features by considering the part-of-speech tag of the head word and the surface form of the left-most child of the head word, respectively.

3.2 Path-based features

Between pairs of potentially coreferring mentions, we also considered the path from the head word of the anaphor to the head word of the antecedent in the syntactic dependency tree. If the mentions are not in the same sentence, this is the path from the anaphor to the root of its sentence, followed by the path from the root to the antecedent in its sentence. We differentiate between the features depending on whether they are in the same sentence or in different sentences. The names of these features are prefixed with SS and DS, respectively.

Following the path in the dependency tree, we concatenated either the surface form, the part-of-speech tag, or the grammatical function label with the direction of the edge to the next token, i.e. up or down. This way, we built six feature templates. For instance, DSPATHFORM is the concatenation of the surface forms of the tokens along the path between mentions in different sentences.

Bergsma and Lin (2006) built a statistical model from paths that include the lemma of the intermediate tokens, but replace the end nodes with *noun*, *pronoun*, or *pronoun-self* for nouns, pronouns, and reflexive pronouns, respectively. They used this model to define a measure of coreference likelihood to resolve pronouns within the same sentence. Rather than building an explicit model, we simply included these paths as features in our set. We refer to this feature template as BERGSMALINPATH in Table 3.

3.3 Semantic role features

We tried to exploit the semantic roles that were included in the CoNLL 2011 data set. Ponzetto and Strube (2006) suggested using the concatenation of the predicate and the role label for a mention that has a semantic role in a predicate. They introduced two new features, I_SEMROLE and J_SEMROLE, that correspond to the semantic roles filled by each of the mentions in a pair. We included these features in our pool of feature templates, but we could not see any contribution from them during the feature selection.

We also introduced a number of feature templates that only applied to pairs of mentions that occur in the same semantic role proposition. These templates included the concatenation of the two labels of the arguments and the predicate sense label, and variations of these that also included the head words of either the antecedent or anaphor, or both. The only feature that was selected during our feature selection procedure corresponds to the concatenation of the argument labels, the predicate sense, and the head word of the anaphor: SEMROLEPROPJHD in Table 3. In the sentence *A lone protestor parked*

[1]We use the term governor in order not to confuse it with head word of an NP.

herself outside the UN, the predicate *park* has the arguments *A lone protestor*, labeled ARG0, and *herself*, labeled ARG1. The corresponding value of this feature would be *ARG0-park.01-ARG1-herself*.

3.4 Feature selection

Starting from Soon et al. (2001)'s feature set, we performed a greedy forward selection. The feature selection used a 5-fold cross-validation over the training set, where we evaluated the features using the arithmetic mean of MUC, BCUB, and CEAFE. After reaching a maximal score using forward selection, we reversed the process using a backward elimination, leaving out each feature and removing the one that had the worst impact on performance. This backwards procedure was carried out until the score no longer increased. We repeated this forward-backward procedure until there was no increase in performance. Table 3 shows the final feature set.

Feature bigrams are often used to increase the separability of linear classifiers. Ideally, we would have generated a complete bigram set from our features. However, as this set is quadratic in nature and due to time constraints, we included only a subset of it in the selection procedure. Some of them, most notably the bigram of mention head words (I-HDFORM+J-HDFORM) were selected in the procedure and appear in Table 3.

4 Evaluation

Table 1 shows some baseline figures using the binary features STRINGMATCH and ALIAS as sole coreference properties, as well as our baseline system using Soon et al. (2001)'s features.

	MD	MUC	BCUB
STRINGMATCH	59.91	44.43	63.65
ALIAS	19.25	16.77	48.07
Soon baseline/LR	60.79	47.50	63.97
Soon baseline/C4.5	58.96	47.02	65.36

Table 1: Baseline figures using string match and alias properties, and our Soon baseline using decision trees with the C4.5 induction program and logistic regression (LR). MD stands for mention detection.

4.1 Contribution of postprocessing

The postprocessing step described in Sec. 2.4 proved effective, contributing from 0.21 to up to 1 point to the final score across the metrics. Table 2 shows the detailed impacts on the development set.

	MD	MUC	BCUB	CEAFE
No postproc.	66.56	54.61	65.93	40.46
With postproc.	67.21	55.62	66.29	40.67
Increase	0.65	1.01	0.36	0.21

Table 2: Impact of the postprocessing step on the development set.

4.2 Contribution of features

The lack of time prevented us from running a complete selection from scratch and describing the contribution of each feature on a clean slate. Nonetheless, we computed the scores when one feature is removed from the final feature set. Table 3 shows the performance degradation observed on the development set, which gives an indication of the importance of each feature. In these runs, no postprocessing was not used.

Toward the end of the table, some features show a negative contribution to the score on the development set. This is explained by the fact that our feature selection was carried out in a cross-validated manner over the training set.

4.3 Results on the test set

Table 4 shows the results we obtained on the test set. The figures are consistent with the performance on the development set across the three official metrics, with an increase of the MUC score and a decrease of both BCUB and CEAFE. The official score in the shared task is computed as the mean of these three metrics.

The shared task organizers also provided a test set with given mention boundaries. The given boundaries included nonanaphoric and singleton mentions as well. Using this test set, we replaced our mention extraction step and used the given mention boundaries instead. Table 4 shows the results with this setup. As mention boundaries were given, we turned off our postprocessing module for this run.

Metric\Corpus	Development set			Test set			Test set with gold mentions		
	R	P	F1	R	P	F1	R	P	F1
Mention detection	65.68	68.82	67.21	69.87	68.08	68.96	74.18	70.74	72.42
MUC	55.26	55.98	55.62	60.20	57.10	58.61	64.33	60.05	62.12
BCUB	65.07	67.56	66.29	66.74	64.23	65.46	68.26	65.17	66.68
CEAFM	52.51	52.51	52.51	51.45	51.45	51.45	53.84	53.84	53.84
CEAFE	41.02	40.33	40.67	38.09	41.06	39.52	39.86	44.23	41.93
BLANC	69.6	70.41	70	71.99	70.31	71.11	72.53	71.04	71.75
Official CoNLL score	53.78	54.62	54.19	55.01	54.13	54.53	57.38	56.48	56.91

Table 4: Scores on development set, on the test set, and on the test set with given mention boundaries: recall (R), precision (P), and harmonic mean (F1). The official CoNLL score is computed as the mean of MUC, BCUB, and CEAFE.

	MD	MUC	BCUB
All features	66.56	54.61	65.93
I-HdForm+J-HdForm	-1.35	-2.66	-1.82
StringMatch†	-1.12	-1.32	-1.55
Distance†	-0.16	-0.62	-0.59
J-HdGovPos	-0.51	-0.49	-0.13
I-HdRmcFun	-0.27	-0.39	-0.2
Alias†	-0.47	-0.36	-0.06
I-HdForm	-0.42	-0.18	0.04
I-Gender+J-Gender	-0.3	-0.15	0.05
NumberAgreement†	0.01	-0.14	-0.41
I-HdPos	-0.32	-0.14	0.05
J-Pronoun†	-0.25	-0.08	-0.09
I-HdLmcForm+ J-HdLmcForm	-0.41	-0.04	0.08
I-HdLsForm	-0.01	0.01	0
SsBergsmaLinPath	-0.04	0.02	-0.13
I-HdGovFun	-0.09	0.09	0.01
J-HdFun	-0.01	0.13	-0.04
I-HdLmcPos	-0.08	0.13	-0.09
DsPathForm	-0.03	0.16	-0.02
J-HdGovFun	-0.04	0.16	-0.05
J-Demonstrative†	-0.03	0.18	0.03
GenderAgreement†	0	0.18	-0.01
SemRolePropJHd	0.01	0.2	0.01
I-Pronoun†	0.01	0.22	0.04
I-HdFun	0.05	0.22	-0.06

Table 3: The final feature set and, for each feature, the degradation in performance when leaving out this feature from the set. All evaluations were carried out on the development set. The features marked with a dagger † originate from the Soon et al. (2001) baseline feature set.

5 Conclusions

The main conclusions and contributions of our work to the CoNLL 2011 shared task concern the detection of mention boundaries, feature lexicalization, and dependency features.

The mention boundaries are relatively difficult to identify. Although far from perfect, we applied a direct mapping from constituents to extract the mentions used in the resolution procedure. We then reclaimed some mentions involving proper nouns in a postprocessing step. Using the gold-standard mention boundaries in the test set, we saw an increase in all metrics with up to 3.51 for the MUC score.

The lexicalization of the feature set brings a significant improvement to the scores. By order of performance loss in Table 3, the first feature of our model is a lexical one. This property does not seem to have been systematically explored before, possibly because of a tradition of using corpora of modest sizes in coreference resolution.

Grammatical dependencies seem to play an important role in the anaphoric expressions. Results in Table 3 also show this, although in a less pronounced manner than lexicalization. Features extracted from dependencies are implicit in many systems, but are not explicitly mentioned as such. We hope our work helped clarified this point through a more systematic exploration of this class of features.

Acknowledgements

This research was supported by Vetenskapsrådet, the Swedish research council, under grant 621-2010-4800.

References

Shane Bergsma and Dekang Lin. 2006. Bootstrapping path-based pronoun resolution. In *Proceedings of the*

21st International Conference on Computational Linguistics and 44th Annual Meeting of the ACL, pages 33–40, July.

Rong-En Fan, Kai-Wei Chang, Cho-Jui Hsieh, Xiang-Rui Wang, and Chih-Jen Lin. 2008. LIBLINEAR: A library for large linear classification. *Journal of Machine Learning Research*, 9:1871–1874.

Mark Hall, Eibe Frank, Geoffrey Holmes, Bernhard Pfahringer, Peter Reutemann, and Ian H. Witten. 2009. The WEKA data mining software: An update. *SIGKDD Explorations*, 11(1):10–18, July.

Richard Johansson and Pierre Nugues. 2007. Extended constituent-to-dependency conversion for English. In Joakim Nivre, Heiki-Jaan Kaalep, Kadri Muischnek, and Mare Koit, editors, *NODALIDA 2007 Conference Proceedings*, pages 105–112, Tartu, May 25-26.

Vincent Ng and Claire Cardie. 2002. Improving machine learning approaches to coreference resolution. In *Proceedings of the 40th Annual Meeting of the Association for Computational Linguistics*, pages 104–111.

Simone Paolo Ponzetto and Michael Strube. 2006. Semantic role labeling for coreference resolution. In *Proceedings of the 11th Conference of EACL: Posters and Demonstrations*, pages 143–146, April.

Sameer Pradhan, Lance Ramshaw, Ralph Weischedel, Jessica MacBride, and Linnea Micciulla. 2007. Unrestricted coreference: Identifying entities and events in OntoNotes. In *Proceedings of the IEEE International Conference on Semantic Computing (ICSC)*, Irvine, CA, September 17-19.

Sameer Pradhan, Lance Ramshaw, Mitchell Marcus, Martha Palmer, Ralph Weischedel, and Nianwen Xue. 2011. CoNLL-2011 shared task: Modeling unrestricted coreference in OntoNotes. In *Proceedings of the Fifteenth Conference on Computational Natural Language Learning (CoNLL 2011)*, Portland, Oregon, June.

Wee Meng Soon, Hwee Tou Ng, and Daniel Chung Yong Lim. 2001. A machine learning approach to coreference resolution of noun phrases. *Computational Linguistics*, 27(4):521–544.

Rule and Tree Ensembles for Unrestricted Coreference Resolution*

Cicero Nogueira dos Santos
Universidade de Fortaleza – UNIFOR
Informática Aplicada – PPGIA
Fortaleza, Brazil
cnogueira@unifor.br

Davi Lopes Carvalho
Universidade de Fortaleza – UNIFOR
Informática Aplicada – PPGIA
Fortaleza, Brazil
davi.carvalho@gmail.com

Abstract

In this paper, we describe a machine learning system based on rule and tree ensembles for unrestricted coreference resolution. We use Entropy Guided Transformation Learning (ETL) and Decision Trees as the base learners, and, respectively, ETL Committee and Random Forest as ensemble algorithms. Our system is evaluated on the closed track of the CoNLL 2011 shared task: Modeling Unrestricted Coreference in OntoNotes. A preliminary version of our system achieves the 6th best score out of 21 competitors in the CoNLL 2011 shared task. Here, we depict the system architecture and our experimental results and findings.

1 Introduction

Unrestricted coreference resolution consists in identifying coreferring entities and events in texts. For instance, in the sentence

"She had *a good suggestion* and *it* was unanimously accepted."

there is a coreference between the pronoun "*it*" and the noun phrase "*a good suggestion*". In the following sentence

"Sales of passenger cars *grew* 22%. *The strong growth* followed year-to-year increases."

there is a coreference between the noun phrase "*the strong growth*" and the event "*grew*". Throughout this paper, we use the term *mention* to mean a reference to an entity or event.

The CoNLL 2011 Shared Task (Pradhan et al., 2011) is dedicated to modeling unrestricted coreference in OntoNotes. The participants are provided with a large corpus that contains various annotation layers such as part-of-speech (POS) tagging, parsing, named entities and semantic role labeling. The task consists in the automatic identification of coreferring entities and events given predicted information on other OntoNotes layers. A previous work on modeling unrestricted coreference using an earlier version of this corpus is presented in (Pradhan et al., 2007).

In this paper, we describe the machine learning approach that we used to the closed track of the CoNLL 2011 Shared Task. Our system follows the common strategy of recasting the problem as a classification task. First, in a preprocessing step, a set of candidate mentions is constructed. Next, also in the preprocessing step, pairs of candidate coreferring mentions are generated. Then, each candidate pair of mentions is classified as co-referring or not using a classifier learned from the annotated corpus. Finally, a postprocessing step (clustering) removes inconsistencies that would result of the pairwise classifications and constructs a partition on the set of mentions. In our system, the learning module is based on ensemble learning. We use Entropy Guided Transformation Learning (ETL) (Milidiú et al., 2008) and Decision Trees (DT) (Quinlan, 1993) as base learners, and, respectively, ETL Committee (dos Santos et al., 2010) and Random Forest (Breiman, 2001) as ensemble algorithms.

* This work is partially funded by the FUNCAP grant 0011-00147.01.00/09.

Proceedings of the 15th Conference on Computational Natural Language Learning: Shared Task, pages 51–55, Portland, Oregon, 23-24 June 2011. ©2011 Association for Computational Linguistics

The remainder of this paper is organized as follows. In Section 2, we present the corpus preprocessing and postprocessing steps. Our machine learning modeling for the unrestricted coreference resolution task is presented in Section 3. The experimental findings are depicted in Section 4. Finally, in Section 5, we present our final remarks.

2 Corpus Processing

In this section we describe some preprocessing and postprocessing steps used in the proposed system.

2.1 Candidate Mention Extraction

For each text document, we generate a list of candidate mentions in the following way:

- all the noun phrases (NP) identified in the provided parsing tree are considered as candidate mentions;
- each pronoun is isolatedly considered as a candidate mention even if it is inside a larger NP;
- named entities in the categories Person (PERSON), Organization (ORG) and Geo-Political Entity (GPE) are isolatedly considered as candidate mentions even if they are inside larger NPs. Additionally, in order to better align with the OntoNotes mention annotation, a processing is performed to include possessive marks "'s" and premodifiers such as "Mr.".

In the current version, our system does not consider verbs when creating candidate mentions. Therefore, the system does not resolve coreferences involving events.

2.2 Candidate Co-referring Pairs Generation

In the training phase, we generate positive and negative examples of co-referring pairs using a strategy similar to the one of Soon et al. (2001). In their method, the text is examined in a left-to-right manner. For each anaphoric mention m_j, is generated a positive example pair that includes m_j and its closest preceding antecedent, m_i. A negative example is created for m_j paired with each of the intervening mentions, m_{i+1}, m_{i+2}, ..., m_{j-1}. We extend the Soon et al. (2001) approach by also including all positive and negative pairs that can be formed with *the mentions in the sentence of the closest preceding antecedent*, m_i.

In the classification phase, the text is also examined in a left-to-right manner. For each mention m_j, candidate co-referring pairs are generated by pairing it with a limited number of preceding mentions. When using predicted mentions, we set this limit to 60 (sixty). For the gold-mentions track, the limit is set to 40 (forty).

2.3 Feature Engineering

We use a set of 80 features to describe each pair of mentions (m_i, m_j). The feature set includes lexical, morphological, syntactic, semantic and positional information. Most of them are borrowed from the works of Ng and Cardie (2002) and Sapena et al. (2010). However, we also propose some new features. In the following, due to space constraints, we briefly describe some of them. The features marked with * are the new proposed ones.

Lexical: *head word* of $m_{i/j}$; *String matching* of (head word of) m_i and m_j (y/n); *Both are pronouns* and their strings match (y/n); *Previous/Next two words* of $m_{i/j}$; *Length* of $m_{i/j}$; *Edit distance* of head words; $m_{i/j}$ is a definitive NP (y/n); $m_{i/j}$ is a demonstrative NP (y/n).

Morphological: *Both are proper names* and their strings match (y/n); *Basic gender agreement**, which use a list of proper names extracted from the training corpus (y/n); *Gender/Number* of $m_{i/j}$; *Gender/Number agreement*(y/n), this and the previous feature are generated using the number and gender data provided by Bergsma and Lin (2006).

Syntactic: *POS tag* of the $m_{i/j}$ head word; *Previous/Next two POS tags* of $m_{i/j}$; m_i and m_j are *both pronouns / proper names* (y/n); *Previous/Next predicate* of $m_{i/j}$*; *Compatible pronouns*, which checks whether two pronouns agree in number, gender and person (y/n)*; *NP embedding level*; *Number of embedded NPs* in $m_{i/j}$*.

Semantic: the result of a *baseline system*; *sense* of the $m_{i/j}$ head word; *Named entity* type of $m_{i/j}$; m_i and m_j have the *same named entity*; *Semantic role of* $m_{i/j}$ for the prev/next predicate*; *Concatenation of semantic roles of* m_i *and* m_j for the same predicate (if they are in the same sentence)*; *Same speaker** (y/n); *Alias* (y/n); m_i and m_j have a *hypernym/hyponym* relation (y/n); m_i and m_j have the same semantic class (y/n); *sum of distances* between m_i and m_j to their class. The last three features are generated using WordNet 3.0 (Miller, 1995).

Distance and Position: Distance between m_i and m_j in sentences; Distance in number of mentions; Distance in number of person names (applies only for the cases where m_i and m_j are both pronouns or one of them is a person name)*; One mention is in apposition to the other (y/n).

2.4 Clustering Strategy

In order to generate the coreference chains, it is needed a strategy to create a partition in the mentions using the predictions for the candidate coreferent pairs. This part of the coreference resolution system is frequently called *clustering strategy* (Ng and Cardie, 2002). Our system uses an aggressive-merge clustering approach similar to the one proposed by Mccarthy and Lehnert (1995). In this strategy, each mention is merged with all of its preceding mentions that are classified as coreferent with it.

Additionally, a postprocessing step is employed to remove inconsistencies that would result of the clustering processing, such as an NP being coreferent to its embedded NP.

3 Machine Learning Modeling

In this section we briefly describes the machine learning approaches used in our experiments. We also describe a baseline system (BLS) that is used by ETL for the learning of correction rules. The classification produced by the BLS is also used as a feature for the other experimented learning strategies.

ETL: Entropy Guided Transformation Learning (ETL) is a correction rule learning algorithm. It extends Transformation Based Learning (TBL) by automatically generating rule templates using Decision Trees (DT) (Milidiú et al., 2008). We use an in-house implementation of ETL.

ETL Committee: is an ensemble method that uses ETL as the base learner (dos Santos et al., 2010). This approach combines the main ideas of Bagging and Random Subspaces, as well as rule redundancy and template sampling to generate diverse ETL classifiers. We use an in-house implementation of ETL Committee.

Decision Trees: the C4.5 (Quinlan, 1993) system is one of the most popular DT induction implementation. It induces a tree based classifier using the training data information gain. In our experiments, we use the J48 tool, which is a DT induction system similar to C4.5. J48 is part of the WEKA data mining toolkit (Hall et al., 2009).

Random Forest: is an ensemble method that uses DT as the base learner. In the Random Forest learning process (Breiman, 2001), first, bootstrap sampling is employed to generate multiple replicates of the training set. Then, a decision tree is grown for each training set replicate. When growing a tree, a subset of the available features is randomly selected at each node, the best split available within those features is selected for that node. In our experiments, the WEKA's Random Forest implementation is used.

Baseline System: the BLS classifies a candidate co-referring pair (m_i, m_j) as co-referring when one of the following conditions occur:

- m_j is an alias of m_i;
- m_j and m_i are 3rd person pronouns and there is no person name between them;
- the pair is composed of a person name and a 3rd person pronoun and there is no person name between them;
- removing determiners, m_i matches m_j;
- the feature *basic gender agreement* is true.

The parameters of each algorithm are tuned using the development set. For both, ETL Committee and Random Forest the ensemble size is set to 50.

4 Experiments and Results

We train models for two different CoNLL 2011 shared task closed tracks: (a) using candidate mentions whose boundaries are automatically extracted (see Section 2.1); and (b) using candidate mentions whose boundaries are provided. In the training phase, the gold standard OntoNotes annotation layers are used. For the development and test sets the automatically generated OntoNotes annotation layers are used.

For all experiments, results are reported using three metrics: MUC, B^3 and CEAF(E). We also report the average F_1 score for these three metrics, which is the official CoNLL 2011 shared task metric. Additionally, results for the test set are also reported using the CEAF(M) and BLANC metrics.

4.1 Automatic Mention Boundaries

In Table 1, we show machine learning system results for unrestricted coreference resolution using the development set. As we can see in Table 1, the results of ensemble methods are better than ones of the base learners, which is the expected result. ETL Committee is the classifier that achieve the best results, closely followed by Random Forest.

All the experimented ML systems achieve results better than the baseline. However, the improvement provided by ML is more expressive only for the MUC metric. For instance, ETL Committee provides an improvement over the baseline of about 6.5 points in the MUC F1-score, while the improvement for the other two metrics is only about 2 points.

We run an additional experiment by constructing a heterogeneous committee composed by the three best classifiers: (1) ETL Committee, (2) Random Forest and (3) ETL. The results for this system is shown in table line with ML Model name "(1) + (2) + (3)". This heterogeneous committee provides our best experimental results for the development set, which is slightly better than ETL Committee results.

Due to deadline constraints, the system output that we have submitted to the CoNLL 2011 shared task is a majority voting committee of three different ETL classifiers. These three ETL classifiers slightly differs in the used feature sets. In Table 1, the results of the Submitted System is presented for the development set. Table 2 presents the Submitted System results for the test set. Our system achieves the 6th best score out of 21 competitors in the closed track of the CoNLL 2011 shared task.

4.2 Gold Mention Boundaries

For the gold mention boundaries task, we were not able to assess system performances on the development set. This is due to the fact that not all gold mentions are annotated in the development set.

We have submitted two outputs for the CoNLL 2011 shared task gold mentions closed track. These

Metric	R	P	F_1
MUC	59.21	54.30	56.65
BCUBED	68.79	62.81	65.66
CEAF (M)	49.54	49.54	49.54
CEAF (E)	35.86	40.21	37.91
BLANC	73.37	66.91	69.46
(MUC + B^3 + CEAF(E))/3			53.41

Table 2: Submitted System results for the test set using automatically extracted mention boundaries.

outputs were generated by two systems described in the previous subsection: (a) the Submitted System; and (b) the heterogeneous committee (ETL Committee + Random Forest + ETL). In Table 3, we show the system results for the test set with gold standard mentions. Again, the heterogeneous committee provides our best results.

At the moment of writing this paper, the scoreboard for this task has not yet been released by the CoNLL 2011 shared task committee.

5 Conclusion

In this paper, we describe a machine learning system based on rule and tree ensembles for unrestricted coreference resolution. The system uses Entropy Guided Transformation Learning and Decision Trees as the base learners. ETL Committee and Random Forest are the used ensemble algorithms. We depict the system architecture and present experimental results and findings of our participation in the CoNLL 2011 shared task.

We present results for two closed tasks: (a) using automatically extracted mention boundaries; and (b) using gold mention boundaries. For both tasks, ensemble classifiers have better results than the base classifiers. This is the expected outcome, since ensemble classifiers tend to be more accurate than the base classifiers. We also experiment heterogeneous committees that combines the three best classifier for the first task. Heterogeneous committees provide our best scoring results for both tasks. Using a preliminary version of our system, we achieve the 6th best score out of 21 competitors in the closed track of the CoNLL 2011 shared task.

One of the possible future works, is to investigate the impact of the new features that we propose.

	MUC			B^3			CEAF(E)			(MUC + B^3 + CEAF(E))/3
ML Model	R	P	F_1	R	P	F_1	R	P	F_1	F_1
(1) ETL Committee	52.31	**57.51**	54.78	63.62	70.42	66.84	42.64	37.99	40.18	53.93
(2) Random Forest	53.31	54.91	54.10	65.23	67.31	66.25	40.47	39.05	39.75	53.37
(3) ETL	**54.80**	52.24	53.49	67.56	62.19	64.77	37.22	39.55	38.35	52.20
(4) Decision Trees	57.51	49.12	52.98	**71.23**	58.94	64.50	34.84	**42.25**	38.19	51.89
(5) Baseline System	43.04	55.13	48.34	57.82	**74.21**	64.99	**43.63**	33.62	37.98	50.43
(1) + (2) + (3)	52.77	57.44	**55.00**	64.09	70.58	**67.18**	42.67	38.48	**40.47**	**54.21**
Submitted System	54.65	53.25	53.94	67.15	63.86	65.46	38.3	39.56	38.92	52.45

Table 1: System results for the development set using automatically extracted mention boundaries.

	Submitted System			(1) + (2) + (3)		
Metric	R	P	F_1	R	P	F_1
MUC	**58.77**	56.54	57.64	57.76	**61.39**	**59.52**
BCUBED	**67.05**	64.84	65.92	64.49	**70.27**	**67.26**
CEAF (M)	50.05	50.05	50.05	**51.87**	**51.87**	**51.87**
CEAF (E)	37.61	**39.62**	38.59	**41.42**	38.16	**39.72**
BLANC	72.59	67.76	69.80	**72.72**	**71.97**	**72.34**
(MUC + B^3 + CEAF(E))/3			54.05			**55.50**

Table 3: System results for the test set using gold mention boundaries.

References

Shane Bergsma and Dekang Lin. 2006. Bootstrapping path-based pronoun resolution. In *Proceedings of ACL2006*, ACL–44, pages 33–40, Stroudsburg, PA, USA. Association for Computational Linguistics.

Leo Breiman. 2001. Random forests. *Machine Learning*, 45(1):5–32.

Cícero Nogueira dos Santos, Ruy Luiz Milidiú, Carlos E. M. Crestana, and Eraldo R. Fernandes. 2010. ETL ensembles for chunking, NER and SRL. In *11th International Conference on Computational Linguistics and Intelligent Text Processing, CICLing*, pages 100–112.

Mark Hall, Eibe Frank, Geoffrey Holmes, Bernhard Pfahringer, Peter Reutemann, and Ian H. Witten. 2009. The weka data mining software: an update. *Sigkdd Explorations*, 11:10–18.

Joseph F Mccarthy and Wendy G Lehnert. 1995. Using decision trees for coreference resolution. In *In Proceedings of the Fourteenth International Joint Conference on Artificial Intelligence*, pages 1050–1055.

Ruy L. Milidiú, Cícero N. dos Santos, and Julio C. Duarte. 2008. Phrase chunking using entropy guided transformation learning. In *Proceedings of ACL2008*, Columbus, Ohio.

George A. Miller. 1995. Wordnet: A lexical database for english. *Communications of the ACM*, 38:39–41.

Vincent Ng and Claire Cardie. 2002. Improving machine learning approaches to coreference resolution. In *Proceedings of the 40th Annual Meeting on Association for Computational Linguistics*, ACL '02, pages 104–111, Stroudsburg, PA, USA. Association for Computational Linguistics.

Sameer Pradhan, Lance Ramshaw, Ralph Weischedel, Jessica MacBride, and Linnea Micciulla. 2007. Unrestricted Coreference: Identifying Entities and Events in OntoNotes. In *in Proceedings of the IEEE International Conference on Semantic Computing (ICSC)*, September 17–19.

Sameer Pradhan, Lance Ramshaw, Mitchell Marcus, Martha Palmer, Ralph Weischedel, and Nianwen Xue. 2011. CoNLL-2011 shared task: Modeling unrestricted coreference in ontonotes. In *Proceedings of the Fifteenth Conference on Computational Natural Language Learning (CoNLL 2011)*, Portland, Oregon, June.

J. Ross Quinlan. 1993. *C4.5: programs for machine learning*. Morgan Kaufmann Publishers Inc., San Francisco, CA, USA.

Emili Sapena, Lluís Padró, and Jordi Turmo. 2010. Relaxcor: A global relaxation labeling approach to coreference resolution. In *Proceedings of the 5th International Workshop on Semantic Evaluation*, SemEval '10, pages 88–91, Stroudsburg, PA, USA. Association for Computational Linguistics.

Wee Meng Soon, Hwee Tou Ng, and Daniel Chung Yong Lim. 2001. A machine learning approach to coreference resolution of noun phrases. *Computational Linguistics*, 27:521–544, December.

Unrestricted Coreference Resolution via Global Hypergraph Partitioning

Jie Cai and **Éva Mújdricza-Maydt** and **Michael Strube**
Natural Language Processing Group
Heidelberg Institute for Theoretical Studies gGmbH
Heidelberg, Germany
(jie.cai|eva.mujdriczamaydt|michael.strube)@h-its.org

Abstract

We present our end-to-end coreference resolution system, *COPA*, which implements a global decision via hypergraph partitioning. In constrast to almost all previous approaches, we do not rely on separate classification and clustering steps, but perform coreference resolution globally in one step. *COPA* represents each document as a hypergraph and partitions it with a spectral clustering algorithm. Various types of relational features can be easily incorporated in this framwork. *COPA* has participated in the *open* setting of the CoNLL shared task on modeling unrestricted coreference.

1 Introduction

Coreference resolution is the task of grouping mentions of entities into sets so that all mentions in one set refer to the same entity. Most recent approaches to coreference resolution divide this task into two steps: (1) a classification step which determines whether a pair of mentions is coreferent or which outputs a confidence value, and (2) a clustering step which groups mentions into entities based on the output of step 1.

In this paper we present an end-to-end coreference resolution system, *COPA*, which avoids the division into two steps and instead performs a global decision in one step. The system presents a document as a hypergraph, where the vertices denote mentions and the edges denote relational features between mentions. Coreference resolution is then performed globally in one step by partitioning the hypergraph into subhypergraphs so that all mentions in one subhypergraph refer to the same entity (Cai and Strube, 2010). *COPA* assigns edge weights by applying simple descriptive statistics on the tranining data. Since *COPA* does not need to learn an explicit model, we used only 30% of the CoNLL shared task training data. We did this not for efficiency reasons, only for convenience.

While *COPA* has been developed originally to perform coreference resolution on MUC and ACE data (Cai and Strube, 2010), the move to the OntoNotes data (Weischedel et al., 2011) required mainly to update the mention detector and the feature set. Since several off-the-shelf preprocessing components are used, *COPA* participated in the *open* setting of the CoNLL shared task on modeling unrestricted coreference (Pradhan et al., 2011). We did not make extensive use of information beyond information from the closed class setting.

2 Preprocessing

COPA is implemented on top of the *BART*-toolkit (Versley et al., 2008). Documents are transformed into the *MMAX2*-format (Müller and Strube, 2006) which allows for easy visualization and (linguistic) debugging. Each document is stored in several XML-files representing different layers of annotations. These annotations are created by a pipeline of preprocessing components. We use the *Stanford MaxentTagger* (Toutanova et al., 2003) for part-of-speech tagging, and the *Stanford Named Entity Recognizer* (Finkel et al., 2005) for annotating named entities. In order to derive syntactic information, we use the *Charniak/Johnson reranking parser* (Charniak and Johnson, 2005) com-

Proceedings of the 15th Conference on Computational Natural Language Learning: Shared Task, pages 56–60,
Portland, Oregon, 23-24 June 2011. ©2011 Association for Computational Linguistics

bined with a constituent-to-dependency conversion Tool (`http://nlp.cs.lth.se/software/treebank_converter`). The preprocessing models are not trained on CoNLL data, so we only participated in the open task.

We have implemented an in-house mention detector, which makes use of the parsing output, the part-of-speech tags, as well as the chunks from the *Yamcha Chunker* (Kudoh and Matsumoto, 2000). For the OntoNotes data, the mention detector annotates the biggest noun phrase spans.

3 COPA: Coreference Partitioner

The *COPA* system consists of modules which derive hyperedges from features and assign edge weights indicating a positive correlation with the coreference relation, and resolution modules which create a hypergraph representation for the testing data and perform partitioning to produce subhypergraphs, each of which represents an entity.

3.1 HyperEdgeCreator

COPA needs training data only for computing the hyperedge weights. Hyperedges represent features. Each hyperedge corresponds to a feature instance modeling a simple relation between two or more mentions. This leads to initially overlapping sets of mentions. Hyperedges are assigned weights which are calculated on the training data as the percentage of the initial edges being in fact coreferent. Due to the simple strategy of assigning edge weights, only a reasonable size of training data is needed.

3.2 Coreference Resolution Modules

Unlike pairwise models, *COPA* processes a document globally in one step, taking care of the preference information among all the mentions simultaneously and clustering them into sets directly. A document is represented as a single hypergraph with multiple edges. The hypergraph resolver partitions the hypergraph into several sub-hypergraphs, each corresponding to one set of coreferent mentions.

3.2.1 HGModelBuilder

A single document is represented in a hypergraph with basic relational features. Each hyperedge in a graph corresponds to an instance of one of those features with the weight assigned by the *HyperEdgeLearner*. Instead of connecting nodes with the target relation as usually done in graph models, *COPA* builds the graph directly out of low dimensional features without assuming a distance metric.

3.2.2 HGResolver

In order to partition the hypergraph we adopt a spectral clustering algorithm (Agarwal et al., 2005). All experimental results are obtained using symmetric Laplacians (L_{sym}) (von Luxburg, 2007).

We apply the recursive variant of spectral clustering, *recursive 2-way partitioning (R2 partitioner)* (Cai and Strube, 2010). This method does not need any information about the number of target sets (the number k of clusters). Instead a stopping criterion $\alpha^\star$ has to be provided which is adjusted on development data.

3.3 Complexity of HGResolver

Since edge weights are assigned using simple descriptive statistics, the time HGResolver needs for building the graph Laplacian matrix is not substantial. For eigensolving, we use an open source library provided by the Colt project[1]which implements a Householder-QL algorithm to solve the eigenvalue decomposition. When applied to the symmetric graph Laplacian, the complexity of the eigensolving is given by $O(n^3)$, where n is the number of mentions in a hypergraph. Since there are only a few hundred mentions per document in our data, this complexity is not an issue. Spectral clustering gets problematic when applied to millions of data points.

4 Features

In our system, features are represented as types of hyperedges. Any realized edge is an instance of the corresponding edge type. All instances derived from the same type have the same weight, but they may get reweighed by the distance feature (see Cai and Strube (2010)). We use three types of features:

negative: prevent edges between mentions;

positive: generate strong edges between mentions;

weak: add edges to an existing graph without introducing new vertices;

[1] `http://acs.lbl.gov/~hoschek/colt/`

In the following subsections we describe the features used in our experiments. Some of the features described in Cai and Strube (2010) had to be changed to cope with the OntoNotes data. We also introduced a few more features (in particular in order to deal with the dialogue section in the data).

4.1 Negative Features

Negative features describe pairwise relations which are most likely not coreferent. While we implemented this information as weak positive features in Cai and Strube (2010), here we apply these features before graph construction as global variables.

When two mentions are connected by a negative relation, no edges will be built between them in the graph. For instance, no edges are allowed between the mention *Hillary Clinton* and the mention *he* due to incompatible gender.

(1) N_Gender, (2) N_Number: Two mentions do not agree in gender or number.

(3) N_SemanticClass: Two mentions do not agree in semantic class (only the *Object*, *Date* and *Person* top categories derived from WordNet (Fellbaum, 1998) are used).

(4) N_Mod: Two mentions have the same syntactic heads, and the anaphor has a pre-modifier which does not occur in the antecedent and does not contradict the antecedent.

(5) N_DSPrn: Two first person pronouns in direct speeches assigned to different speakers.

(6) N_ContraSubjObj: Two mentions are in the subject and object positions of the same verb, and the anaphor is a non-possesive pronoun.

4.2 Positive Features

The majority of well studied coreference features (e.g. Stoyanov et al. (2009)) are actually positive coreference indicators. In our system, the mentions which participate in positive relations are included in the graph representation.

(7) StrMatch_Npron & (8) StrMatch_Pron: After discarding stop words, if the strings of mentions completely match and are not pronouns, they are put into edges of the *StrMatch_Npron* type. When the matched mentions are pronouns, they are put into the *StrMatch_Pron* type edges.

(9) Alias: After discarding stop words, if mentions are aliases of each other (i.e. proper names with partial match, full names and acronyms, etc.).

(10) HeadMatch: If the syntactic heads of mentions match.

(11) Nprn_Prn: If the antecedent is not a pronoun and the anaphor is a pronoun. This feature is restricted to a sentence distance of 2. Though it is not highly weighted, it is crucial for integrating pronouns into the graph.

(12) Speaker12Prn: If the speaker of the second person pronoun is talking to the speaker of the first person pronoun. The mentions contain only first or second person pronouns.

(13) DSPrn: If one of the mentions is the subject of a *speak* verb, and other mentions are first person pronouns within the corresponding direct speech.

(14) ReflexivePrn: If the anaphor is a reflexive pronoun, and the antecedent is subject of the sentence.

(15) PossPrn: If the anaphor is a possesive pronoun, and the antecedent is the subject of the sentence or the subclause.

(16) GPEIsA: If the antecedent is a Named Entity of GPE entity type (i.e. one of the ACE entity type (NIST, 2004)), and the anaphor is a definite expression of the same type.

(17) OrgIsA: If the antecedent is a Named Entity of Organization entity type, and the anaphor is a definite expression of the same type.

4.3 Weak Features

Weak features are weak coreference indicators. Using them as positive features would introduce too much noise to the graph (i.e. a graph with too many singletons). We apply weak features only to mentions already integrated in the graph, so that weak information provides it with a richer structure.

(18) W_Speak: If mentions occur with a word meaning *to say* in a window size of two words.

(19) W_Subject: If mentions are subjects.

(20) W_Synonym: If mentions are synonymous as indicated by WordNet.

5 Results

We submitted *COPA*'s results to the *open* setting in the CoNLL shared task on modeling unrestricted coreference. We used only 30% of the training data (randomly selected) and the 20 features described in Section 4.

The stopping criterion $\alpha*$ (see Section 3) is tuned on development data to optimize the final coreference scores. A value of 0.06 is chosen for testing.

COPA's results on development set (which consists of 202 files) and on testing set are displayed in Table 1 and Table 2 respectively. The *Overall* numbers in both tables are the average scores of MUC, $BCUBED$ and $CEAF(E)$.

Metric	R	P	F1
MUC	52.69	57.94	55.19
$BCUBED$	64.26	73.39	68.52
$CEAF(M)$	54.44	54.44	54.44
$CEAF(E)$	45.73	40.92	43.19
$BLANC$	69.78	75.26	72.13
$Overall$			55.63

Table 1: *COPA*'s results on CoNLL development set

Metric	R	P	F1
MUC	56.73	58.90	57.80
$BCUBED$	64.60	71.03	67.66
$CEAF(M)$	53.37	53.37	53.37
$CEAF(E)$	42.71	40.68	41.67
$BLANC$	69.77	73.96	71.62
$Overall$			55.71

Table 2: *COPA*'s results on CoNLL testing set

6 Mention Detection Errors

As described in Section 2, our mention detection is based on automatically extracted information, such as syntactic parses and basic noun phrase chunks. Since there is no *minimum span* information provided in the OntoNotes data (in constrast to the previous standard corpus, ACE), exact mention boundary detection is required. A lot of the spurious mentions in our system are generated due to mismatches of ending or starting punctuations, and the OntoNotes annotation is also not consistent in this regard. Our current mention detector does not extract verb phrases. Therefore it misses all the *Event* mentions in the OntoNotes corpus.

We are planning to include idiomatic expression identification into our mention detector, which will help to avoid detecting a lot of spurious mentions, such as *God* in the phrase *for God's sake*.

7 *COPA* Errors

Besides the fact that the current *COPA* is not resolving any *event coreferences*, our in-house mention detector performs weakly in extracting *date* mentions too. As a result, the system outputs several spurious coreference sets, for instance a set containing the *September* from the mention *15th September*.

A large amount of the recall loss in our system is due to the lack of the world knowledge. For example, *COPA* does not resolve the mention *the Europe station* correctly into the entity *Radio Free Europe*, for it has no knowledge that the entity is a station.

Some more difficult coreference phenomena in *OntoNotes* data might require a reasoning mechanism. To be able to connect the mention *the victim* with the mention *the groom's brother*, the event of the brother being killed needs to be intepreted by the system.

We also observed from the experiments that the resolution of the *it* mentions are quite inaccurate. Although our mention detector takes care of discarding pleonastic *it*'s, there are still a lot of them left which introduce wrong coreference sets. Since the *it*'s do not contain enough information by themselves, more features exploring their local syntax are necessary.

8 Conclusions

In this paper we described a coreference resolution system, *COPA*, which implements a global decision in one step via hypergraph partitioning. *COPA*'s hypergraph-based strategy is a general preference model, where the preference for one mention depends on information on all other mentions.

The system implements three types of relational features — negative, positive and weak features, and assigns the edge weights according to the statitics from the training data. Since the weights are robust with respect to the amount of training data we used only 30% of the training data.

Acknowledgements. This work has been funded by the Klaus Tschira Foundation, Heidelberg, Germany. The first author has been supported by a HITS PhD. scholarship.

References

Sameer Agarwal, Jonwoo Lim, Lihi Zelnik-Manor, Pietro Perona, David Kriegman, and Serge Belongie. 2005. Beyond pairwise clustering. In *Proceedings of the IEEE Computer Society Conference on Computer Vision and Pattern Recognition (CVPR'05)*, volume 2, pages 838–845.

Jie Cai and Michael Strube. 2010. End-to-end coreference resolution via hypergraph partitioning. In *Proceedings of the 23rd International Conference on Computational Linguistics,* Beijing, China, 23–27 August 2010, pages 143–151.

Eugene Charniak and Mark Johnson. 2005. Coarse-to-fine n-best parsing and MaxEent discriminative reranking. In *Proceedings of the 43rd Annual Meeting of the Association for Computational Linguistics,* Ann Arbor, Mich., 25–30 June 2005, pages 173–180.

Christiane Fellbaum, editor. 1998. *WordNet: An Electronic Lexical Database.* MIT Press, Cambridge, Mass.

Jenny Rose Finkel, Trond Grenager, and Christopher Manning. 2005. Incorporating non-local information into information extraction systems by Gibbs sampling. In *Proceedings of the 43rd Annual Meeting of the Association for Computational Linguistics,* Ann Arbor, Mich., 25–30 June 2005, pages 363–370.

Taku Kudoh and Yuji Matsumoto. 2000. Use of Support Vector Machines for chunk identification. In *Proceedings of the 4th Conference on Computational Natural Language Learning,* Lisbon, Portugal, 13–14 September 2000, pages 142–144.

Christoph Müller and Michael Strube. 2006. Multi-level annotation of linguistic data with MMAX2. In Sabine Braun, Kurt Kohn, and Joybrato Mukherjee, editors, *Corpus Technology and Language Pedagogy: New Resources, New Tools, New Methods*, pages 197–214. Peter Lang: Frankfurt a.M., Germany.

NIST. 2004. The ACE evaluation plan: Evaluation of the recognition of ACE entities, ACE relations and ACE events. http://www.itl.nist.gov/iad/mig//tests/ace/2004/doc/ace04-evalplan-v7.pdf.

Sameer Pradhan, Lance Ramshaw, Mitchell Marcus, Martha Palmer, Ralph Weischedel, and Nianwen Xue. 2011. CoNLL-2011 Shared Task: Modeling unrestricted coreference in OntoNotes. In *Proceedings of the Shared Task of 15th Conference on Computational Natural Language Learning,* Portland, Oreg., 23–24 June 2011.

Veselin Stoyanov, Nathan Gilbert, Claire Cardie, and Ellen Riloff. 2009. Conundrums in noun phrase coreference resolution: Making sense of the state-of-the-art. In *Proceedings of the Joint Conference of the 47th Annual Meeting of the Association for Computational Linguistics and the 4th International Joint Conference on Natural Language Processing,* Singapore, 2–7 August 2009, pages 656–664.

Kristina Toutanova, Dan Klein, Christopher D. Manning, and Yoram Singer. 2003. Feature-rich part-of-speech tagging with a cyclic dependency network. In *Proceedings of the Human Language Technology Conference of the North American Chapter of the Association for Computational Linguistics,* Edmonton, Alberta, Canada, 27 May –1 June 2003, pages 252–259.

Yannick Versley, Simone Paolo Ponzetto, Massimo Poesio, Vladimir Eidelman, Alan Jern, Jason Smith, Xiaofeng Yang, and Alessandro Moschitti. 2008. BART: A modular toolkit for coreference resolution. In *Companion Volume to the Proceedings of the 46th Annual Meeting of the Association for Computational Linguistics,* Columbus, Ohio, 15–20 June 2008, pages 9–12.

Ulrike von Luxburg. 2007. A tutorial on spectral clustering. *Statistics and Computing*, 17(4):395–416.

Ralph Weischedel, Martha Palmer, Mitchell Marcus, Eduard Hovy, Sameer Pradhan, Lance Ramshaw, Nianwen Xue, Ann Taylor, Jeff Kaufman, Michelle Franchini, Mohammed El-Bachouti, Robert Belvin, and Ann Houston. 2011. OntoNotes release 4.0. LDC2011T03, Philadelphia, Penn.: Linguistic Data Consortium.

Multi-metric optimization for coreference: The UniTN / IITP / Essex submission to the 2011 CONLL Shared Task

Olga Uryupina[‡] **Sriparna Saha**[†] **Asif Ekbal**[†] **Massimo Poesio**[*‡]
[‡]University of Trento
[†]Indian Institute of Technology Patna
[*] University of Essex
uryupina@gmail.com, sriparna@iitp.ac.in,
asif@iitp.ac.in, massimo.poesio@unitn.it

Abstract

Because there is no generally accepted metric for measuring the performance of anaphora resolution systems, a combination of metrics was proposed to evaluate submissions to the 2011 CONLL Shared Task (Pradhan et al., 2011). We investigate therefore Multi-objective function Optimization (MOO) techniques based on Genetic Algorithms to optimize models according to multiple metrics simultaneously.

1 Introduction

Many evaluation metrics have been proposed for anaphora resolution (Vilain et al., 1995; Bagga and Baldwin, 1998; Doddington et al., 2000; Luo, 2005; Recasens and Hovy, 2011). Each of these metrics seems to capture some genuine intuition about the the task, so that, unlike in other areas of HLT, none has really taken over. This makes it difficult to compare systems, as dramatically demonstrated by the results of the Coreference Task at SEMEVAL 2010 (Recasens et al., 2010). It was therefore wise of the CONLL organizers to use a basket of metrics to assess performance instead of a single one.

This situation suggests using methods to optimize systems according to more than one metric at once. And as it happens, techniques for doing just that have been developed in the area of Genetic Algorithms—so-called **multi-objective optimization** techniques (MOO) (Deb, 2001). The key idea of our submission is to use MOO techniques to optimize our anaphora resolution system according to three metrics simultaneously: the MUC scorer (a member of what one might call the 'link-based' cluster of metrics) and the two CEAF metrics (representative of the 'entity-based' cluster). In a previous study (Saha et al., 2011), we show that our MOO-based approach yields more robust results than single-objective optimization.

We test two types of optimization: feature selection and architecture–whether to learn a single model for all types of anaphors, or to learn separate models for pronouns and for other nominals. We also discuss how the default mention extraction techniques of the system we used for this submission, BART (Versley et al., 2008), were modified to handle the all-mention annotation in the OntoNotes corpus.

In this paper, we first briefly provide some background on optimization for anaphora resolution, on genetic algorithms, and on the method for multi-objective optimization we used, Non-Dominated Sorting Genetic Algorithm II (Deb et al., 2002). After that we discuss our experiments, and present our results.

2 Background

2.1 Optimization for Anaphora Resolution

There have only been few attempts at optimization for anaphora resolution, and with a few exceptions, this was done by hand.

The first systematic attempt at automatic optimization of anaphora resolution we are aware of was carried out by Hoste (2005), who used genetic algorithms for automatic optimization of both feature selection and of learning parameters, also considering

Proceedings of the 15th Conference on Computational Natural Language Learning: Shared Task, pages 61–65,
Portland, Oregon, 23-24 June 2011. ©2011 Association for Computational Linguistics

two different machine learners, TimBL and Ripper. Her results suggest that such techniques yield improvements on the MUC-6/7 datasets. Recasens and Hovy (2009) carried out an investigation of feature selection for Spanish using the ANCORA corpus.

A form of multi-objective optimization was applied to coreference by Munson et al. (2005). Munson et al. (2005) did not propose to train models so as to simultaneously optimize according to multiple metrics; instead, they used ensemble selection to learn to choose among previously trained models the best model for each example. Their general conclusion was negative, stating that "ensemble selection seems too unreliable for use in NLP", but they did see some improvements for coreference.

2.2 Genetic Algorithms

Genetic algorithms (GAs) (Goldberg, 1989) are randomized search and optimization techniques guided by the principles of evolution and natural genetics. In GAs the parameters of the search space are encoded in the form of strings called *chromosomes*. A collection of such strings is called a *population*. An *objective* or *fitness* function is associated with each chromosome that represents the degree of *goodness* of that chromosome. A few of the chromosomes are selected on the basis of the principle of survival of the fittest, and assigned a number of copies that go into the mating pool. Biologically inspired operators like *crossover* and *mutation* are applied on these chromosomes to yield a new generation of strings. The processes of selection, crossover and mutation continues for a fixed number of generations or till a termination condition is satisfied.

2.3 Multi-objective Optimization

Multi-objective optimization (MOO) can be formally stated as follows (Deb, 2001). Find the vectors $\overline{x}^* = [x_1^*, x_2^*, \ldots, x_n^*]^T$ of decision variables that simultaneously optimize the M objective values

$$\{f_1(\overline{x}), f_2(\overline{x}), \ldots, f_M(\overline{x})\}$$

while satisfying the constraints, if any.

An important concept in MOO is that of **domination**. In the context of a maximization problem, a solution $\overline{x_i}$ is said to dominate $\overline{x_j}$ if $\forall k \in 1, 2, \ldots, M$, $f_k(\overline{x_i}) \geq f_k(\overline{x_j})$ and $\exists k \in 1, 2, \ldots, M$, such that $f_k(\overline{x_i}) > f_k(\overline{x_j})$.

Genetic algorithms are known to be more effective for solving MOO than classical methods such as weighted metrics, goal programming (Deb, 2001), because of their population-based nature. A particularly popular genetic algorithm of this type is NSGA-II (Deb et al., 2002), which we used for our runs.

3 Using MOO for Optimization in Anaphora Resolution

We used multi-objective optimization techniques for feature selection and for identifying the optimal architecture for the CONLL data. In this section we briefly discuss each aspect of the methodology.

3.1 The BART System

For our experiments, we use BART (Versley et al., 2008), a modular toolkit for anaphora resolution that supports state-of-the-art statistical approaches to the task and enables efficient feature engineering. BART comes with a set of already implemented features, along with the possibility to design new ones. It also implements different models of anaphora resolution, allowing the choice between single and split classifiers that we explore in our runs, as well as between mention-pair and entity-mention, and between best-first and ranking. It also has interfaces to different machine learners (MaxEnt, SVM, decision trees). It is thus ideally suited for experimenting with feature selection and other aspects of optimization. However, considering all the parameters, it was unfeasible to run an optimization on the amount of data available on CONLL; we focused therefore on feature selection and the choice between single and split classifiers. We considered 42 features, including 7 classifying mention type, 8 for string matching of different subparts and different levels of exactness, 2 for aliasing, 4 for agreement, 12 for syntactic information including also binding constraints, 3 encoding salience, 1 encoding patterns extracted from the Web, 3 for proximity, and 2 for 1st and 2nd person pronouns. Again because of time considerations, we used decision trees as implemented in Weka as our classification model instead of maximum-entropy or SVMs. Finally, we used a simple mention-pair model without ranking as in (Soon et al., 2001).

3.2 Mention detection

BART supports several solutions to the mention detection (MD) task. The users can input precomputed mentions, thus, experimenting with *gold* boundaries or *system* boundaries computed by external modules (e.g., CARAFE). BART also has a built-in mention extraction module, computing boundaries heuristically from the output of a parser.

For the CoNLL shared task, we use the BART internal MD module, as it corresponds better to the mention detection guidelines of the OntoNotes dataset. We have further adjusted this module to improve the MD accuracy. The process of mention detection involves two steps.

First, we create a list of *candidate mentions* by merging basic NP chunks with named entities. NP chunks are computed from the parse trees provided in the CoNLL distribution, Named entities are extracted with the Stanford NER tool (Finkel et al., 2005). For each candidate mention, we store it minimal and maximal span. The former is used for computing feature values (e.g., for string matching); it corresponds to either the basic NP chunk or the NE, depending on the mention type. The latter is used for alignment with CoNLL mentions; it is computed by climbing up the parse tree.

This procedure, combined with the perfect (gold) coreference resolution, gives us an F-score of 91.56% for the mention detection task on the CoNLL development set[1].

At the second step, we aim at discarding mentions that are unlikely to participate in coreference chains. We have identified several groups of such mentions: erroneous ("[uh]"), (parts of) multiword expressions ("for [example]"), web addresses, emails ("[http://conll.bbn.com]"), time/date expressions ("two times [a year]"), non-referring pronouns ("[there]","[nobody]"), pronouns that are unlikely to participate in a chain ("[somebody]", "[that]"), time/date expressions that are unlikely to participate in a chain ("[this time]"), and expletive "it".

Our experiments on the development data show that the first five groups can be reliably identified and safely discarded from the processing: even with the perfect resolution, we observe virtually no performance loss (the F-score for our MD module with the gold coreference resolution remains at 91.45% once we discard mentions from groups 1-5).

The remaining groups are more problematic: when we eliminate such mentions, we see performance drops with the gold resolution. The exact impact of discarding those mentions can only be assessed once we have trained the classifier.

In practice, we have performed our optimization experiments, selected the best classifier and then have done additional runs to fine-tune the mention detection module.

3.3 Using NSGA-II

Chromosome Representation of Feature and Architecture Parameters We used chromosomes of length 43, each binary gene encoding whether or not to use a particular feature in constructing the classifier, plus one gene set to 1 to use a split classifier, 0 to use a single classifier for all types of anaphors.

Fitness Computation and Mutations For fitness computation, the following procedure is executed.

1. Suppose there are N number of features present in a particular chromosome (i.e., there are total N number of 1's in that chromosome).

2. Construct the coreference resolution system (i.e., BART) with only these N features.

3. This coreference system is evaluated on the development data. The recall, precision and F-measure values of three metrics are calculated.

For MOO, the objective functions corresponding to a particular chromosome are F_1 = F-measure$_{MUC}$ (for the MUC metric), F_2 = F-measure$_{\phi_3}$ (for CEAF using the ϕ_3 entity alignment function (Luo, 2005)) and F_3 = F-measure$_{\phi_4}$ (for CEAF using the ϕ_3 entity alignment function). The objective is to: $max[F_1, F_2, F_3]$: i.e., these three objective functions are simultaneously optimized using the search capability of NSGA-II.

We use crowded binary tournament selection as in NSGA-II, followed by conventional crossover and mutation for the MOO based optimization. The most characteristic part of NSGA-II is its elitism operation, where the non-dominated solutions (Deb,

[1]Note that, due to the fact that OntoNotes guidelines exclude singleton mentions, it is impossible to evaluate the MD component independently from coreference resolution.

2001) among the parent and child populations are propagated to the next generation. The near-Pareto-optimal strings of the last generation provide the different solutions to the feature selection problem.

Genetic Algorithms Parameters Using the CONLL development set, we set the following parameter values for MOO (i.e., NSGA-II): population size=20, number of generations=20, probability of mutation=0.1 and probability of crossover=0.9.

3.4 Running the Optimization

Considering the size of the OntoNotes corpus, it would be very time-consuming to run an optimization experiment on the whole dataset. We have therefore split the data into 3 sub-samples and performed separate MOO experiments on each one.

The MOO approach provides a set of non-dominated solutions on the final Pareto optimal front. All the solutions are equally important from the algorithmic point of view. We have collected sets of chromosomes for each sub-sample and evaluated them on the whole train/development set, picking the solution with the highest FINAL[2] score for our CoNLL submission.

4 Results

4.1 Development set

Table 1 compares the performance level obtained using all the features with that of loose re-implementations of the systems proposed by Soon et al. (2001) and Ng and Cardie (2002), commonly used as baselines. Our reimplementation of the Ng & Cardie model uses only a subset of features.

The results in Table 1 show that our system with a rich feature set does not outperform simpler baselines (and, in fact, yields poorer results). A similar trend has been observed by Ng and Cardie (2002), where the improvement was only possible after manual feature selection.

The last line of Table 1 shows the performance level of the best chromosome found through the MOO technique. As it can be seen, it outperforms all the baselines according to all the measures, leading to an improvement of 2-5 percentage points in the FINAL score.

This suggests that automatic feature selection is essential to improve performance – i.e., that an efficient coreference resolution system should combine rich linguistic feature sets with automatic feature selection mechanisms.

4.2 Test set

We have re-trained our best solution on the combined train and development set, running it on the test data. This system has showed the following performance in the official evaluation (open track): the FINAL score of 54.32, $F_{MUC} = 57.53\%$, $F_{B3} = 65.18\%$, $F_{CEAFE} = 40.16\%$.

5 Conclusion

Our results on the development set suggest that a linguistically-rich system for coreference resolution might benefit a lot from feature selection. In particular, we have investigated Non-Dominated Sorting Genetic Algorithm II (Deb et al., 2002) for multi-objective optimization.

In subsequent work, we plan to expand the optimization technique to consider also learning parameters optimization, classifier selection, and learning model selection.

Acknowledgments

This work was in part supported by the Provincia di Trento Grande Progetto LiveMemories, in part by an Erasmus Mundus scholarship for Asif Ekbal and Sriparna Saha.

[2]The FINAL score is an average of F_{MUC}, F_{B3} and F_{CEAFE}.

Features	F_{MUC}	F_{CEAFE}	F_{B3}	FINAL
following Soon et al. (2001)	54.12	41.08	66.67	53.42
-*-, with splitting	53.81	41.03	66.70	53.31
following Ng & Cardie (2002)	52.97	42.40	66.18	53.31
-*-, with splitting	53.28	40.46	66.03	52.72
All features	50.18	38.54	63.79	50.33
-*-, with splitting	50.19	39.47	65.38	51.16
Optimized feature set (splitting)	57.05	42.61	67.46	55.15

Table 1: Performance on the development set

References

A. Bagga and B. Baldwin. 1998. Algorithms for scoring coreference chains. In *Proc. of the LREC workshop on Linguistic Coreference*, pages 563–566, Granada.

Kalyanmoy Deb, Amrit Pratap, Sameer Agarwal, and T. Meyarivan. 2002. A fast and elitist multiobjective genetic algorithm: NSGA-II. *IEEE Transactions on Evolutionary Computation*, 6(2):181–197.

Kalyanmoy Deb. 2001. *Multi-objective Optimization Using Evolutionary Algorithms*. John Wiley and Sons, Ltd, England.

G. Doddington, A. Mitchell, M. Przybocki, L. Ramshaw, S. Strassell, and R. Weischedel. 2000. The automatic content extraction (ACE) program–tasks, data, and evaluation. In *Proc. of LREC*.

Jenny Rose Finkel, Trond Grenager, and Christopher Manning. 2005. Incorporating non-local information into information extraction systems by Gibbs sampling. In *Proceedings of the 43rd Annual Meeting of the Association for Computational Linguistics*, pages 363–370.

D. E. Goldberg. 1989. *Genetic Algorithms in Search, Optimization and Machine Learning*. Addison-Wesley, New York.

Veronique Hoste. 2005. *Optimization Issues in Machine Learning of Coreference Resolution*. Ph.D. thesis, Antwerp University.

X. Luo. 2005. On coreference resolution performance metrics. In *Proc. NAACL / EMNLP*, Vancouver.

Art Munson, Claire Cardie, and Rich Caruana. 2005. Optimizing to arbitrary NLP metrics using ensemble selection. In *Proceedings of Human Language Technology Conference and Conference on Empirical Methods in Natural Language Processing (HLT/EMNLP)*, pages 539–546.

Vincent Ng and Claire Cardie. 2002. Improving machine learning approaches to coreference resolution. In *Proceedings of the 40th Annual Meeting on Association for C omputational Linguistics*, pages 104–111.

Sameer Pradhan, Lance Ramshaw, Mitchell Marcus, Martha Palmer, Ralph Weischedel, and Nianwen Xue. 2011. Conll-2011 shared task: Modeling unrestricted coreference in ontonotes. In *Proceedings of the Fifteenth Conference on Computational Natural Language Learning (CoNLL 2011)*, Portland, Oregon, June.

M. Recasens and E. Hovy. 2009. A deeper look into features for coreference resolution. In S. Lalitha Devi, A. Branco, and R. Mitkov, editors, *Anaphora Processing and Applications (DAARC 2009*, number 5847 in LNAI, pages 29–42, Berlin / Heidelberg. Springer-Verlag.

M. Recasens and E. Hovy. 2011. Blanc: Implementing the rand index for coreference evaluation. *Natural Language Engineering*.

M. Recasens, L. Màrquez, E. Sapena, M. A. Martí, M. Taulé, V. Hoste, M. Poesio, and Y. Versley. 2010. Semeval-2010 task 1: Coreference resolution in multiple languages. In *Proc. SEMEVAL 2010*, Uppsala.

Sriparna Saha, Massimo Poesio, Asif Ekbal, and Olga Uryupina. 2011. Single and multi-objective optimization for feature selection in anaphora resolution. Submitted.

Wee Meng Soon, Hwee Tou Ng, and Daniel Chung Yong Lim. 2001. A machine learning approach to coreference resolution of noun phrases. *Computational Linguistic*, 27(4):521–544.

Yannick Versley, Simone Paolo Ponzetto, Massimo Poesio, Vladimir Eidelman, Alan Jern, Jason Smith, Xiaofeng Yang, and Alessandro Moschitti. 2008. BART: a modular toolkit for coreference resolution. In *Proceedings of the 46th Annual Meeting of the Association for Computational Linguistics on Human Language Technologies*, pages 9–12.

M. Vilain, J. Burger, J. Aberdeen, D. Connolly, and L. Hirschman. 1995. A model-theoretic coreference scoring scheme. In *Proc. of the Sixth Message Understanding Conference*, pages 45–52.

Combining Syntactic and Semantic Features by SVM for Unrestricted Coreference Resolution

Huiwei Zhou[1], Yao Li[2], Degen Huang[3], Yan Zhang[4], Chunlong Wu[5], Yuansheng Yang[6]
Dalian University of Technology
Dalian, Liaoning, China
{[1]zhouhuiwei, [3]huangdg, [6]yangys}@dlut.edu.cn
[2]tianshanyao@mail.dlut.edu.cn
[4]zhangyan_zyzy@yeah.net
[5]wuchunlong@gmail.com

Abstract

The paper presents a system for the CoNLL-2011 share task of coreference resolution. The system composes of two components: one for mentions detection and another one for their coreference resolution. For mentions detection, we adopted a number of heuristic rules from syntactic parse tree perspective. For coreference resolution, we apply SVM by exploiting multiple syntactic and semantic features. The experiments on the CoNLL-2011 corpus show that our rule-based mention identification system obtains a recall of 87.69%, and the best result of the SVM-based coreference resolution system is an average F-score 50.92% of the MUC, B-CUBED and CEAFE metrics.

1 Introduction

Coreference resolution, defined as finding the different mentions in a document which refer to the same entity in reality, is an important subject in Natural Language Processing. In particular, coreference resolution is a critical component of information extraction systems (Chinchor and Nancy, 1998; Sundheim and Beth, 1995) and a series of coreference resolution tasks have been introduced and evaluated from MUC (MUC-6, 1995). Some machine learning approaches have been applied to coreference resolution (Soon et al., 2001; Ng and Cardie, 2002; Bengtson and Roth, 2008; Stoyanov et al., 2009). Soon et al.(2001) use a decision tree classifier to decide whether two mentions in a document are coreferent. Bergsma and Lin (2006) exploit an effective feature of gender and number to a pronoun resolution system and improve the performance significantly, which is also appeared in our feature set. However, automatic coreference resolution is a hard task since it needs both syntactic and semantic knowledge and some intra-document knowledge. To improve the performance further, many deep knowledge resources like shallow syntactic and semantic knowledge are exploited for coreference resolution (Harabagiu et al., 2001; McCallum and Wellner, 2004; Denis and Baldridge, 2007; Ponzetto and Strube, 2005; Versley, 2007; Ng, 2007). In order to make use of more syntactic information, Kong et al. (2010) employ a tree kernel to anaphoricity determination for coreference resolution and show that applying proper tree structure in corefernce resolution can achieve a good performance.

The CoNLL-2011 Share Task (Pradhan et al., 2011) "Modeling Unrestricted Coreference in OntoNotes" proposes a task about unrestricted coreference resolution, which aims to recognize mentions and find coreference chains in one document. We participate in the closed test.

In this paper, we exploit multi-features to a coreference resolution system for the CONLL-2011 Share Task, including flat features and a tree structure feature. The task is divided into two steps in our system. In the first step, we adopt some heuristic rules to recognize mentions which may be in a coreference chain; in the second step, we exploit a number of features to a support vector machine (SVM) classifier to resolute unrestricted coreference. The experiments show that our system gets a reasonable result.

The rest of the paper is organized as follows. In

Proceedings of the 15th Conference on Computational Natural Language Learning: Shared Task, pages 66–70,
Portland, Oregon, 23-24 June 2011.

Section 2, we describe in detail how our system does the work of coreference resolution, including how we recognize mentions and how we mark the coreference chains. The experimental results are discussed in Section 3. Finally in Section 4, we give some conclusion.

2 The Coreference Resolution System

The task of coreference resolution is divided into two steps in our system: mentions detection and coreference resolution. In the first step, we use some heuristic rules to extract mentions which may refer to an entity. In the second step, we make up mention-pairs with the mentions extracted in the first step, and then classify the mention-pairs into two groups with an SVM model: Coreferent or NotCoreferent. Finally we get several coreference chains in a document according to the result of classification. Each coreference chain stands for one entity.

2.1 Rule-based Identification of Mentions

The first step for coreference resolution is to identify mentions from a sequence of words. We have tried the machine learning method detecting the boundary of a mention. But the recall cannot reach a high level, which will lead to bad performance of coreference resolution. So we replace it with a rule-based method. After a comprehensive study, we find that mentions are always relating to pronouns, named entities, definite noun phrases or demonstrative noun phrases. So we adopt the following 5 heuristic rules to extract predicted mentions:

1. If a word is a pronoun, then it is a mention.
2. If a word is a possessive pronoun or a possessive, then the smallest noun phrase containing this word is a mention.
3. If a word string is a named entity, then it is a mention.
4. If a word string is a named entity, then the smallest noun phrase containing it is a mention.
5. If a word is a determiner (a, an, the, this, these, that, etc.), then all the noun phrase beginning with this word is a mention.

2.2 Coreference Resolution with Multi-Features

The second step is to mark the coreference chain using the model trained by an SVM classifier. We extract the marked mentions from the training data and take mention-pairs in one document as instances to train the SVM classifier like Soon et al.(2001) . The mentions with the same coreference id form the positive instances while those between the nearest positive mention-pair form the negative instance with the second mention of the mention-pair.

The following features are commonly used in NLP processes, which are also used in our system:

- i-NamedEntity/j-NamedEntity: the named entity the mention i/j belongs to
- i-SemanticRole/j-SemanticRole: the semantic role the mention i/j belongs to which
- i-POSChain/j-POSChain: the POS chain of the mention i/j
- i-Verb/j-Verb: the verb of the mention i/j
- i-VerbFramesetID/j-VerbFramesetID: the verb frameset ID of the mention i/j, which works together with i/j-Verb

All the 5 kinds of features above belong to a single mention. For mention-pairs, there are another 4 kinds of features as below:

- StringMatch: after cutting the articles, 1 if the two mentions can match completely, 2 if one is a substring of the other, 3 if they partly match, 4 else.
- IsAlias: after cutting the articles, 1 if one mention is the name alias or the abbreviation of the other one, 0 else
- Distance: it is the number of sentences between two mentions, 0 if the two mentions are from one sentenci-Verb/j-Verb: the verb of the mention i/j
- SpeakerAgreement: 1 if both the speakers of the two mentions are unknown, 2 if both the two mentions come from the same speaker, 3 if the mentions comes from different speakers.

All of the 14 simple and effective features above are applied in the baseline system, which use the same method with our system. But coreference resolution needs more features to make full use of the intra-documental knowledge, so we employ the following 3 kinds of features to our system to catch more information about the context.

- i-GenderNumber/j-GenderNumber (GN): 7 values: masculine, feminine, neutral, plural, ?rst-person singular, ?rst-person plural, second-person.

- SemanticRelation (SR): the semantic relation in WordNet between the head words of the two mentions: synonym, hyponym, no relation, unknown.

- MinimumTree (MT): a parse tree represents the syntactic structure of a sentence, but coreference resolution needs the overall context in a document. So we add a super root to the forest of all the parse trees in one document, and then we get a super parse tree. The minimum tree (MT) of a mention-pair in a super parse tree is the minimum sub-tree from the common parent mention to the two mentions, just like the method uesd by Zhou(2009). And the similarity of two trees is calculated using a convolution tree kernel (Collins and Duffy, 2001), which counts the number of common sub-trees.

We try all the features in our system, and get some interesting results which is given in Experiments and Results Section.

3 Experiments and Results

Our experiments are all carried out on CONLL-2011 share task data set (Pradhan et al., 2007).

The result of mention identification in the first step is evaluated through mention recall. And the performance of coreference resolution in the second step is measured using the average F1-measures of MUC, B-CUBED and CEAFE metrics (Recasens et al., 2010). All the evaluations are implemented using the scorer downloaded from the CONLL-2011 share task website [1] .

[1]http://conll.bbn.com/index.php/software.html

3.1 Rule-based Identification of Mentions

The mention recall of our system in the mention identification step reaches 87.69%, which can result in a good performance of the coreference resolution step. We also do comparative experiments to investigate the effect of our rule-based mention identification. The result is shown in Table 1. The CRF-based method in Table 1 is to train a conditional random field (CRF) model with 6 basic features, including Word, Pos, Word_ID, Syntactic parse label, Named entity, Semantic role.

Method	Recall	Precision	F-score
Rule-based	87.69	32.16	47.06
CRF-based	59.66	50.06	54.44

Table 1: comparative experiments of CRF-based and rule-based methods of mention identification(%)

Table 1 only shows one kind of basic machine-learning methods performs not so well as our rule-based method in recall measure in mention identification, but the F1-measure of the CRF-based method is higher than that of the rule-based method. In our system, the mention identification step should provide as many anaphoricities as possible to the coreference resolution step to avoid losing coreferent mentions, which means that the higher the recall of mention identification is, the better the system performs.

3.2 Coreference Resolution with Multi-Features

In the second step of our system, SVM-LIGHT-TK1.2 implementation is employed to coreference resolution. We apply the polynomial kernel for the flat features and the convolution tree kernel for the minimum tree feature to the SVM classifier, in which the parameter d of the polynomial kernel is set to 3 (polynomial $(a * b + c)^d$) and the combining parameter r is set to 0.2 ($K = tree - forest - kernel * r + vector - kernel$). All the other parameters are set to the default value. All the experiments are done on the broadcast conversations part of CoNLL-2011 corpus as the calculating time of SVM-LIGHT-TK1.2 is so long.

Experimental result using the baseline method with the GenderNumber feature added is shown in

d=?	MUC	B^3	CEAFE	AVE
2	47.49	61.14	36.15	48.26
3	51.37	62.82	38.26	50.82

Table 2: parameter d in polynomial kernel in coreference resolution using the baseline method with the GN feature(%)

Talbe 2. The result shows that the parameter d in polynomial kernel plays an important role in our coreference resolution system. The score when d is 3 is 2.56% higher than when d is 2, but the running time becomes longer, too.

r=?	MUC	B^3	CEAFE	AVE
1	31.41	45.08	22.72	33.07
0.25	34.15	46.87	23.63	34.88
0	51.37	62.82	38.26	50.82

Table 3: combining parameter r ($K = tree - forest - kernel * r + vector - kernel$) in coreference resolution using the baseline with the GN and MT features(%)

In Table 3, we can find that the lower the combining parameter r is, the better the system performs, which indicates that the MT feature plays a negative role in our system. There are 2 possible reasons for that: the MT structure is not proper for our coreference resolution system, or the simple method of adding a super root to the parse forest of a document is not effective.

Method	MUC	B^3	CEAFE	AVE
baseline	42.19	58.12	33.6	44.64
+GN	51.37	62.82	38.26	50.82
+GN+SR	49.61	64.18	38.13	50.64
+GN +SEMCLASS	50.97	62.53	37.96	50.49

Table 4: effect of GN and SR features in coreference resolution using no MT feature (%)

Table 4 shows the effect of GenderNumber feature and SemanticRelation feature, and the last item is the method using the SemanticClassAgreementFeature (SEMCLASS) used by (Soon et al., 2001) instead of the SR feature of our system. The GN feature significantly improves the performance of our system by 6.18% of the average score, which may be greater if we break up the gender and number feature into two features. As the time limits, we haven't separated them until the deadline of the paper. The effect of the SR feature is not as good as we think. The score is lower than the method without SR feature, but is higher than the method using SEMCLASS feature. The decreasing caused by S-R feature may be due to that the searching depth in WordNet is limited to one to shorten running time.

To investigate the performance of the second step, we do an experiment for the SVM-based coreference resolution using just all the anaphoricities as the mention collection input. The result is shown in Table 5. As the mention collection includes no incorrect anaphoricity, any mistake in coreference resolution step has double effect, which may lead to a relatively lower result than we expect.

MUC	B^3	CEAFE	AVE
65.55	58.77	39.96	54.76

Table 5: using just all the anaphoricities as the mention collection input in coreference resolution step (%)

In the three additional features, only the GN feature significantly improves the performance of the coreference resolution system, the result we finally submitted is to use the baseline method with GN feature added. The official result is shown in Table 6. The average score achieves 50.92%.

MUC	B^3	CEAFE	AVE
48.96	64.07	39.74	50.92

Table 6: official result in CoNLL-2011 Share Task using baseline method with GN feature added (%)

4 Conclusion

This paper proposes a system using multi-features for the CONLL-2011 share task. Some syntactic and semantic information is used in our SVM-based system. The best result (also the official result) achieves an average score of 50.92%. As the MT and S-R features play negative roles in the system, future work will focus on finding a proper tree structure for the intra-documental coreference resolution and combining the parse forest of a document into a tree to make good use of the convolution tree kernel.

References

A. McCallum and B. Wellner. 2004. Conditional models of identity uncertainty with application to noun coreference. *In Advances in Neural Information Processing Systems (NIPS)*, 2004.

Chinchor, Nancy A. 1998. Overview of MUC-7/MET-2. *In Proceedings of the Seventh Message Understanding Conference (MUC-7).*

Eric Bengtson, Dan Roth. 2008. Understanding the Value of Features for Coreference Resolution *Proceedings of the 2008 Conferenceon Empirical Methods in Natural Language Processing*, pages294C303.

Fang Kong, Guodong Zhou, Longhua Qian, Qiaoming Zhu. 2010. Dependency-driven Anaphoricity Determination for Coreference Resolution *Proceedings of the 23rd International Conferenceon Computational Linguistics (Coling2010)*, pages599C607.

Guodong Zhou, Fang Kong. 2009. Global Learning of Noun Phrase Anaphoricity in Coreference Resolution via Label Propagation. *In Proceedings of the 2009 Coreference on Empirical Methods in Natural Language Processing*, pages 978-986, 2009.

M. Collins, N.Duffy. 2001. Convolution Kernels for Natural Language Resolution *NIPS' 2001.*

Marta Recasens, Lluts Mrquez, Emili Sapena, M. Antnia Martł, Mariona Taul, Vronique Hoste, Massimo Poesio, Yannick Versley 2010. SemEval-2010 Task 1: Coreference Resolutionin Multiple Languages *In Proceeding SemEval 2010 Proceedings of the 5th International Workshop on Semantic Evaluation*, 2010.

MUC-6. 1995. Coreference task definition (v2.3, 8 Sep 95) *In Proceedings of the Sixth Message Understanding Conference (MUC-6)*, pages 335-344.

P.Denis, J.Baldridge. 2007. Joint determination of anaphoricity and coreference resolution using integer programming. *In Proceedings of HLT/NAACL*, 2007.

V. Ng and C. Cardie. 2002. Improving machine learning approaches to coreference resolution. *In Proceedings of ACL*, 2002.

V. Ng. 2007. Shallow semantics for coreference resolution. *In Proceedings of IJCAI*, 2007.

Veselin Stoyanov, Nathan Gilbert, Claire Cardie, Ellen Riloff. 2009. Conundrums in Noun Phrase Coreference Resolution: Making Sense of the State-of-the-Art *Proceeding ACL '09 Proceedings of the Joint Conference of the 47th Annual Meeting of the ACL.*

W.Soon,H.Ng,and D.Lim. 2001. A machine learning approach to coreference resolution of noun phrase. *Computational Linguistics*, 27(4):521-544,2001.

S. M.Harabagiu,R.C.Bunescu,and S.J. Maiorano. 2001. Text and knowledge mining for coreference resolution. *In Proceedings of NAACL*, 2001.

S.Ponzetto, M.Strube. 2005. Semantic role labeling for coreference resolution. *In Proceedings of EACL*, Italy, April 2005.

Sameer Pradhan, Lance Ramshaw, Mitchell Marcus, Martha Palmer, Ralph Weischedel, Nianwen Xue. 2011. CoNLL-2011 Shared Task: Modeling Unrestricted Coreference in OntoNotes. *Proceedings of the Fifteenth Conference on Computational Natural Language Learning (CoNLL 2011).*

Sameer S. Pradhan, Lance Ramshaw, Ralph Weischedel, Jessica MacBride, Linnea Micciulla. 2007. Unrestricted Coreference: Identifying Entities and Events in OntoNotes. *In International Conference on Semantic Computing*, 2007.

Shane Bergsma, Dekang Lin. 2006. Bootstrapping Path-Based Pronoun Resolution. *In Proceedings of the 21st International Conference on Computational Linguistics*, 2006.

Sundheim, Beth M. 1995. Overview of results of the MUC-6 evaluation. *In Proceedings of the Sixth Message Understanding Conference (MUC-6)*, pages 13-31.

Y.Versley. 2007. Antecedent selection techniques for high-recall coreference resolution. *In Proceedings of EMNLP/CoNLL*, 2007.

Supervised Coreference Resolution with SUCRE

Hamidreza Kobdani and Hinrich Schütze
Institute for Natural Language Processing
University of Stuttgart, Germany
kobdani@ims.uni-stuttgart.de

Abstract

In this paper we present SUCRE (Kobdani and Schütze, 2010) that is a modular coreference resolution system participating in the CoNLL-2011 Shared Task: Modeling Unrestricted Coreference in OntoNote (Pradhan et al., 2011). The SUCRE's modular architecture provides a clean separation between data storage, feature engineering and machine learning algorithms.

1 Introduction

Noun phrase coreference resolution is the process of finding markables (noun phrase) referring to the same real world entity or concept. In other words, this process groups the markables of a document into entities (equivalence classes) so that all markables in an entity are coreferent. Examples of applications of coreference resolution are Information Extraction, Question Answering and Automatic Summarization.

Coreference is an equivalence relation between two markables, i.e., it is reflexive, symmetric and transitive. The first solution that intuitively comes to mind is binary classification of markable pairs (links). Therefore at the heart of most existing approaches there is a binary classifier that classifies links to coreferent/disreferent. One can also use the transitive property of coreference relation to build the entities; this is done using a clustering method.

Our approach in this paper consist of the above mentioned steps, namely:

1. Classification of links to coreferent/disreferent.
2. Clustering of links which are classified as coreferent.

This paper is organized as follows. In Section 2, we present our feature engineering approach. Section 3 presents the system architecture. Data set is described in Section 4. Sections 5 and 6 present results and conclusions.

2 Feature Engineering

In recent years there has been substantial work on the problem of coreference resolution. Most methods present and report on the benchmark data sets for *English*. The feature sets they use are based on (Soon et al., 2001). These features consist of string-based features, distance features, span features, part-of-speech features, grammatical features, and agreement features.

We defined a comprehensive set of features based on previous coreference resolution systems for English, e.g. (Bengtson and Roth, 2008). In the common approach to coreference resolution we have chosen, features are **link features**, i.e., features are defined over a pair of markables. For link feature definition and extraction, the head words of markables are usually used, but in some cases the head word is not a suitable choice. For example, consider these two markables: *the book* and *a book*, in both cases *book* is the head word but to distinguish which markable is definite and which indefinite additional information about the markables has to be taken into account. Now consider these two markables: *the university students in Germany* and *the university students in France* in this case the head words and the first four words of each markable are the same but they cannot be coreferent, and this could be detected only by looking at the entire noun phrase. Some features require complex preprocess-

Proceedings of the 15th Conference on Computational Natural Language Learning: Shared Task, pages 71–75,
Portland, Oregon, 23-24 June 2011. ©2011 Association for Computational Linguistics

ing or complex definitions. Consider the two markables *the members of parliament* and *the members of the European Union*. The semantic class of *members* is *person* in the first case and *country* in the second. To cover all such cases, we introduced a feature definition language (Kobdani et al., 2010). With the feature definition language we will be able to access all information that is connected to a markable, including the first, last and head words of the two markables; all other words of the two markables; and the two markables as atomic elements.

After defining new features (new definition from scratch or definition by combination of existing features), we have to evaluate them. In principle, we could use any figure of merit to evaluate the usefulness of a feature or to compare two similar features, including Gini coefficient, mutual information, and correlation coefficient. In our current system, expected information gain (IG) and information gain ratio (IGR) are used.

As an example, consider the following two features, which can be considered different attempts to formalize the same linguistic property:

1. The noun phrase has a subject role and is *definite* (e.g. markable begins with a *definite* article)
2. The noun phrase has a subject role and is *not indefinite* (e.g. markable begins with an *indefinite* article)

The information gain ratios of the above mentioned features are equal to 0.0026 for the first and 0.0051 for the second one – this shows that the second one is a better choice. We now define IG and IGR.

The change in entropy from a prior state to a state that takes some information is the expected information gain (Mitchell, 1997):

$$IG\left(f\right) = H\left(C\right) - H_f\left(C\right) \tag{1}$$

Where f is the feature value, C its corresponding class, and entropy is defined as follows:

$$H\left(C\right) = -\sum_i P\left(C_i\right) log_2 P\left(C_i\right) \tag{2}$$

$$H_f(C) = \sum_f \frac{|C_f|}{|C|} H\left(C_f\right) \tag{3}$$

If a feature takes a large number of distinct values, the information gain would not be a good measure for deciding its relevance. In such cases the information gain ratio is used instead. The information gain ratio for a feature is calculated as follows:

$$IGR\left(f\right) = \frac{IG\left(f\right)}{SInf\left(C\right)} \tag{4}$$

$$SInf(C) = -\sum_i \frac{|C_i|}{|C|} log_2 \frac{|C_i|}{|C|} \tag{5}$$

Equation (4) can be used as an indicator for which features are likely to improve classification accuracy.

3 System Architecture

The architecture of the system has two main parts: preprocessing and coreference resolution.

In preprocessing the text corpus is converted to a relational data model. The main purpose of the relational model in our system is the use of a feature definition language (Kobdani et al., 2010). After modeling the text corpus, coreference resolution can be performed.

The main steps of the system are presented as follows.

3.1 Preliminary text conversion

In this step, tokens are extracted from the corpus. In the CoNLL-2011 Shared Task this step is as simple as reading each line of the input data set and extracting its corresponding token.

3.2 Atomic attributes of tokens

Atomic features of the tokens are extracted in this step. The extracted atomic features are: part of speech, number, pronoun person (first, second and third), pronoun type (subjective,,predeterminer,reflexive,objective and possessive), WordNet semantic class and gender.

We use a rather simple method to extract semantic class of each token from WordNet. We look at the synonyms of the token and if one of them is in the predefined keyword set, we take it as its corresponding semantic class. The example of the keywords are person, time, abstraction, device, human action, organization, place and animal.

3.3 Markable Detection

In this step all noun phrases from the parse tree are extracted. After clustering step all markables which are not included in a chain are deleted from the list of markables. In other word we will not have any cluster with less than 2 members.

Figure 1 presents the simple markable detection method which we used in the SUCRE.

3.4 Atomic attributes of markables

In this step, the atomic attributes of the markables are extracted. In the data set of the CoNLL-2011 shared task the named entity property of a markable can be used as its atomic attribute.

3.5 Link Generator

For training, the system generates a positive training instance for an adjacent coreferent markable pair (m, n) and negative training instances for the markable m and all markables disreferent with m that occur before n (Soon et al., 2001). For decoding it generates all the possible links inside a window of 100 markables.

3.6 Link feature definition and extraction

The output of the link generator, which is the list of the generated links, is the input to the link feature extractor for creating train and test data sets. To do this, the feature definitions are used to extract the feature values of the links (Kobdani et al., 2011).

3.7 Learning

For learning we implemented a decision tree classifier (Quinlan, 1993). To achieve state-of-the-art performance, in addition to decision tree we also tried support vector machine and maximum entropy that did not perform better than decision tree.

3.8 Classification and Clustering

In this part, the links inside one document are classified then the coreference chains are created. We use *best-first clustering* for this purpose. It searches for the best predicted antecedent from right to left starting from the end of the document. For the documents with more than a predefined number of markables we apply a limit for searching. In this way, in addition to better efficiency, the results also improve.

Markable_Detection_PSG_A $(W_1, W_2, \ldots, W_n)$

1. A markable M is presented by a set of three words:
   Begin (M_b), End (M_e) and Head (M_h).
2. Let DM be the set of detected markables.
3. Let T_i be the node i in the parse tree with label L_i
   (if node is a word then L_i is equal to W_i).
4. Start from parse tree root T_r:
   Find_Markables(T_r,L_r,DM)

Find_Markables(T,L,DM)

1. If L is equal to noun phrase, then extract the markable M:
   (a) Set the begin word of the markable:
   M_b = Noun_Phrase_Begin(T,L)
   (b) Set the end word of the markable:
   M_e = Noun_Phrase_End(T,L)
   (c) Set the head word of the markable:
   M_h = Noun_Phrase_Head(T,L)
   (d) Add the markable M to the set of detected markables DM.
2. Repeat for all T_i the daughters of T:
   Find_Markables(T_i,L_i,DM)

Noun_Phrase_Begin(T,L)

If T has no daughter then return L;
else set T_b to the first daughter of T and return Noun_Phrase_Begin(T_b,L_b).

Noun_Phrase_End(T,L)

If T has no daughter then return L;
else set T_b to the last daughter of T and return Noun_Phrase_End(T_b,L_b).

Noun_Phrase_Head(T,L)

If T has no daughter then return L;
else set T_h to the biggest noun phrase daughter of T and return Noun_Phrase_Head(T_h,L_h).

Figure 1: Markable Detection from Parse Tree (all possible markables) .

	Automatic			Gold		
	Rec.	Prec.	F_1	Rec.	Prec.	F_1
MD	60.17	60.92	60.55	62.50	61.62	62.06
MUC	54.30	51.84	53.06	57.44	53.15	55.21
B^3	71.39	64.68	67.87	74.07	64.39	68.89
$CEAF_M$	46.36	46.36	46.36	47.07	47.07	47.07
$CEAF_E$	35.38	37.26	35.30	35.19	38.44	36.74
BLANC	65.01	64.93	64.97	66.23	65.16	65.67

Table 1: Results of SUCRE on the development data set for the automatically detected markables. MD: Markable Detection.

	Automatic			Gold		
	Rec.	Prec.	F_1	Rec.	Prec.	F_1
MUC	58.63	87.88	70.34	60.48	88.25	71.78
B^3	57.91	86.47	69.36	59.21	86.25	70.22
$CEAF_M$	59.81	59.81	59.81	60.91	60.91	60.91
$CEAF_E$	70.49	36.43	48.04	71.09	37.73	49.30
BLANC	69.67	76.27	72.34	70.34	76.01	72.71

Table 2: Results of SUCRE on the development data set for the true markables (i.e. no singletone is included).

4 Data Sets

OntoNotes has been used for the CoNLL-2011 shared task. The OntoNotes project [1] is to provide a large-scale, accurate corpus for general anaphoric coreference. It aims to cover entities and events (i.e. it is not limited to noun phrases or a limited set of entity types) (Pradhan et al., 2007).

For training we used 4674 documents containing a total of 1909175 tokens, 190700 markables and 50612 chains.

SUCRE participated in the closed track of the shared task. Experiments have been performed for the two kind of documents, namely, the automatically preprocessed documents and the gold preprocessed documents. In this paper, we report only the scores on the development data set using the official scorer of the shared task. The automatically preprocessed part consists of 303 documents containing a total of 136257 tokens, 52189 automatically detected markables, 14291 true markables and 3752 chains. The gold preprocessed part consists of 303 documents containing a total of 136257 tokens, 52262 automatically detected markables, 13789 true markables and 3752 chains.

5 Results

We report recall, precision, and F_1 for MUC (Vilain et al., 1995), B^3 (Bagga and Baldwin, 1998), $CEAF_M$/$CEAF_E$ (Luo, 2005) and BLANC (Recasens et al., 2010).

Table 1 presents results of our system for the automatically detected markables. It is apparent from this table that the application of the gold preprocessed documents slightly improves the performance (MD-F1: +1.51; MUC-F1: +2.15; B^3-F1: +1.02; $CEAF_M$-F1: +0.71; $CEAF_E$-F1: +1.44; BLANC-F1: +0.70).

Table 2 presents results of our system for the true markables that were all and only part of coreference chains. Again the results show that the application of gold preprocessed documents slightly improves the performance (MUC-F1: +1.44; B^3-F1: +0.86; $CEAF_M$-F1: +1.1; $CEAF_E$-F1: +1.26; BLANC-F1: +0.37).

Comparing the results of tables 1 and 2, there is a significant difference between the scores on the automatically detected markables and the scores on the true markables (e.g. for the automatically preprocessed documents: MUC-F1: +17.28; $CEAF_M$-F1: +13.45; $CEAF_E$-F1: +12.74; BLANC-F1: +7.37). No significant improvement in B^3 is seen (automatic: +1.49; gold: +1.33). We suspect that this is partly due to the very sensitive nature of B^3 against the singleton chains. Because in the implementation of scorer for the CoNLL-2011 shared task the non-detected key markables are automatically included into the response as singletons.

6 Conclusion

In this paper, we have presented our system SUCRE participated in the CoNLL-2011 shared task. We took a deeper look at the feature engineering of SUCRE. We presented the markable detection method we applied.

We showed that the application of the gold preprocessed documents improves the performance. It has been demonstrated that the availability of the true markables significantly improves the results. Also it has been shown that the singletons have a large impact on the B^3 scores.

[1] http://www.bbn.com/ontonotes/

References

Amit Bagga and Breck Baldwin. 1998. Algorithms for scoring coreference chains. In *LREC Workshop on Linguistics Coreference '98*, pages 563–566.

Eric Bengtson and Dan Roth. 2008. Understanding the value of features for coreference resolution. In *EMNLP '08*, pages 294–303.

Hamidreza Kobdani and Hinrich Schütze. 2010. Sucre: A modular system for coreference resolution. In *SemEval '10*, pages 92–95.

Hamidreza Kobdani, Hinrich Schütze, Andre Burkovski, Wiltrud Kessler, and Gunther Heidemann. 2010. Relational feature engineering of natural language processing. In *CIKM '10*. ACM.

Hamidreza Kobdani, Hinrich Schütze, Michael Schiehlen, and Hans Kamp. 2011. Bootstrapping coreference resolution using word associations. In *Proceedings of the 49th Annual Meeting of the Association for Computational Linguistics*, ACL '11. Association for Computational Linguistics.

Xiaoqiang Luo. 2005. On coreference resolution performance metrics. In *HLT '05*, pages 25–32.

Tom M. Mitchell. 1997. *Machine Learning*. McGraw-Hill, New York.

Sameer Pradhan, Lance Ramshaw, Ralph Weischedel, Jessica MacBride, and Linnea Micciulla. 2007. Unrestricted Coreference: Identifying Entities and Events in OntoNotes. In *in Proceedings of the IEEE International Conference on Semantic Computing (ICSC)*, September 17-19.

Sameer Pradhan, Lance Ramshaw, Mitchell Marcus, Martha Palmer, Ralph Weischedel, and Nianwen Xue. 2011. Conll-2011 shared task: Modeling unrestricted coreference in ontonotes. In *Proceedings of the Fifteenth Conference on Computational Natural Language Learning (CoNLL 2011)*, Portland, Oregon, June.

J. Ross Quinlan. 1993. *C4.5: Programs for machine learning*. Morgan Kaufmann Publishers Inc., San Francisco, CA, USA.

Marta Recasens, Lluís Màrquez, Emili Sapena, M.Antònia Martí, Mariona Taulé, Véronique Hoste, Massimo Poesio, and Yannick Versley. 2010. SemEval-2010 Task 1: Coreference resolution in multiple languages. In *SemEval '10*, pages 70–75.

Wee Meng Soon, Hwee Tou Ng, and Daniel Chung Yong Lim. 2001. A machine learning approach to coreference resolution of noun phrases. In *CL '01*, pages 521–544.

Marc Vilain, John Burger, John Aberdeen, Dennis Connolly, and Lynette Hirschman. 1995. A model-theoretic coreference scoring scheme. In *MUC6 '95*, pages 45–52.

ETS: An Error Tolerable System for Coreference Resolution

Hao Xiong , Linfeng Song , Fandong Meng , Yang Liu , Qun Liu and Yajuan Lü
Key Lab. of Intelligent Information Processing
Institute of Computing Technology
Chinese Academy of Sciences
P.O. Box 2704, Beijing 100190, China
{xionghao,songlinfeng,mengfandong,yliu,liuqun,lvyajuan}@ict.ac.cn

Abstract

This paper presents our error tolerable system for coreference resolution in CoNLL-2011(Pradhan et al., 2011) shared task (closed track). Different from most previous reported work, we detect mention candidates based on packed forest instead of single parse tree, and we use beam search algorithm based on the Bell Tree to create entities. Experimental results show that our methods achieve promising results on the development set.

1 Introduction

Over last decades, there has been increasing interest on coreference resolution within NLP community. The task of coreference resolution is to identify expressions in a text that refer to the same discourse entity. This year, CoNLL[1] holds a shared task aiming to model unrestricted coreference in OntoNotes.[2] The OntoNotes project has created a large-scale, accurate corpus for general anaphoric coreference that covers entities and events not limited to noun phrases or a limited set of entity types. And Pradhan et al. (2007) have ever used this corpus for similar unrestricted coreference task.

Our approach to this year's task could be divided into two steps: mention identification and creation of entities. The first stage is conducted on the analysis of parse trees produced by input data. The official data have provided gold and automatic parse trees for each sentences in training and development set. However, according to statistics, almost 3% mentions have no corresponding constituents in automatic parse trees. Since only automatic parse trees will be provided in the final test set, the effect of parsing errors are inevitable. To alleviate this issue, based on given automatic parse trees, we modify a state-of-the-art parser (Charniak and Johnson, 2005) to generate packed forest, and determine mention candidates among all constituents from both given parse tree and packed forest. The packed forest is a compact representation of all parse trees for a given sentence. Readers can refer to (Mi et al., 2008) for detailed definitions.

Once the mentions are identified, the left step is to group mentions referring to same object into similar entity. This problem can be viewed as binary classification problem of determining whether each mention pairs corefer. We use a Maximum Entropy classifier to predict the possibility that two mentions refer to the similar entity. And mainly following the work of Luo et al. (2004), we use a beam search algorithm based on Bell Tree to obtain the global optimal classification.

As this is the first time we participate competition of coreference resolution, we mainly concentrate on developing fault tolerant capability of our system while omitting feature engineering and other helpful technologies.

2 Mention Detection

The first step of the coreference resolution tries to recognize occurrences of mentions in documents. Note that we recognize mention boundaries only on development and test set while generating training

[1] http://conll.bbn.com/
[2] http://www.bbn.com/ontonotes/

Proceedings of the 15th Conference on Computational Natural Language Learning: Shared Task, pages 76–80,
Portland, Oregon, 23-24 June 2011. ©2011 Association for Computational Linguistics

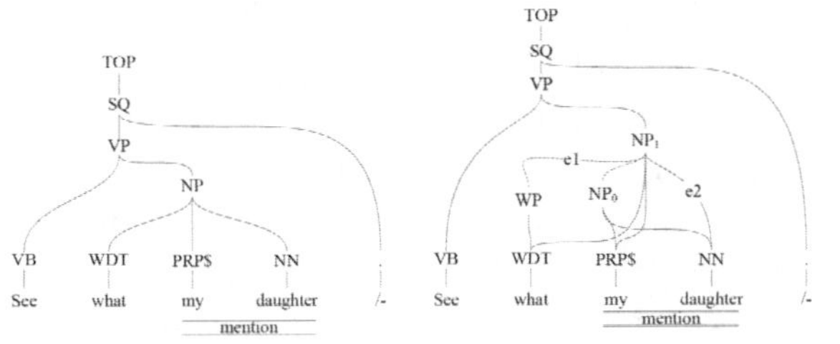

Figure 1: Left side is parse tree extracted from development set, and right side is a forest. "*my daughter*" is a mention in this discourse, however it has no corresponding constituent in parse tree, but it has a corresponding constituent NP_0 in forest.

instances using gold boundaries provided by official data.

The first stage of our system consists of following three successive steps:

- Extracting constituents annotated with *NP*, *NNP*, *PRP*, *PRP$* and *VBD* **POS tags** from single parse tree.
- Extracting constituents with the same tags as the last step from packed forest.
- Extracting Named Entity recognized by given data.

It is worth mentioning that above three steps will produce duplicated mentions, we hence collect all mentions into a list and discard duplicated candidates. The contribution of using packed forest is that it extends the searching space of mention candidates. Figure 1 presents an example to explain the advantage of employing packed forest to enhance the mention detection process. The left side of Figure 1 is the automatic parse tree extracted from development set, in which mention "*my daughter*" has no corresponding constituent in its parse tree. Under normal strategy, such mention will not be recognized and be absent in the clustering stage. However, we find that mention has its constituent NP_0 in packed forest. According to statistics, when using packed forest, only 0.5% mentions could not be recognized while the traditional method is 3%, that means the theoretical upper bound of our system reaches 99% compared to baseline's 97%.

Since the requirement of this year's task is to model unrestricted coreference, intuitively, we should not constraint in recognizing only noun phrases but also adjective phrase, verb and so on. However, we find that most mentions appeared in corpus are noun phrases, and our experimental results indicate that considering constituents annotated with above proposed POS tags achieve the best performance.

3 Determining Coreference

This stage is to determine which mentions belong to the same entity. We train a Maximum Entropy classifier (Le, 2004) to decide whether two mentions are coreferent. We use the method proposed by Soon, et al.'s to generate the training instances, where a positive instance is formed between current mention M_j and its closest preceding antecedent M_i, and a negative instance is created by paring M_j with each of the intervening mentions, M_{i+1}, M_{i+2},...,M_{j-1}.

We use the following features to train our classifier.

Features in Soon et al.'s work (Soon et al., 2001)

Lexical features

IS_PREFIX: whether the string of one mention is prefix of the other;

IS_SUFFIX: whether the string of one mention is suffix of the other;

ACRONYM: whether one mention is the acronym of the other;

Distance features

SENT_DIST: distance between the sentences containing the two mentions;

MEN_DIST: number of mentions between two mentions;

Grammatical features

IJ_PRONOUN: whether both mentions are pronoun;

I_NESTED: whether mention i is nested in another mention;

J_NESTED: whether mention j is nested in another mention;

Syntax features

HEAD: whether the heads of two mentions have the same string;

HEAD_POS: whether the heads of two mentions have the same POS;

HEA_POS_PAIRS: pairs of POS of the two mentions' heads;

Semantic features

WNDIST: distance between two mentions in WordNet;

I_ARG0: whether mention i has the semantic role of Arg0;

J_ARG0: whether mention j has the semantic role of Arg0;

IJ_ARGS: whether two mentions have the semantic roles for similar predicate;

In the submitted results, we use the L-BFGS parameter estimation algorithm with gaussian prior smoothing (Chen and Rosenfeld, 1999). We set the gaussian prior to 2 and train the model in 100 iterations.

3.1 Creation of Entities

This stage aims to create the mentions detected in the first stage into entities, according to the prediction of classifier. One simple method is to use a greedy algorithm, by comparing each mention to its previous mentions and refer to the one that has the highest probability. In principle, this algorithm is too greedy and sometimes results in unreasonable partition (Ng, 2010). To address this problem, we follow the literature (Luo et al., 2004) and propose to use beam search to find global optimal partition.

Intuitively, creation of entities can be casted as partition problem. And the number of partitions equals the Bell Number (Bell, 1934), which has a "closed" formula $B(n) = \frac{1}{e}\sum_{k=0}^{\infty}\frac{k^n}{k!}$. Clearly, this number is very huge when n is large, enumeration of all partitions is impossible, so we instead designing a beam search algorithm to find the best partition.

Formally, the task is to optimize the following objective,

$$\hat{y} = \arg\max_{\phi \in P} \sum_{e \in \phi} Prob(e) \qquad (1)$$

where P is all partitions, $Prob(e)$ is the cost of entity e. And we can use the following formula to calculate the $Prob(e)$,

$$\begin{aligned} Prob(e) = & \sum_{i \in e, j \in e} pos(m_i, m_j) \\ & + \sum_{i \in e, j \notin e} neg(m_i, m_j) \end{aligned} \qquad (2)$$

where $pos(m_i, m_j)$ is the score predicted by classifier that the possibility two mentions m_i and m_j group into one entity, and $neg(m_i, m_j)$ is the score that two mentions are not coreferent.

Theoretically, we can design a dynamic algorithm to obtain the best partition schema. Providing there are four mentions from A to D, and we have obtained the partitions of A, B and C. To incorporate D, we should consider assigning D to each entity of every partition, and generate the partitions of four mentions. For detailed explanation, the partitions of three mentions are [A][B][C], [AB][C], [A][BC] and [ABC], when considering the forth mention D, we generate the following partitions:

- [A][B][C][D], [AD][B][C], [A][BD][C], [A][B][CD]
- [AB][C][D], [ABD][C],[AB][CD]
- [A][BC][D], [AD][BC], [A][BCD]
- [ABC][D], [ABCD]

The score of partition [AD][B][C] can be calculated by $score([A][B][C]) + pos(A, D) + neg(B, D) + neg(C, D)$. Since we can computer pos and neg score between any two mentions in advance, this problem can be efficiently solved by dynamic algorithm. However, in practice, enumerating the whole partitions is intractable, we instead exploiting a beam with size k to store the top k partitions of current mention size, according to the score the partition obtain. Due to the scope limitation, we omit the detailed algorithm, readers can refer to Luo et al. (2004) for detailed description, since our approach is almost similar to theirs.

4 Experiments

4.1 Data Preparation

The shared task provided data includes information of lemma, POS, parse tree, word sense, predicate arguments, named entity and so on. In addition to those information, we use a modified in house parser to generate packed forest for each sentence in development set, and prune the packed forest with threshold p=3 (Huang, 2008). Since the OntoNotes involves multiple genre data, we merge all files and

	Mention	MUC	BCUBED	CEAFM	CEAFE	BLANC
baseline	58.97%	44.17%	63.24%	45.08%	37.13%	62.44%
baseline_gold	59.18%	44.48%	63.46%	45.37%	37.47%	62.36%
sys_forest	59.07%	44.4%	63.39%	45.29%	37.41%	62.41%
sys_btree	59.44%	44.66%	63.77%	45.62%	37.82%	62.47%
sys_forest_btree	59.71%	44.97%	63.95%	45.91%	37.96%	62.52%

Table 1: Experimental results on development set (F score).

	Mention	MUC	BCUBED	CEAFM	CEAFE	BLANC
sys1	54.5%	39.15%	63.91%	45.32%	37.16%	63.18%
sys2	53.06%	35.55%	59.68%	38.24%	32.03%	50.13%

Table 2: Experimental results on development set with different training division (F score).

take it as our training corpus. We use the supplied score toolkit [3] to compute MUC, BCUBED, CEAFM, CEAFE and BLANC metrics.

4.2 Experimental Results

We first implement a baseline system (*baseline*) that use single parse tree for mention detection and greedy algorithm for creation of entities. We also run the baseline system using gold parse tree, namely *baseline_gold*. To investigate the contribution of packed forest, we design a reinforced system, namely *sys_forest*. And another system, named as *sys_btree*, is used to see the contribution of beam search with beam size k=10. Lastly, we combine two technologies and obtain system *sys_forest_btree*.

Table 1 shows the experimental results on development data. We find that the system using beam search achieve promising improvement over baseline. The reason for that has been discussed in last section. We also find that compared to *baseline*, *sys_forest* and *baseline_gold* both achieve improvement in term of some metrics. And we are glad to find that using forest, the performance of our system is approaching the system based on gold parse tree. But even using the gold parse tree, the improvement is slight. [4] One reason is that we used some lexical and grammar features which are dominant during prediction, and another explanation is that packed forest enlarges the size of mentions but brings difficulty to resolve them.

To investigate the effect of different genres to develop set, we also perform following compared experiments:

- *sys1:* all training corpus + WSJ development corpus
- *sys2:* WSJ training corpus + WSJ development corpus

Table 2 indicates that knowledge from other genres can help coreference resolution. Perhaps the reason is the same as last experiments, where syntax diversity affects the task not very seriously.

5 Conclusion

In this paper, we describe our system for CoNLL-2011 shared task. We propose to use packed forest and beam search to improve the performance of coreference resolution. Multiple experiments prove that such improvements do help the task.

6 Acknowledgement

The authors were supported by National Natural Science Foundation of China, Contracts 90920004. We would like to thank the anonymous reviewers for suggestions, and SHUGUANG COMPUTING PLATFORM for supporting experimental platform.

[3] http://conll.bbn.com/download/scorer.v4.tar.gz

[4] Since under task requirement, singleton mentions are filtered out, it is hard to recognize the contribution of packed forest to mention detection, while we may incorrectly resolve some mentions into singletons that affects the score of mention detection.

References

E.T. Bell. 1934. Exponential numbers. *The American Mathematical Monthly*, 41(7):411–419.

E. Charniak and M. Johnson. 2005. Coarse-to-fine n-best parsing and maxent discriminative reranking. In *Proceedings of the 43rd Annual Meeting on Association for Computational Linguistics*, pages 173–180. Association for Computational Linguistics.

Stanley F. Chen and Ronald Rosenfeld. 1999. A gaussian prior for smoothing maximum entropy models. Technical report, CMU-CS-99-108.

Liang Huang. 2008. Forest reranking: Discriminative parsing with non-local features. In *Proceedings of ACL-08: HLT*, pages 586–594, Columbus, Ohio, June.

Z. Le. 2004. Maximum entropy modeling toolkit for Python and C++.

X. Luo, A. Ittycheriah, H. Jing, N. Kambhatla, and S. Roukos. 2004. A mention-synchronous coreference resolution algorithm based on the bell tree. In *Proceedings of the 42nd Annual Meeting on Association for Computational Linguistics*, pages 135–es. Association for Computational Linguistics.

H. Mi, L. Huang, and Q. Liu. 2008. Forestbased translation. In *Proceedings of ACL-08: HLT*, pages 192–199. Citeseer.

Vincent Ng. 2010. Supervised noun phrase coreference research: The first fifteen years. In *Proceedings of the 48th Annual Meeting of the Association for Computational Linguistics*, pages 1396–1411, Uppsala, Sweden, July. Association for Computational Linguistics.

Sameer Pradhan, Lance Ramshaw, Ralph Weischedel, Jessica MacBride, and Linnea Micciulla. 2007. Unrestricted Coreference: Identifying Entities and Events in OntoNotes. In *in Proceedings of the IEEE International Conference on Semantic Computing (ICSC)*, September 17-19.

Sameer Pradhan, Lance Ramshaw, Mitchell Marcus, Martha Palmer, Ralph Weischedel, and Nianwen Xue. 2011. Conll-2011 shared task: Modeling unrestricted coreference in ontonotes. In *Proceedings of the Fifteenth Conference on Computational Natural Language Learning (CoNLL 2011)*, Portland, Oregon, June.

W.M. Soon, H.T. Ng, and D.C.Y. Lim. 2001. A machine learning approach to coreference resolution of noun phrases. *Computational Linguistics*, 27(4):521–544.

An Incremental Model for Coreference Resolution with Restrictive Antecedent Accessibility

Manfred Klenner
Institute of Computational Linguistics
University of Zurich
klenner@cl.uzh.ch

Don Tuggener
Institute of Computational Linguistics
University of Zurich
tuggener@cl.uzh.ch

Abstract

We introduce an incremental model for coreference resolution that competed in the CoNLL 2011 shared task (open regular). We decided to participate with our *baseline* model, since it worked well with two other datasets. The benefits of an incremental over a mention-pair architecture are: a drastic reduction of the number of candidate pairs, a means to overcome the problem of underspecified items in pairwise classification and the natural integration of global constraints such as transitivity. We do not apply machine learning, instead the system uses an empirically derived salience measure based on the dependency labels of the true mentions. Our experiments seem to indicate that such a system already is on par with machine learning approaches.

1 Introduction

With notable exceptions (Luo et al., 2004; Yang et al., 2004; Daume III and Marcu, 2005; Culotta et al., 2007; Klenner, 2007; Rahman and Ng, 2009; Klenner and Ailloud, 2009; Cai and Strube, 2010; Raghunathan et al., 2010) supervised approaches to coreference resolution are often realized by pairwise classification of anaphor-antecedent candidates. A popular and often reimplemented approach is presented in (Soon et al., 2001). As recently discussed in (Ng, 2010), the so called mention-pair model suffers from several design flaws which originate from the locally confined perspective of the model:

- Generation of (transitively) redundant pairs, as the formation of coreference sets (coreference clustering) is done after pairwise classification
- Thereby generation of skewed training sets which lead to classifiers biased towards negative classification
- No means to enforce global constraints such as transitivity
- Underspecification of antecedent candidates

These problems can be remedied by an incremental entity-mention model, where candidate pairs are evaluated on the basis of the emerging coreference sets. A clustering phase on top of the pairwise classifier no longer is needed and the number of candidate pairs is reduced, since from each coreference set (be it large or small) only one mention (the most representative one) needs to be compared to a new anaphor candidate. We form a 'virtual prototype' that collects information from all the members of each coreference set in order to maximize 'representativeness'. Constraints such as transitivity and morphological agreement can be assured by just a single comparison. If an anaphor candidate is compatible with the virtual prototype, then it is by definition compatible with all members of the coreference set.

We designed our system to work purely with a simple, yet empirically derived salience measure. It turned out that it outperformed (for German and English, using CEAF, B-cubed and Blanc) the systems from the 2010's SemEval shared task[1] on 'coreference resolution in multiple languages'. Only with the more and more questioned (Luo, 2005; Cai and

[1]We have carried out a post task evaluation with the data provided on the SemEval web page.

Proceedings of the 15th Conference on Computational Natural Language Learning: Shared Task, pages 81–85,
Portland, Oregon, 23-24 June 2011. ©2011 Association for Computational Linguistics

Strube, 2010) MUC measure our system performed worse (at least for English). Our system uses real preprocessing (i.e. a dependency parser (Schneider, 2008)) and extracts markables (nouns, named entities and pronouns) from the chunks and based on POS tags delivered by the preprocessing pipeline. Since we are using a parser, we automatically take part in the *open regular session*. Please note that the dependency labels are the only additional information being used by our system.

2 Our Incremental Model

Fig. 1 shows the basic algorithm. Let I be the chronologically ordered list of markables, C be the set of coreference sets (i.e. the coreference partition) and B a buffer, where markables are stored, if they are not found to be anaphoric (but might be valid antecedents, still). Furthermore m_i is the current markable and $\oplus$ means concatenation of a list and a single item. The algorithm proceeds as follows: a set of antecedent candidates is determined for each markable m_i (steps 1 to 7) from the coreference sets and the buffer. A valid candidate r_j or b_k must be compatible with m_i. The definition of compatibility depends on the POS tags of the anaphor-antecedent pair (in order to be coreferent, e.g. two pronouns must agree in person, number and gender etc.).

In order to reduce underspecification, m_i is compared to a virtual prototype of each coreference set. The virtual prototype bears information accumulated from all elements of the coreference set. For instance, assume a candidate pair 'she .. Clinton'. Since the gender of 'Clinton' is unspecified, the pair might or might not be a good candidate. But if there is a coreference set already including 'Clinton', let's say: {'Hilary Clinton', her, she} then we know the gender from the other members and are more save in our decision. The virtual prototype here would be something like: singular, feminine, human.

From the set of candidates, Cand, the most salient $ante_i \in$ Cand is selected (step 10) and the coreference partition is augmented (step 11). If $ante_i$ comes from a coreference set, m_i is added to that set. Otherwise ($ante_i$ is from the buffer), a new set is formed, $\{ante_i, m_i\}$, and added to the set of coreference sets.

2.1 Restricted Accessibility of Antecedent Candidates

As already discussed, access to coreference sets is restricted to the virtual prototype - the concrete members are invisible. This reduces the number of considered pairs (from the cardinality of a set to 1).

Moreover, we also restrict the access to buffer elements: if an antecedent candidate, r_j, from a coreference set exists, then elements from the buffer, b_k, are only licensed if they are more recent than r_j. If both appear in the same sentence, the buffer element must be more salient in order to get licensed.

2.2 Filtering based on Anaphora Type

There is a number of conditions not shown in the basic algorithm from Fig. 1 that define compatibility of antecedent and anaphor candidates based on POS tags. Reflexive pronouns must be bound in the subclause they occur, more specifically to the subject governed by the same verb. Personal and possessive pronouns are licensed to bind to morphologically compatible antecedent candidates (named entities, nouns[2] and pronouns) within a window of three sentences.

We use the information given by CoNLL input data to identify 'speaker' and the person adressed by 'you'. 'I' refers to one of the coreference sets whose speaker is the person who, according to the CoNLL data, is the producer of the sentence. 'You' refers to the producer of the last sentence not being produced by the current 'speaker'. If one didn't have access to these data, it would be impossible to correctly identify the reference of 'I', since turn taking is not indicated in the pure textual data.

As we do not use machine learning, we only apply string matching techniques to match nominal NPs and leave out bridging anaphora (i.e. anaphoric nouns that are connected to their antecedents through a semantic relation such as hyponymy and cannot be identified by string matching therefore). Named entities must either match completely or the antecedent must be longer than one token and all tokens of the anaphor must be contained in the antecedent (to capture relations such

[2]To identify animacy and gender of NEs we use a list of known first names annotated with gender information. To obtain animacy information for common nouns we conduct a WordNet lookup.

for i=1 to length(I)
    for j=1 to length(C)
        r_j := virtual prototype of coreference set C_j
        Cand := Cand $\oplus$ r_j if compatible(r_j, m_i)
    for k= length(B) to 1
        b_k:= the k-th licensed buffer element
        Cand := Cand $\oplus$ b_k if compatible(b_k, m_i)
if Cand = {} then B := B $\oplus$ m_i
if Cand $\neq$ {} then
    $ante_i$:= most salient element of Cand
    C := augment(C,$ante_i$,m_i)

Figure 1: Incremental Model: Base Algorithm

as 'Hillary Clinton ... Clinton'). Demonstrative NPs are mapped to nominal NPs by matching their heads. Definite NPs match with noun chunks that are longer than one token[3] and must be contained completely without the determiner (e.g. 'Recent events ... the events'). From the candidates that pass these filters the most salient one is selected as antecedent. If two or more candidates with equal salience are available, the closest one is chosen.

2.3 Binding Theory as a Filter

There is another principle that help reduce the number of candidates even further: binding theory. We know that 'He' and 'him' cannot be coreferent in the sentence 'He gave him the book'. Thus, the pair 'He'-'him' need not be considered at all. Actually, there are subtle restrictions to be captured here. We have not implemented a full-blown binding theory on top of our dependency parser, yet. Instead, we approximated binding restrictions by subclause detection. 'He' and 'him' in the example above are in the same subclause (the main clause) and are, thus, exclusive. This is true for nouns and personal pronouns, only. Possesive and reflexive pronouns are allowed to be bound in the same subclause.

2.4 An Empirically-based Salience Measure

Since we look for a simple and fast salience measure and do not apply machine learning in our baseline system, our measure is solely based on the grammatical functions (given by the dependency labels) of the true mentions. Grammatical functions have played a major role in calculating salience, especially in rule based system such as (Hobbs, 1976; Lappin and Leass, 1994; Mitkov et al., 2002; Siddharthan, 2003). Instead of manually specifying the weights for the dependency labels like (Lappin and Leass, 1994), we derived them empirically from the coreference CoNLL 2011 gold standard (training data). The salience of a dependency label, D, is estimated by the number of true mentions in the gold standard that bear D (i.e. are connected to their heads with D), divided by the total number of true mentions. The salience of the label *subject* is thus calculated by:

$$\frac{Number\,of\,true\,mentions\,bearing\,subject}{Total\,number\,of\,true\,mentions}$$

For a given dependency label, this fraction indicates how strong is the label a clue for bearing an antecedent. This way, we get a hierarchical ordering of the dependency labels (subject > object > pobject > ...) according to which antecedents are ranked. Clearly, future work will have to establish a more elaborate calculation of salience. To our surprise, however, this salience measure performed quite well, at least together with our incremental architeture.

3 Evaluation

The results of our evaluation over the CoNLL 2011 shared task development set are given in Fig. 2 (development set) and 3 (official results on the test set).

The official overall score of our system in the open regular setting is 51.77.

Our results are mediocre. There are several rea-

[3] If we do not apply this restriction too many false positives are produced.

Metric	R	P	F1
CEAFM	49.73	49.73	49.73
CEAFE	44.26	37.70	40.72
BCUB	59.17	71.66	66.06
BLANC	62.70	72.74	64.82
MUC	42.20	49.21	45.44

Figure 2: CoNLL 2011 Development Set Results

Metric	R	P	F1
CEAFM	50.03	50.03	50.03
CEAFE	41.28	39.70	40.48
BCUB	61.70	68.61	64.97
BLANC	66.05	73.90	69.05
MUC	49.04	50.71	49.86

Figure 3: CoNLL 2011 Test Set Results

sons for that. First and foremost, the scorer requires chunk extensions to match perfectly. That is, even if the head of an antecedent is found, this does not count if the chunk extension of that noun phrase was not correctly identified. Since chunks do not play a major role in depencendy parsing, our approximation might be faulty[4]. Another shortcomming are nominal anaphora that can not be identified by string matching (e.g. Obama ... The president). Our simple salience-based approach does not cope at all with this type of anaphora.

4 Related Work

(Ng, 2010) discusses the entity-mention model which operates on emerging coreference sets to create features describing the relation of an anaphor candidate and established coreference sets. (Luo et al., 2004) implemented such a model but it performed worse than the mention-pair model. (Yang et al., 2004) presented an incremental model which used some coreference set specific features, namely introducing the number of mentions in a set as a feature besides checking for morphological compatibility with all mentions in a set. They also report that the set size feature only marginally improves or in some combinations even worsens system performance. (Daume III and Marcu, 2005) introduced a wide range of set specific features, capturing set count, size and distribution amongst others, in a joint model for the ACE data.

All the above mentioned systems use an incremental model to generate features describing the emerging coreference sets and the anaphor candidate. In contrast, we use an incremental architecture to control pair generation in order to prevent generation of either redundant or irrelevant pairs.

5 Conclusions

We have introduced an incremental model for coreference resolution based on an empirically derived salience measure that is meant as a simple and very fast baseline system. We do not use machine learning, nor do we resolve more complex nominal anaphora such as 'Obama ... The president' (but we handle those that can be resolved by simple pattern matching, e.g. Hilary Clinton .. Clinton). Given these restrictions, our system performed well.

The central idea of our approach is that the evolving coreference sets should restrict the access to antecedent candidates in a twofold way: by use of virtual prototypes that accumulate the properties of all members of a coreference set (e.g. wrt. animacy), but also by restricting reachable buffer elements (i.e. yet unattached markables).

The benefits of our incremental model are:

- due to the restricted access to antecedent candidates, the number of generated candidate pairs can be reduced drastically[5]
- no coreference clustering phase is needed
- the problem of underspecification that exists for any pair-wise model can be compensated by a virtual prototype that accumulates the properties of the elements of a coreference set

These benefits are independent of the underlying classification scheme, be it a simple salience-based one or a more advanced machine learning one. The work presented here thus would like to opt for further research based on incremental architectures. Web demos for English and German are available[6].

[4]Especially Asiatic names pose problems to our parser, quite often the extensions could not get correctly fixed.

[5]We observed a reduction over 75% in some experiments when moving from a mention-pair to an incremental entity-mention model.

[6]http://kitt.cl.uzh.ch/kitt/coref/

References

Jie Cai and Michael Strube. 2010. Evaluation metrics for end-to-end coreference resolution systems. In *Proceedings of the SIGdial 2010 Conference: The 11th Annual Meeting of the Special Interest Group on Discourse and Dialogue*.

Aron Culotta, Michael Wick, and Andrew McCallum. 2007. First-order probabilistic models for coreference resolution. In *Human Language Technologies 2007: The Conference of the North American Chapter of the Association for Computational Linguistics; Proceedings of the Main Conference*, pages 81–88, Rochester, New York, April. Association for Computational Linguistics.

Hal Daume III and Daniel Marcu. 2005. A large-scale exploration of effective global features for a joint entity detection and tracking model. In *HLT '05: Proceedings of the conference on Human Language Technology and Empirical Methods in Natural Language Processing*, pages 97–104, Morristown, NJ, USA. Association for Computational Linguistics.

Jerry R. Hobbs. 1976. Pronoun resolution. Technical Report 76-1, Research Report, Department of Computer Sciences, City College, City University of New York.

Manfred Klenner and Etienne Ailloud. 2009. Optimization in Coreference Resolution Is Not Needed: A Nearly-Optimal Zero-One ILP Algorithm with Intensional Constraints. In *Proc. of the EACL*.

Manfred Klenner. 2007. Enforcing consistency on coreference sets. In *In Recent Advances in Natural Language Processing (RANLP)*, pages 323–328.

Shalom Lappin and Herbert J Leass. 1994. An algorithm for pronominal anaphora resolution. *Computational Linguistics*, 20:535–561.

Xiaoqiang Luo, Abe Ittycheriah, Hongyan Jing, Nanda Kambhatla, and Salim Roukos. 2004. A mention-synchronous coreference resolution algorithm based on the bell tree. In *Proceedings of the 42nd Annual Meeting on Association for Computational Linguistics*.

Xiaoqiang Luo. 2005. On coreference resolution performance metrics. In *HLT '05: Proceedings of the conference on Human Language Technology and Empirical Methods in Natural Language Processing*, pages 25–32, Morristown, NJ, USA. Association for Computational Linguistics.

Ruslan Mitkov, Richard Evans, and Constantin Orasan. 2002. A new, fully automatic version of mitkov's knowledge-poor pronoun resolution method. In *CICLing '02: Proceedings of the Third International Conference on Computational Linguistics and Intelligent Text Processing*, pages 168–186, London, UK. Springer-Verlag.

Vincent Ng. 2010. Supervised noun phrase coreference research: The first fifteen years. In *Proceedings of the 48th Annual Meeting of the Association for Computational Linguistics*.

Karthik Raghunathan, Heeyoung Lee, Sudarshan Rangarajan, Nathanael Chambers, Mihai Surdeanu, Dan Jurafsky, and Christopher Manning. 2010. A multi-pass sieve for coreference resolution. In *Proceedings of the 2010 Conference on Empirical Methods in Natural Language Processing*, EMNLP '10, pages 492–501, Stroudsburg, PA, USA. Association for Computational Linguistics.

Altaf Rahman and Vincent Ng. 2009. Supervised models for coreference resolution. In *Proceedings of the 2009 Conference on Empirical Methods in Natural Language Processing: Volume 2 - Volume 2*, EMNLP '09, pages 968–977, Stroudsburg, PA, USA. Association for Computational Linguistics.

Gerold Schneider. 2008. *Hybrid Long-Distance Functional Dependency Parsing*. Doctoral Thesis, Institute of Computational Linguistics, Univ. of Zurich.

Advaith Siddharthan. 2003. Resolving pronouns robustly: Plumbing the depths of shallowness. In *Proceedings of the Workshop on Computational Treatments of Anaphora, 11th Conference of the European Chapter of the Association for Computational Linguistics (EACL 2003)*.

Wee M. Soon, Hwee T. Ng, and Daniel. 2001. A machine learning approach to coreference resolution of noun phrases. *Computational Linguistics*, 27(4):521–544, December.

Xiaofeng Yang, Jian Su, Guodong Zhou, and Chew Lim Tan. 2004. An np-cluster based approach to coreference resolution. In *Proceedings of the 20th international conference on Computational Linguistics*.

Narrative Schema as World Knowledge for Coreference Resolution

Joseph Irwin
Nara Institute of
Science and Technology
Nara Prefecture, Japan
joseph-i@is.naist.jp

Mamoru Komachi
Nara Institute of
Science and Technology
Nara Prefecture, Japan
komachi@is.naist.jp

Yuji Matsumoto
Nara Institute of
Science and Technology
Nara Prefecture, Japan
matsu@is.naist.jp

Abstract

In this paper we describe the system with which we participated in the CoNLL-2011 Shared Task on modelling coreference. Our system is based on a cluster-ranking model proposed by Rahman and Ng (2009), with novel semantic features based on recent research on narrative event schema (Chambers and Jurafsky, 2009). We demonstrate some improvements over the baseline when using schema information, although the effect varied between the metrics used. We also explore the impact of various features on our system's performance.

1 Introduction

Coreference resolution is a problem for automated document understanding. We say two segments of a natural-language document *corefer* when they refer to the same real-world entity. The segments of a document which refer to an *entity* are called *mentions*. In coreference resolution tasks, mentions are usually restricted to noun phrases.

The goal of the CoNLL-2011 Shared Task (Pradhan et al., 2011) is to model unrestricted coreference using the OntoNotes corpus. The OntoNotes corpus is annotated with several layers of syntactic and semantic information, making it a rich resource for investigating coreference resolution (Pradhan et al., 2007).

We participated in both the "open" and "closed" tracks. The "closed" track requires systems to only use the provided data, while the "open" track allows use of external data. We created a baseline system based on the cluster-ranking model proposed by Rahman and Ng (2009). We then experimented with adding novel semantic features derived from co-referring predicate-argument chains. These *narrative schema* were developed by Chambers and Jurafsky (2009). They are described in more detail in a later section.

2 Related Work

Supervised machine-learning approaches to coreference resolution have been researched for almost two decades. Recently, the state of the art seems to be moving away from the early mention-pair classification model toward entity-based models. Ng (2010) provides an excellent overview of the history and recent developments within the field.

Both entity-mention and mention-pair models are formulated as binary classification problems; however, ranking may be a more natural approach to coreference resolution (Ng, 2010; Rahman and Ng, 2009). Rahman and Ng (2009) in particular propose the cluster-ranking model which we used in our baseline. In another approach, Daumé and Marcu (2005) apply their Learning as Search Optimization framework to coreference resolution, and show good results.

Feature selection is important for good performance in coreference resolution. Ng (2010) discusses commonly used features, and analyses of the contribution of various features can be found in (Daumé and Marcu, 2005; Rahman and Ng, 2011; Ponzetto and Strube, 2006b). Surprisingly, Rahman and Ng (2011) demonstrated that a system using almost exclusively lexical features could outperform

Proceedings of the 15th Conference on Computational Natural Language Learning: Shared Task, pages 86–92,
Portland, Oregon, 23-24 June 2011. ©2011 Association for Computational Linguistics

systems which used more traditional sets of features.

Although string features have a large effect on performance, it is recognized that the use of semantic information is important for further improvement (Ng, 2010; Ponzetto and Strube, 2006a; Ponzetto and Strube, 2006b; Haghighi and Klein, 2010). The use of predicate-argument structure has been explored by Ponzetto and Strube (2006b; 2006a).

3 Narrative Schema for Coreference

Narrative schema are extracted from large-scale corpora using coreference information to identify predicates whose arguments often corefer. Similarity measures are used to build up schema consisting of one or more *event chains* – chains of typically-coreferring predicate arguments (Chambers and Jurafsky, 2009). Each chain corresponds to a *role* in the schema.

A role defines a class of participants in the schema. Conceptually, if a schema is present in a document, than each role in the schema corresponds to an entity in the document. An example schema is shown with some typical participants in Figure 1. In this paper the temporal order of events in the schema is not considered.

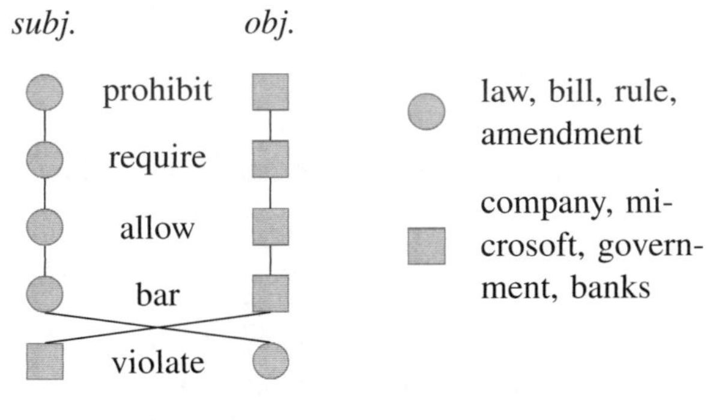

Figure 1: An example narrative schema with two roles.

Narrative schema are similar to the *script* concept put forth by Schank and Abelson (1977). Like scripts, narrative schema can capture complex structured information about events described in natural language documents (Schank and Abelson, 1977; Abelson, 1981; Chambers and Jurafsky, 2009).

We hypothesize that narrative schema can be a good source of information for making coreference decisions. One reason they could be useful is that they can directly capture the fact that arguments of certain predicates are relatively more likely to refer to the same entity. In fact, they can capture global information about verbs ranging over the entire document, which we expect may lead to greater accuracy when combined with the incremental clustering algorithm we employ.

Additionally, the information that two predicates often share arguments yields semantic information about the argument words themselves. For example, if the subjects of the verbs *eat* and *drink* often corefer, we may be able to infer that words which occur in the subject position of these verbs share some property (e.g., animacy). This last conjecture is somewhat validated by Ponzetto and Strube (2006b), who reported that including predicate-argument pairs as features improved the performance of a coreference resolver.

4 System Description

4.1 Overview

We built a coreference resolution system based on the cluster-ranking algorithm proposed by Rahman and Ng (2009). During document processing maintains a list of clusters of coreferring mentions which are created iteratively. Our system uses a deterministic mention-detection algorithm that extracts candidate NPs from a document. We process the mentions in order of appearance in the document. For each mention a ranking query is created, with features generated from the clusters created so far. In each query we include a null-cluster instance, to allow joint learning of discourse-new detection, following (Rahman and Ng, 2009).

For training, each mention is assigned to its correct cluster according to the coreference annotation. The resulting queries are used to train a classification-based ranker.

In testing, the ranking model thus learned is used to rank the clusters in each query as it is created; the active mention is assigned to the cluster with the highest rank.

A data-flow diagram for our system is shown in Figure 2.

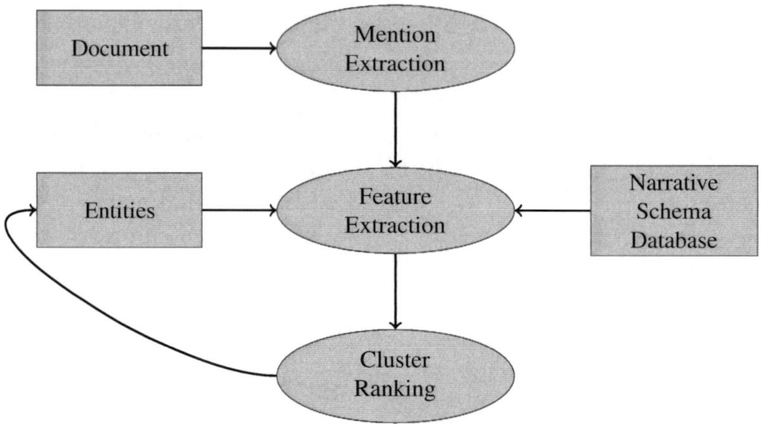

Figure 2: System execution flow

4.2 Cluster-ranking Model

Our baseline system uses a cluster-ranking model proposed by Rahman and Ng (2009; 2011). In this model, clusters are iteratively constructed after considering each active mention in a document in order. During training, features are created between the active mention and each cluster created so far. A rank is assigned such that the cluster which is coreferent to the active mention has the highest value, and each non-coreferent cluster is assigned the same, lower rank (The exact values are irrelevant to learning a ranking; for the experiments in this paper we used the values 2 and 1). In this way it is possible to learn to preferentially rank correct clustering decisions higher.

For classification, instances are constructed exactly the same way as for training, except that for each active mention, a query must be constructed and ranked by the classifier in order to proceed with the clustering. After the query for each active mention has been ranked, the mention is assigned to the cluster with the highest ranking, and the algorithm proceeds to the next mention.

4.3 Notation

In the following sections, m_k is the active mention currently being considered, m_j is a candidate antecedent mention, and c_j is the cluster to which it belongs. Most of the features used in our system actually apply to a pair of mentions (i.e., m_k and m_j) or to a single mention (either m_k or m_j). To create a training or test instance using m_k and c_j, the features which apply to m_j are converted to cluster-level features by a procedure described in 4.6.

4.4 Joint Anaphoric Mention Detection

We follow Rahman and Ng (2009) in jointly learning to detect anaphoric mentions along with resolving coreference relations. For each active mention m_k, an instance for a 'null' cluster is also created, with rank 2 if the mention is not coreferent with any preceding mention, or rank 1 if it has an antecedent. This allows the ranker the option of making m_k discourse-new. To create this instance, only the features which involve just m_k are used.

4.5 Features

The features used in our system are shown in Table 1. For the NE features we directly use the types from the OntoNotes annotation. [1]

4.6 Making Cluster-Level Features

Each feature which applies to m_j must be converted to a cluster-level feature. We follow the procedure described in (Rahman and Ng, 2009). This procedure uses binary features whose values correspond to being logically true or false. Multi-valued features are first converted into equivalent sets of binary-valued features. For each binary-valued feature, four corresponding cluster-level features are created, whose values are determined by four logical

[1]The set of types is: PERSON, NORP, FACILITY, ORGANIZATION, GPE, LOCATION, PRODUCT, EVENT, WORK, LAW, LANGUAGE, DATE, TIME, PERCENT, MONEY, QUANTITY, ORDINAL, CARDINAL

Features involving m_j only	
SUBJECT	Y if m_j is the grammatical subject of a verb; N otherwise
*NE_TYPE1	the NE label for m_j if there is one else NONE
Features involving m_k only	
DEFINITE	Y if the first word of m_k is *the*; N otherwise
DEMONSTRATIVE	Y if the first word of m_k is one of *this, that, these*, or *those*; N otherwise
DEF_DEM_NA	Y if neither DEFINITE nor DEMONSTRATIVE is Y; N otherwise
PRONOUN2	Y if m_k is a personal pronoun; N otherwise
PROTYPE2	nominative case of m_k if m_k is a pronoun or NA if it is not (e.g., HE if m_k is *him*)
NE_TYPE2	the NE label for m_k if there is one
Features involving both m_j and m_k	
DISTANCE	how many sentences separate m_j and m_k; the values are A) same sentence, B) previous sentence, and C) two sentences ago or more
HEAD_MATCH	Y if the head words are the same; N otherwise
PRONOUN_MATCH	if either of m_j and m_k is not a pronoun, NA; if the nominative case of m_j and m_k is the same, C; I otherwise
*NE_TYPE′	the concatenation of the NE labels of m_j and m_k (if either or both are not labelled NEs, the feature is created using NONE as the corresponding label)
SCHEMA_PAIR_MATCH	Y if m_j and m_k appear in the same role in a schema, and N if they do not
Features involving c_j and m_k	
SCHEMA_CLUSTER_MATCH	a cluster-level feature between m_k and c_j (details in Section 4.7)

Table 1: Features implemented in our coreference resolver. Binary-valued features have values of **YES** or **NO**. Multi-valued features are converted into equivalent sets of binary-valued features before being used to create the cluster-level features used by the ranker.

predicates: NONE, MOST-FALSE, MOST-TRUE, and ALL.

To be precise, a feature F may be thought of as a function taking m_j as a parameter, e.g., $F(m_j)$. To simplify notation, features which apply to the *pair* m_j,m_k take m_k as an implicit parameter. The logical predicates then compare the two counts $n = |\{m_j \mid F(m_j) = true\}|$ and $C = |c_j|$. The resulting features are shown in Table 2.

NONE_F	TRUE iff $n = 0$
MOST-FALSE_F	TRUE iff $n < \frac{C}{2}$
MOST-TRUE_F	TRUE iff $\frac{C}{2} \leq n < C$
ALL_F	TRUE iff $n = C$

Table 2: Cluster-level features created from binary-valued feature F

The two features marked with * are treated differently. For each value of NE_TYPE1 and NE_TYPE′, a new cluster-level feature is created whose value is the number of times that feature/value appeared in the cluster (i.e., if there were two PERSON NEs in a cluster then the feature NE_TYPE1_PERSON would have the value 2).

4.7 SCHEMA_CLUSTER_MATCH

The SCHEMA_CLUSTER_MATCH feature is actually three features, which are calculated over an entire candidate antecedent cluster c_j. First a list is created of all of the schema roles which the mentions in c_j participate in, and sorted in decreasing order according to how many mentions in c_j participate in each. Then, the value of the feature SCHEMA_CLUSTER_MATCH$_n$ is Y if mention m_k also participates in the nth schema role in the list, for $n = 1, 2, 3$. If it does not, or if the corresponding n_{th} schema role has fewer than two participants in c_j, the value of this feature is N.

4.8 Implementation Details

Our system was implemented in Python, in order to make use of the NLTK library[2]. For the ranker we used SVM^{rank}, an efficient implementation for training ranking SVMs (Joachims, 2006) [3].

[2]http://www.nltk.org/
[3]http://svmlight.joachims.org/

		R	P	F_1
CLOSED	MUC	12.45%	50.60%	19.98
	B^3	35.07%	89.90%	50.46
	CEAF	45.84%	17.38%	25.21
			Overall score:	31.88
OPEN	MUC	18.56%	51.01%	27.21
	B^3	38.97%	85.57%	53.55
	CEAF	43.33%	19.36%	26.76
			Overall score:	35.84

Table 3: Official system results

5 Experiments and Results

5.1 CoNLL System Submission

We submitted two results to the CoNLL-2011 Shared Task. In the "closed" track we submitted the results of our baseline system without the schema features, trained on all documents in both the training and development portions of the OntoNotes corpus.

We also submitted a result in the "open" track: a version of our system with the schema features added. Due to issues with the implementation of this second version, however, we were only able to submit results from a model trained on just the WSJ portion of the training dataset. For the schema features, we used a database of narrative schema released by Chambers and Jurafsky (2010) – specifically the list of schemas of size 12. [4]

The official system scores for our system are listed in Table 3. We can attribute some of the low performance of our system to features which are too noisy, and to having not enough features compared to the large size of the dataset. It is likely that these two factors adversely impact the ability of the SVM to learn effectively. In fact, the features which we introduced partially to provide more features to learn with, the NE features, had the worst impact on performance according to later analysis. Because of a problem with our implementation, we were unable to get an accurate idea of our system's performance until after the submission deadline.

[4]Available at http://cs.stanford.edu/people/nc/schemas/

		R	P	F_1
Baseline	MUC	12.77%	57.66%	20.91
	B^3	35.1%	91.05%	50.67
	CEAF	47.80%	17.29%	25.40
+SCHEMA	MUC	12.78%	54.84%	20.73
	B^3	35.75%	90.39%	51.24
	CEAF	46.62%	17.43%	25.38

Table 4: Schema features evaluated on the development set. Training used the entire training dataset.

5.2 Using Narrative Schema as World Knowledge for Coreference Resolution

We conducted an evaluation of the baseline without schema features against a model with both schema features added. The results are shown in Table 4.

The results were mixed, with B^3 going up and MUC and CEAF falling slightly. Cross-validation using just the development set showed a more positive picture, however, with both MUC and B^3 scores increasing more than 1 point ($p = 0.06$ and $p < 0.01$, respectively), and CEAF increasing about 0.5 points as well (although this was not significant at $p > 0.1$). [5]

One problem with the schema features that we had anticipated was that they may have a problem with sparseness. We had originally intended to extract schema using the coreference annotation in OntoNotes, predicting that this would help alleviate the problem; however, due to time constraints we were unable to complete this effort.

5.3 Feature Analysis

We conducted a feature ablation analysis on our baseline system to better understand the contribution of each feature to overall performance. The results are shown in Table 5. We removed features in blocks of related features; -HEAD removes HEAD_MATCH; -DIST removes the DISTANCE feature; -SUBJ is the baseline system without SUBJECT; -PRO is the baseline system without PRONOUN2, PROTYPE2, and PRONOUN_MATCH; -DEF_DEM removes DEFINITE, DEMONSTRATIVE, and DEF_DEM_NA; and -NE removes the named entity features.

[5]All significance tests were performed with a two-tailed t-test.

Baseline	MUC	12.77%	57.66%	20.91	
	B^3	35.1%	91.05%	50.67	
	CEAF	47.80%	17.29%	25.40	
		R	P	F_1	ΔF_1
-HEAD	MUC	0.00%	33.33%	0.01	-20.90
	B^3	26.27%	99.98%	41.61	-9.06
	CEAF	52.88%	13.89%	22.00	-3.40
-DIST	MUC	0.39%	60.86%	0.79	-20.12
	B^3	26.59%	99.72%	41.99	-8.68
	CEAF	52.76%	13.99%	22.11	-3.29
-SUBJ	MUC	12.47%	47.69%	19.78	-1.13
	B^3	36.54%	87.80%	51.61	0.94
	CEAF	43.75%	17.22%	24.72	-0.68
-PRO	MUC	18.36%	55.98%	27.65	6.74
	B^3	37.45%	85.78%	52.14	1.47
	CEAF	47.86%	19.19%	27.40	2.00
-DEF_DEM	MUC	18.90%	51.72%	27.68	6.77
	B^3	41.65%	86.11%	56.14	5.47
	CEAF	46.39%	21.61%	29.48	4.08
-NE	MUC	22.76%	49.5%	31.18	10.27
	B^3	46.78%	84.92%	60.33	9.66
	CEAF	45.65%	25.19%	32.46	7.06

Table 5: Effect of each feature on performance.

The fact that for three of the features, removing the feature actually improved performance is troubling. Possibly these features were too noisy; we need to improve the baseline features for future experiments.

6 Conclusions

Semantic information is necessary for many tasks in natural language processing. Most often this information is used in the form of relationships between words – for example, how semantically similar two words are, or which nouns are the objects of a verb. However, it is likely that humans make use of much higher-level information than the similarity between two concepts when processing language (Abelson, 1981). We attempted to take advantage of recent developments in automatically aquiring just this sort of information, and demonstrated the possibility of making use of it in NLP tasks such as coreference. However, we need to improve both the implementation and data for this approach to be practical.

For future work, we intend to investigate avenues for improving the aquisition and use of the narrative schema information, and also compare narrative schema with other types of semantic information in coreference resolution. Because coreference information is central to the extraction of narrative schema, the joint learning of coreference resolution and narrative schema is another area we would like to explore.

References

Robert P. Abelson. 1981. Psychological status of the script concept. *American Psychologist*, 36(7):715–729.

Nathanael Chambers and Dan Jurafsky. 2009. Unsupervised Learning of Narrative Schemas and their Participants. In *Proceedings of the Joint Conference of the 47th Annual Meeting of the ACL and the 4th International Joint Conference on Natural Language Processing of the AFNLP*, pages 602–610, Suntec, Singapore.

Nathanael Chambers and Dan Jurafsky. 2010. A database of narrative schemas. In *Proceedings of the Seventh International Conference on Language Resources and Evaluation (LREC 2010)*, Malta.

Hal Daumé and Daniel Marcu. 2005. A large-scale exploration of effective global features for a joint entity detection and tracking model. In *Proceedings of the Conference on Human Language Technology and Empirical Methods in Natural Language Processing - HLT '05*, pages 97–104, Morristown, NJ, USA.

Aria Haghighi and Dan Klein. 2010. Coreference resolution in a modular, entity-centered model. In *Human Language Technologies: The 2010 Annual Conference of the North American Chapter of the Association for Computational Linguistics*, pages 385–393.

Thorsten Joachims. 2006. Training linear SVMs in linear time. In *Proceedings of the 12th ACM SIGKDD International Conference on Knowledge Discovery and Data Mining KDD 06*, pages 217–226.

Vincent Ng. 2010. Supervised noun phrase coreference research: the first fifteen years. In *Proceedings of the 48th Annual Meeting of the Association for Computational Linguistics*, pages 1396–1411.

Simone Paolo Ponzetto and Michael Strube. 2006a. Exploiting semantic role labeling, WordNet and Wikipedia for coreference resolution. In *Proceedings of the main conference on Human Language Technology Conference of the North American Chapter of the Association of Computational Linguistics*, pages 192–199.

Simone Paolo Ponzetto and Michael Strube. 2006b. Semantic role labeling for coreference resolution. In *Proceedings of the Eleventh Conference of the European Chapter of the Association for Computational*

Linguistics - EACL '06, pages 143–146, Morristown, NJ, USA.

Sameer Pradhan, Lance Ramshaw, Ralph Weischedel, Jessica MacBride, and Linnea Micciulla. 2007. Unrestricted Coreference: Identifying Entities and Events in OntoNotes. In *International Conference on Semantic Computing (ICSC 2007)*, pages 446–453.

Sameer Pradhan, Lance Ramshaw, Mitchell Marcus, Martha Palmer, Ralph Weischedel, and Nianwen Xue. 2011. CoNLL-2011 Shared Task: Modeling Unrestricted Coreference in OntoNotes. In *Proceedings of the Fifteenth Conference on Computational Natural Language Learning (CoNLL 2011)*, Portland, Oregon.

Altaf Rahman and Vincent Ng. 2009. Supervised Models for Coreference Resolution. In *Proceedings of the 2009 Conference on Empirical Methods in Natural Language Processing*, pages 968–977, Singapore.

Altaf Rahman and Vincent Ng. 2011. Narrowing the Modeling Gap: A Cluster-Ranking Approach to Coreference Resolution. *Journal of Artificial Intelligence Research*, 40:469–521.

Roger C. Schank and Robert P. Abelson. 1977. *Scripts, plans, goals and understanding: An inquiry into human knowledge structures.* Lawrence Erlbaum, Oxford, England.

Hybrid Approach for Coreference Resolution

First Author: Sobha, Lalitha Devi., Pattabhi, RK Rao., Vijay Sundar Ram, R.
Second Author: Malarkodi, CS., Akilandeswari, A.
AU-KBC Research Centre,
MIT Campus of Anna University,
Chrompet, Chennai, India.
sobha@au-kbc.org

Abstract

This paper describes our participation in the CoNLL-2011 shared task for closed task. The approach used combines refined salience measure based pronominal resolution and CRFs for non-pronominal resolution. In this work we also use machine learning based approach for identifying non-anaphoric pronouns.

1 Introduction

In this paper we describe our system, used in the CoNLL-2011 shared task "Modeling Unrestricted Coreference in OntoNotes". The goal of this task is to identify coreference chains in a document. The coreference chains can include names, nominal mentions, pronouns, verbs that are coreferenced with a noun phrases.

The coreferents are classified into two types, pronominal and non-pronominal referents. We use two different approaches using machine learning and salience factor in the resolution of the above two types. Pronominal resolution is done using salience factors and Non-Pronominals using machine learning approach. Pronominal resolution refers to identification of a Noun phrase (NP) that is referred by a pronominal and Non-Pronominals are NP referring to another NP. In the next section we describe the system in detail.

2 System Description

In this section we give a detailed description of our system. The task is divided into two sub-tasks. They are

i) Pronominal resolution
ii) Non-pronominal resolution

2.1 Pronominal Resolution

Here we have identified salience factors and assigned weights for each factor. Before resolving the pronouns we identify whether a given pronoun is anaphoric or not. In example, (1) below, the pronoun "It", does not refer to any entity, and it is a pleonastic "it".

(1) "It will rain today"

In identifying the non-anaphoric pronouns such as "it" we use a CRFs engine, a machine learning approach. We build a language model using the above ML method to identify the non-anaphoric pronouns and the features used in training are word and it's POS in a window of five (two preceding and two following words to the pronoun). After the non-anaphoric pronoun identification, we resolve the anaphoric pronouns using a pronominal resolution system. Though we use salience factors based on the Lappin and Leass (1994), we have substantially deviated from the basic algorithm and have also used factors from Sobha (2008), where named entity and ontology are considered for resolution.

For identifying an antecedent for a pronoun we consider all the noun phrases before the pronoun in

Proceedings of the 15th Conference on Computational Natural Language Learning: Shared Task, pages 93–96,
Portland, Oregon, 23-24 June 2011. ©2011 Association for Computational Linguistics

the current sentence and in the four sentences preceding the current sentence. Those noun phrases which agree in PNG with the pronoun are considered as the possible candidates. The PNG is obtained using the gender data work of Shane Bergsma and Dekang Lin (2006). The possible candidates are scored based on the salience factors and ranked. The salience factors considered here are presented in the table 1.

Salience Factors	Weights
Current Sentence (sentence in which pronoun occurs)	100
For the preceding sentences up to four sentences from the current sentence	Reduce sentence score by 10
Current Clause (clause in which pronoun occurs)	100 – for possessive pronoun 50 – for non-possessive pronouns
Immediate Clause (clause preceding or following the current clause)	50 – for possessive pronoun 100 – for non-possessive pronouns
Non-immediate Clause (neither the current or immediate clause)	50
Possessive NP	65
Existential NP	70
Subject	80
Direct Object	50
Indirect Object	40
Compliment of PP	30

Table 1: Salience Factors and weights

Improving pronominal resolution Using Name Entity (NE) and WordNet: Pronouns such as "He", "She", "I" and "You" can take antecedents which are animate and particularly having the NE tag PERSON. Similarly the pronoun "It" can never take an animate as the antecedent. From the WordNet we obtain the information of noun category such as "person", "object", "artifact", "location" etc. Using the NE information provided in the document and the category information in WordNet, the irrelevant candidates are filtered out from the possible candidates. Thus the antecedent and pronoun category agrees.

The highest ranked candidate is considered as the antecedent for the particular pronoun.

In TC and BC genres, the pronouns "I" and "you" refer to the speakers involved in the conversation. For these pronouns we identify the antecedent using heuristic rules making use of the speaker information provided.

2.2 Non-pronominal Coreference resolution

In identifying the Non-pronominal as said earlier, we have used a CRFs based machine learning approach. CRFs are well known for label sequencing tasks such as Chunking, Named Entity tagging (Lafferty et al, 2001; Taku Kudo 2005). Here we have CRFs for classification task, by using only the current state features and not the features related to state transition. The features used for training are based on Soon et al (2001). We have changed the method of deriving, values of the features such as String match, alias, from the Soon el al method and found that our method is giving more result. The features used in our work are as follows.

a) Distance feature – same as in Soon et al

b) Definite NP - same as in Soon et al

c) Demonstrative NP – same as in Soon et al

d) String match – (Not as Soon et al)the possible values are between 0 and 1. This is calculated as ratio of the number of words matched between the NPs and the total number of words of the anaphor NP. Here we consider the NP on the left side as antecedent NP and NP on the right side as anaphor NP.

e) Number Agreement – We use the gender data file (Bergsma and Lin, 2006) and also the POS information

f) Gender agreement – We use the gender data file (Bergsma and Lin, 2006)

g) Alias feature – (Not as in Soon et al) the alias feature takes the value 0 or 1. This is obtained using three methods,

i) Comparing the head of the NPs, if both are same then scored as 1

ii) If both the NPs start with NNP or NNPS POS tags, and if they are same then scored as 1

iii) Looks for Acronym match, if one is an acronym of other it is scored as 1

h) Both proper NPs – same as Soon et al.

i) NE tag information.

The semantic class information (noun category) obtained from the WordNet is used for the filtering purpose. The pairs which do not have semantic feature match are filtered out. We have not used the appositive feature described in Soon et al (2001), since we are not considering appositives for the coreference chains.

The feature template for CRF is defined in such a way that more importance is given to the features such as the string match, gender agreement and alias feature. The data for training is prepared by taking all NPs between an anaphor and antecedent as negative NPs and the antecedent and anaphor as positive NP.

The core CRFs engine for Non-pronominal resolution system identifies the coreferring pairs of NPs. The Coreferring pairs obtained from pronominal resolution system and Non-pronominal system are merged to generate the complete coreference chains. The merging is done as follows: A member of a coreference pair is compared with all the members of the coreference pairs identified and if it occurs in anyone of the pair, then the two pairs are grouped. This process is done for all the members of the identified pairs and the members in each group are aligned based on their position in the document to form the chain.

3 Evaluation

In this section we present the evaluation of the complete system, which was developed under the closed task, along with the independent evaluation of the two sub-modules.

a) Non-anaphoric detection modules
b) Pronominal resolution module

The data used for training as well as testing was provided CoNLL-2001 shared task (Pradhan et al., 2011), (Pradhan et al., 2007) organizers. The results shown in this paper were obtained for the development data.

The non-anaphoric pronoun detection module is trained using the training data. This module was evaluated using the 91files development data. The training data contained 1326 non-anaphoric pronouns. The development data used for evaluation had 160 non-anaphoric pronouns. The table 2 shows the evaluation, of the non-anaphoric pronoun detection module.

The Pronominal resolution module was also evaluated on the development data. The filtering of non-anaphoric pronouns helped in the increase in precision of the pronoun resolution module. The table 3 shows the evaluation of pronoun resolution module on the development data. Here we show the results without the non-anaphor detection and with non-anaphor detection.

Type of pronoun	Actual (gold standard)	System identified Correctly	Accuracy (%)
Anaphoric Pronouns	939	908	96.6
Non-anaphoric pronouns	160	81	50.6
Total	1099	989	89.9

Table 2: Evaluation of Non-anaphoric pronoun

System type	Total Anaphoric Pronouns	System identified pronouns	System correctly Resolved Pronouns	Precision (%)
Without non-anaphoric pronoun detection	939	1099	693	63.1
With non-anaphoric pronoun detection	939	987	693	70.2

Table 3: Evaluation of Pronominal resolution module

The output of the Non-pronominal resolution module, merged with the output of the pronominal resolution module and it was evaluated using scorer program of the CoNLL-2011. The evaluation was done on the development data, shown in the table 4.

On analysis of the output we found mainly three types of errors. They are

a) Newly invented chains – The system identifies new chains that are not found in the gold standard annotation. This reduces the precision of the system. This is because of the string match as one of the features.

Metric	Mention Detection			Coreference Resolution		
	Rec	Prec	F1	Rec	Prec	F1
MUC	68.1	61.5	64.6	52.1	49.9	50.9
BCUBED	68.1	61.5	64.6	66.6	67.6	67.1
CEAFE	68.1	61.5	64.6	42.8	44.9	43.8
Avg	68.1	61.5	64.6	53.8	54.1	53.9

Table 4: Evaluation of the Complete System

b) Only head nouns in the chain – We observed that system while selecting pair for identifying coreference, the pair has only the head noun instead of the full phrase. In the phrase "the letters sent in recent days", the system identifies "the letters" instead of the whole phrase. This affects both the precision and recall of the system.

c) Incorrect merging of chains – The output chains obtained from the pronominal resolution system and the non-pronominal resolution system are merged to form a complete chain. When the antecedents in the pronominal chain are merged with the non-pronominal chains, certain chains are wrongly merged into single chain. For example "the chairman of the committee" is identified as coreferring with another similar phrase "the chairman of executive board" by the non-pronominal resolution task. Both of these are actually not referring to the same person. This happens because of string similarity feature of the non-pronominal resolution. This merging leads to building a wrong chain. Hence this affects the precision and recall of the system.

4 Conclusion

We have presented a coreference resolution system which combines the pronominal resolution using refined salience based approach with non-pronominal resolution using CRFs, machine learning approach. In the pronominal resolution, initially we identify the non-anaphoric pronouns using CRFs based technique. This helps in improving the precision. In non-pronominal resolution algorithm, the string match feature is an effective feature in identifying coreference. But, this feature is found to introduce errors. We need to add additional contextual and semantic feature to reduce above said errors. The results on the development set are encouraging.

References

Shane Bergsma, and Dekang Lin. 2006. Bootstrapping Path-Based Pronoun Resolution. In Proceedings of the Conference on Computational Linguistics / Association for Computational Linguistics (COLING/ACL-06), Sydney, Australia, July 17-21, 2006.

John Lafferty, Andrew McCallum, Fernando Pereira. 2001. Conditional Random Fields: Probabilistic Models for Segmenting and Labeling Sequence Data. In Proceedings of the Eighteenth International Conference on Machine Learning (ICML-2001). 282-289.

S. Lappin and H. Leass. 1994. An Algorithm for Pronominal Anaphora Resolution. Computational Linguistics, 20(4):535–562, 1994.

Sameer Pradhan, Lance Ramshaw, Mitchell Marcus, Martha Palmer, Ralph Weischedel, Nianwen Xue. 2011. CoNLL-2011 Shared Task: Modeling Unrestricted Coreference in OntoNotes. In Proceedings of the Fifteenth Conference on Computational Natural Language Learning (CoNLL 2011).

Sameer Pradhan and Lance Ramshaw and Ralph Weischedel and Jessica MacBride and Linnea Micciulla. 2007. Unrestricted Coreference: Identifying Entities and Events in OntoNotes. In Proceedings of the IEEE International Conference on Semantic Computing (ICSC)". Irvine, CA, September 17-19, 2007.

Sobha, L. 2008. Anaphora Resolution Using Named Entity and Ontology. In Proceedings of the Second Workshop on Anaphora Resolution (WAR II), Ed Christer Johansson, NEALT Proceedings Series, Vol. 2 (2008) Estonia. 91-96.

W. M. Soon, H. T. Ng, and D. C. Y. Lim. 2001. A Machine Learning Approach to Coreference Resolution of Noun Phrases. Computational Linguistics, 27(4):521–544.

Taku Kudo. 2005. CRF++, an open source toolkit for CRF, http://crfpp.sourceforge.net .

Poly-co: a multilayer perceptron approach for coreference detection

Eric Charton
École Polytechnique de Montréal
2500, chemin de Polytechnique
Montréal (Québec), H3T 1J4
eric.charton@polymtl.ca

Michel Gagnon
École Polytechnique de Montréal
2500, chemin de Polytechnique
Montréal (Québec), H3T 1J4
michel.gagnon@polymtl.ca

Abstract

This paper presents the coreference resolution system Poly-co submitted to the closed track of the CoNLL-2011 Shared Task. Our system integrates a multilayer perceptron classifier in a pipeline approach. We describe the heuristic used to select the pairs of coreference candidates that are feeded to the network for training, and our feature selection method. The features used in our approach are based on similarity and identity measures, filtering informations, like gender and number, and other syntactic information.

1 Introduction

Coreference resolution is the process of determining whether two expressions in natural language refer to the same entity in the world. It is an important subtask in natural language processing systems. In this paper, we present a learning approach to coreference resolution of named entities (NE), pronouns (PRP), noun phrases (NP) in unrestricted text according to the CoNLL-2011 shared task (Pradhan et al., 2011). This system have been used in the context of closed track.

2 Previous propositions

Many learning-based systems have been proposed to solve coreference resolution task, and Soon's (Soon et al., 2001) architecture is one of the most popular ones. In this proposition, all possible mentions in a training document are determined by a pipeline of natural language processing (NLP) modules. Then, training examples are generated as feature vectors. Each feature vector represents a pair of mentions that can potentially corefer. Those vectors are used as training examples given to build a C5 classifier. To determine the coreference chains in a new document, all potential pairs of coreferring mentions are presented to the classifier, which decides whether the two mentions actually corefer. Since then, this dominant architecture has been widely implemented. As it is a very flexible proposition, many families of classifiers have been used, trained with various configurations of feature vectors. Good results are obtained with SVM classifiers, like described in (Versley et al., 2008). Some propositions keep only the principle of feature vectors, associated with more complex coreference detection algorithms. A constraint-based graph partitioning system has been experimented by (Sapena et al., 2010) and a coreference detection system based on Markov logic networks (MLNs) has been proposed by (Poon and Domingos, 2008).

3 Architecture of the proposed system

A considerable engineering effort is needed to achieve the coreference resolution task. A significant part of this effort concerns feature engineering. We decided to keep the well established architecture of (Soon et al., 2001) with a pre-processing NLP pipeline used to prepare pairs of coreference features. The features are then submitted to the classifier for pairing validation. We tested various classifiers on our feature model (see table 2) and finally selected a multilayer perceptron (MLP) classifier to make decision. Since the Ontonotes layers provide syntactic information (Pradhan et al., 2007),

Proceedings of the 15th Conference on Computational Natural Language Learning: Shared Task, pages 97–101,
Portland, Oregon, 23-24 June 2011. ©2011 Association for Computational Linguistics

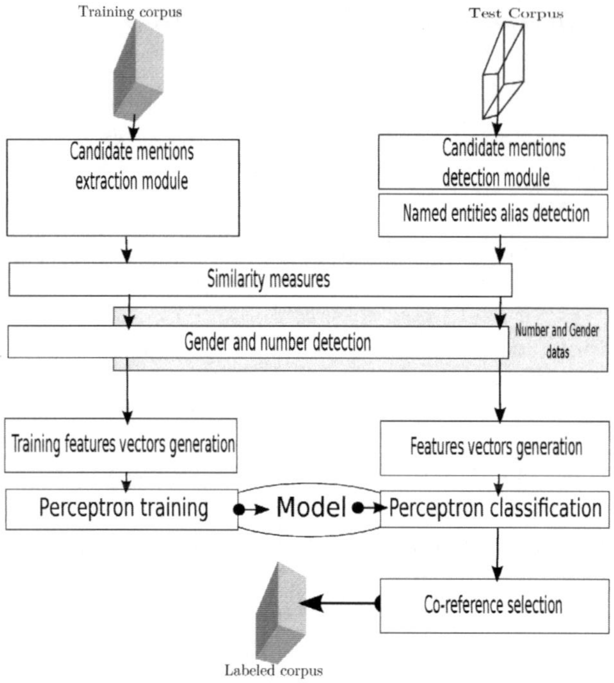

Figure 1: The pipeline architecture of the Poly-co system.

we could concentrate our efforts on the introduction of some complementary high level properties (like mention similarities or gender compatibility) used in the feature vectors given to the classifiers. The global architecture, presented in figure 1, includes two pipelines. One configured for training purposes and the other one for coreference resolution.

3.1 Architecture components

Ontonotes corpus includes part-of-speech tagging, noun phrases identification and named entity labels. We introduce complementary modules to detect gender and number, and evaluate mentions aliasing and similarity. The detection task is composed of 4 modules:

- **Candidate mentions detection module**, based on extraction rules, using Ontonotes layers.
- Named entities **alias detection module**, based on the previous version of Poly-co, described in (Charton et al., 2010). The purpose of this module is to identify variations in names of the same entity by examination of their surface form.
- **Similarity calculation module**, used to evaluate the similarity of two mentions according to a comparison of their string.
- **Gender and number detection module**, which determines gender and number for any candidate mention.

In the training pipeline, the **candidate mentions detection module** and the **alias detection module** are replaced by a unique **candidate mentions extraction module**. This module collects from the training corpus the labeled mentions and their reference numbers and use them to generate aliases and mentions values required to build training features.

As we will see later, similarity calculation and gender and number detection all result in a value that is integrated to the feature vector used to train and apply the classifier. We give below a more detailed description of each module.

3.1.1 Candidate mentions detection module

It is mandatory for coreference resolution to first get all the potential mentions from the input text. To determine the mentions, this module explores the text corpus and extracts a *candidate mentions list*. This list includes, for each mention, its position in the document, its word content and its syntactic category. This module uses simple detection rules to collect the mentions according to their part of speech (POS) and their text content, their syntactic boundaries and their named entity type labels.

When used in classification mode, the detection process is followed by a filtering process, where rules are used to remove mentions that have a very low probability of being involved in coreference. These rules are based on simple word sequence patterns. For example, pronoun *it* is filtered out when immediately followed by verb *to be* and relative pronoun *that* within the next 6 following words.

3.1.2 Alias detection module

This module implements an algorithm that clusters entities by comparing the form of their names. Entities are put in a list, ordered according to their chronological apparition in the text. At the beginning of the process, the first entity in the list is removed and constitutes the first item of a cluster. This entity is compared sequentially, by using similarity and logical rules (i.e, a PERSON can't be an alias of a LOC), with every other entities contained in the list. When there is a match, the entity is removed from the list and transferred to the currently instantiated cluster. This operation is repeated until the list is empty.

At the end of this process, an entity in a cluster is considered to be an alias of every other entity in the same cluster.

The TIME and DATE alias detection is done through a specific heuristic set. Each TIME entity representation is converted in a standardized format (Hour/Minutes). Dates are normalized as a relative amount of days (*"today"* is 1, *"last month"* is -30, etc) or a formal date (Year/Month/Day).

3.1.3 Similarity calculation module

The similarity module is applied on named entities (excepted TIME and DATE) and NP of the *candidate mentions list*. It consists in a text comparison function which returns the number of common words between two mentions. After execution of this module, we obtain a square matrix containing a similarity measure for every pair of mentions.

3.1.4 Gender and number detection module

Gender and number are associated with each entry of the *candidate mentions list*, including PRP and NP. First, this module tries to detect the gender using the gender data provided[1]. Then a set of less than 10 very simple rules is used to avoid anomaly (i.e a PERSON entity associated with the neutral gender). Another set of rules using plural markers of words and POS is used to validate the number.

4 Features definition and production

The feature vector of the Poly-co system (see table 1) consists of a 22 features set, described below. This vector is based on two extracted mentions, A and B, where B is the potential antecedent and A is the anaphor.

Four features are common to A and B (section *A and B properties* of table 1):

- **IsAlias** : this value is binary (yes or no) and provided by the **alias module**. The value is *yes* if A and B have been identified as describing the same entity.

[1]The list allowed by the Shared Task definition and available at http://www.clsp.jhu.edu/ sbergsma/Gender/

Feature Name	Value	value
A and B properties		
IsAlias	yes/no	1/0
IsSimilar	real	0.00 /1.00
Distance	int	0/const(b)
Sent	int	0/x
Reference A		
ISNE	yes/no	1/0
ISPRP	yes/no	1/0
ISNP	yes/no	1/0
NE_SEMANTIC TYPE	null / EN	0 / 1-18
PRP_NAME	null / PRP	0 / 1-30
NP_NAME	null / DT	0 / 1-15
NP_TYPE	null / TYPE	0 / 1-3
GENDER	M/F/N/U	1/2/3/0
NUMBER	S/P/U	1/2/0
Reference B		
Same as Reference A		

Table 1: Feature parameters

- **IsSimilar** : this value is the similarity measure provided by the **similarity module**.
- **Distance** : this indicates the offset distance (in terms of number of items in the *candidate mentions list*) between A and B.
- **Sent** : this indicates the amount of sentences marker (like . ! ?) separating the mentions A and B.

For each candidate A and B, a set containing nine features is added to the vector (in table 1, only properties for A are presented). First, 3 flags determine if mention is a named entity (IsNE), a personal pronoun (IsPRP) or a noun phrase (IsNP). The next six flags define the characteristics of the mention :

- NE_SEMANTIC TYPE is one of the 18 available NE types (PERSON, ORG, TIME, etc)
- PRP_NAME is a value representing 30 possible words (like *my, she, it, etc*) for a PRP.
- NP_NAME is a value indicating the DT used by a NP (like *the*, *this*, *these*, etc).
- NP_TYPE specifies if NP is demonstrative, definite, or a quantifier.
- GENDER and NUMBER flags indicate whether the mention gender (*Male, Female* or *Neutral*)

Poly-co Score	Mentions			B3			CEAF			MUC		
	R	P	F	R	P	F	R	P	F	R	P	F
Multilayer perceptron (MLP)	65.91	64.84	65.37	66.61	62.09	64.27	50.18	50.18	50.18	54.47	50.86	**52.60**
SVM	65.06	66.11	**65.58**	65.28	57.68	61.24	46.31	46.31	46.31	53.30	50.00	51.60
Tree J48	66.06	64.57	65.31	66.53	62.27	**64.33**	50.59	50.59	**50.59**	54.24	50.60	52.36

Table 2: System results obtained with scorer v4 on gold dev-set applying various classifiers on same features vectors.

Poly-co Score	Mentions			B3			CEAF			MUC		
Multilayer perceptron (MLP)	64.53	63.42	**63.97**	66.07	61.65	**63.79**	49.12	49.12	**49.12**	52.70	49.22	**50.90**

Table 3: System results obtained with scorer v4 on predicted dev-set using our system.

and number (***Singular*** or ***Plural***) are known or not (if not, ***U*** is the value for the flag).

A *null* value (0) is used when a flag doesn't have to be defined (i.e PRP flag if the mention is a NE).

5 Classifier training and use

For training, we use an algorithm that selects the more relevant pairs or mentions. Suppose that the *candidate mentions list* contains k mentions $M_1, M_2, \ldots, M_k$, in this order in the document. The algorithm starts with the last mention in the document, that is, M_k. It compares M_k sequentially with preceding mentions, going backward until a coreferring mention M_c is reached, or a maximum of n mentions have been visited (the value of n is fixed to 10 in our experiments). When a coreferring mention M_c has been found, a vector is constructed for every pair of mentions $\langle M_k, M_i \rangle$, where M_i is a mention that has been visited, including the coreferring one. These vectors are added to the training set, M_c being a positive instance, and all the others ones being negative instances. The process is repeated with M_{k-1}, and so on, until every mention has been processed. If none of the n precedent mentions are coreferent to M_1, all the n pairs are rejected and not used as training instance.

During the coreference detection process, a similar algorithm is used. Starting from mention M_k, we compare it with n preceding mentions, until we find one for which the multilayer perceptron classifier gives a coreference probability higher than 0.5[2]. If none is found within the limit of n mentions, M_k is considered as a non coreferring mention. When this has been done for every mention in the document, the detected coreferences are used to construct the coreference chains.

[2]Note that in comparison tests, displayed in table 2, SVM provides a binary decision and J48 a probability value. They are used as the multilayer perceptron ones.

6 Results

The results presented on table 2 are obtained on the dev-set of the Ontonotes corpus. To evaluate the potential of our features model, we trained our system with MLP, SVM and J48 Tree classifiers. We finally chose the MLP models for the test evaluation due to its better performance on the predicted dev-set. However, according to the small difference between MLP and J48 Tree, it's difficult to define clearly wich one is the best choice.

7 Conclusions

We presented Poly-co, a system for coreference resolution in English easy to adapt to other languages. The first version of Poly-co was built to detect only coreferences of persons. As the dataset provided for CoNLL is much more complex, it was an intersting opportunity to evaluate our mention detection algorithms in the perspective of a full task, including difficult coreferences mentions beetween named entities, noun phrases and prepositions. Our comparison of various classifier results on dev-sets have shown that our proposition to use a multilayer perceptron as coreference chain builder can be an intersting solution, but does not introduce an important difference of performance with previously experimented classifiers.

References

Eric Charton, Michel Gagnon, and Benoit Ozell. 2010. Poly-co : an unsupervised co-reference detection system. In *INLG 2010-GREC*, Dublin. ACL SIGGEN.

Hoifung Poon and Pedro Domingos. 2008. Joint unsupervised coreference resolution with Markov logic. In *Proceedings of the Conference on Empirical Methods in Natural Language Processing - EMNLP '08*, page 650, Morristown, NJ, USA. Association for Computational Linguistics.

Sameer Pradhan, Lance Ramshaw, Ralph Weischedel, Jessica MacBride, and Linnea Micciulla. 2007. Unrestricted coreference: Identifying entities and events in OntoNotes. In *International Conference on Semantic Computing, 2007. ICSC 2007.*, pages 446–453. IEEE.

Sameer Pradhan, Lance Ramshaw., Mitchell Marcus, Martha Palmer, Ralph Weischedel, and Xue Nianwen. 2011. CoNLL-2011 Shared Task: Modeling Unrestricted Coreference in OntoNotes. In *Proceedings of the Fifteenth Conference on Computational Natural Language Learning (CoNLL 2011)*, Portland, Oregon.

Emili Sapena, L. Padró, and Jordi Turmo. 2010. RelaxCor: A global relaxation labeling approach to coreference resolution. In *Proceedings of the 5th International Workshop on Semantic Evaluation*, number July, pages 88–91. Association for Computational Linguistics.

Wee Meng Soon, Hwee Tou Ng, and Daniel Chung Yong Lim. 2001. A Machine Learning Approach to Coreference Resolution of Noun Phrases. *Computational Linguistics*, 27(4):521–544, December.

Yannick Versley, S.P. Ponzetto, Massimo Poesio, Vladimir Eidelman, Alan Jern, Jason Smith, Xiaofeng Yang, and Alessandro Moschitti. 2008. BART: A modular toolkit for coreference resolution. In *Proceedings of the Sixth International Language Resources and Evaluation (LREC'08)*, number 2006, pages 9–12, Marrakech. European Language Resources Association (ELRA).

Mention Detection: Heuristics for the OntoNotes annotations

Jonathan K. Kummerfeld, Mohit Bansal, David Burkett and **Dan Klein**
Computer Science Division
University of California at Berkeley
{jkk,mbansal,dburkett,klein}@cs.berkeley.edu

Abstract

Our submission was a reduced version of the system described in Haghighi and Klein (2010), with extensions to improve mention detection to suit the OntoNotes annotation scheme. Including exact matching mention detection in this shared task added a new and challenging dimension to the problem, particularly for our system, which previously used a very permissive detection method. We improved this aspect of the system by adding filters based on the annotation scheme for OntoNotes and analysis of system behavior on the development set. These changes led to improvements in coreference F-score of 10.06, 5.71, 6.78, 6.63 and 3.09 on the MUC, B^3, Ceaf-e, Ceaf-m and Blanc, metrics, respectively, and a final task score of 47.10.

1 Introduction

Coreference resolution is concerned with identifying *mentions* of entities in text and determining which mentions are referring to the same entity. Previously the focus in the field has been on the latter task. Typically, mentions were considered correct if their span was within the true span of a gold mention, and contained the head word. This task (Pradhan et al., 2011) has set a harder challenge by only considering exact matches to be correct.

Our system uses an unsupervised approach based on a generative model. Unlike previous work, we did not use the Bllip or Wikipedia data described in Haghighi and Klein (2010). This was necessary for the system to be eligible for the closed task.

The system detects mentions by finding the maximal projection of every noun and pronoun. For the OntoNotes corpus this approach posed several problems. First, the annotation scheme explicitly rejects noun phrases in certain constructions. And second, it includes coreference for events as well as things. In preliminary experiments on the development set, we found that spurious mentions were our primary source of error. Using an oracle to exclude all spurious mentions at evaluation time yielded improvements ranging from five to thirty percent across the various metrics used in this task. Thus, we decided to focus our efforts on methods for detecting and filtering spurious mentions.

To improve mention detection, we filtered mentions both before and after coreference resolution. Filters prior to coreference resolution were constructed based on the annotation scheme and particular cases that should never be mentions (e.g. single word spans with the EX tag). Filters after coreference resolution were constructed based on analysis of common errors on the development set.

These changes led to considerable improvement in mention detection precision. The heuristics used in post-resolution filtering had a significant negative impact on recall, but this cost was out-weighed by the improvements in precision. Overall, the use of these filters led to a significant improvement in F_1 across all the coreference resolution evaluation metrics considered in the task.

2 Core System

We use a generative approach that is mainly unsupervised, as described in detail in Haghighi and

Proceedings of the 15th Conference on Computational Natural Language Learning: Shared Task, pages 102–106,
Portland, Oregon, 23-24 June 2011. ©2011 Association for Computational Linguistics

Klein (2010), and briefly below.

2.1 Model

The system uses all three of the standard abstractions in coreference resolution; mentions, entities and types. A mention is a span in the text, the entity is the actual object or event the mention refers to, and each type is a group of entities. For example, "the Mountain View based search giant" is a mention that refers to the entity Google, which is of type organization.

At each level we define a set of properties (e.g. proper-head). For mentions, these properties are linked directly to words from the span. For entities, each property corresponds to a list of words, instances of which are seen in specific mentions of that entity. At the type level, we assign a pair of multinomials to each property. The first of these multinomials is a distribution over words, reflecting their occurrence for this property for entities of this type. The second is a distribution over non-negative integers, representing the length of word lists for this property in entities of this type.

The only form of supervision used in the system is at the type level. The set of types is defined and lists of prototype words for each property of each type are provided. We also include a small number of extra types with no prototype words, for entities that do not fit well in any of the specified types.

These abstractions are used to form a generative model with three components; a semantic module, a discourse module and a mention module. In addition to the properties and corresponding parameters described above, the model is specified by a multinomial prior over types (ϕ), log-linear parameters over discourse choices (π), and a small number of hyperparameters (λ).

Entities are generated by the semantic module by drawing a type t according to ϕ, and then using that type's multinomials to populate word lists for each property.

The assignment of entities to mentions is handled by the discourse module. Affinities between mentions are defined by a log-linear model with parameters π for a range of standard features.

Finally, the mention module generates the actual words in the span. Words are drawn for each property from the lists for the relevant entity, with a hyper-parameter for interpolation between a uniform distribution over the words for the entity and the underlying distribution for the type. This allows the model to capture the fact that some properties use words that are very specific to the entity (e.g. proper names) while others are not at all specific (e.g. pronouns).

2.2 Learning and Inference

The learning procedure finds parameters that are likely under the model's posterior distribution. This is achieved with a variational approximation that factors over the parameters of the model. Each set of parameters is optimized in turn, while the rest are held fixed. The specific update methods vary for each set of parameters; for details see Section 4 of Haghighi and Klein (2010).

3 Mention detection extensions

The system described in Haghighi and Klein (2010) includes every NP span as a mention. When run on the OntoNotes data this leads to a large number of spurious mentions, even when ignoring singletons.

One challenge when working with the OntoNotes data is that singleton mentions are not annotated. This makes it difficult to untangle errors in coreference resolution and errors in mention detection. A mention produced by the system might not be in the gold set for one of two reasons; either because it is a spurious mention, or because it is not co-referent. Without manually annotating the singletons in the data, these two cases cannot be easily separated.

3.1 Baseline mention detection

The standard approach used in the system to detect mentions is to consider each word and its maximal projection, accepting it only if the span is an NP or the word is a pronoun. This approach will introduce spurious mentions if the parser makes a mistake, or if the NP is not considered a mention in the OntoNotes corpus. In this work, we considered the provided parses and parses produced by the Berkeley parser (Petrov et al., 2006) trained on the provided training data. We added a set of filters based on the annotation scheme described by Pradhan et al. (2007). Some filters are applied before coreference resolution and others afterward, as described below.

Data Set	Filters	P	R	F
Dev	None	37.59	76.93	50.50
	Pre	39.49	76.83	52.17
	Post	59.05	68.08	63.24
	All	58.69	67.98	63.00
Test	All	56.97	69.77	62.72

Table 1: Mention detection performance with various subsets of the filters.

3.2 Before Coreference Resolution

The pre-resolution filters were based on three reliable features of spurious mentions:

- Appositive constructions
- Attributes signaled by copular verbs
- Single word mentions with a POS tag in the set: EX, IN, WRB, WP

To detect appositive constructions we searched for the following pattern:

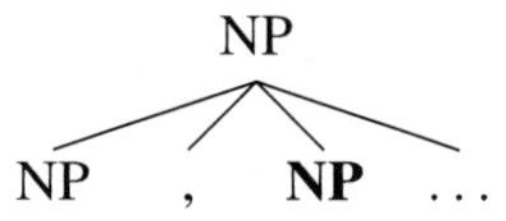

And to detect attributes signaled by copular structures we searched for this pattern:

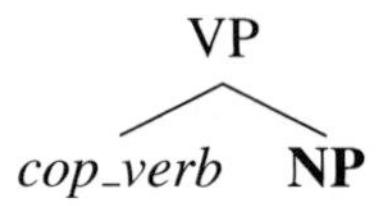

where we used the fairly conservative set of copular verbs: {is, are, was, 'm}. In both cases, any mention whose maximal NP projection appeared as the bold node in a subtree matching the pattern was excluded.

In all three cases, errors from the parser (or POS tagger) may lead to the deletion of valid mentions. However, we found the impact of this was small and was outweighed by the number of spurious mentions removed.

3.3 After Coreference Resolution

To construct the post-coreference filters we analyzed system output on the development set, and tuned

Filters	MUC	B^3	Ceaf-e	Blanc
None	25.24	45.89	50.32	59.12
Pre	27.06	47.71	50.15	60.17
Post	42.08	62.53	43.88	66.54
All	42.03	62.42	43.56	66.60

Table 2: Precision for coreference resolution on the dev set.

Filters	MUC	B^3	Ceaf-e	Blanc
None	50.54	78.54	26.17	62.77
Pre	51.20	77.73	27.23	62.97
Post	45.93	64.72	39.84	61.20
All	46.21	64.96	39.24	61.28

Table 3: Recall for coreference resolution on the dev set.

based on MUC and B^3 performance. The final set of filters used were:

- Filter if the head word is in a gazetteer, which we constructed based on behavior on the development set (head words found using the Collins (1999) rules)
- Filter if the POS tag is one of WDT, NNS, RB, JJ, ADJP
- Filter if the mention is a specific case of `you` or `it` that is more often generic (`you know`, `you can`, `it is`)
- Filter if the mention is any cardinal other than a year

A few other more specific filters were also included (e.g. `'s` when tagged as PRP) and one type of exception (if all words are capitalized, the mention is kept).

4 Other modifications

The parses in the OntoNotes data include the addition of structure within noun phrases. Our system was not designed to handle the NML tag, so we removed such nodes, reverting to the standard flattened NP structures found in the Penn Treebank.

We also trained the Berkeley parser on the provided training data, and used it to label the development and test sets.[1] We found that performance was

[1] In a small number of cases, the Berkeley parser failed, and we used the provided parse tree instead.

Filters	MUC	B^3	Ceaf-e	Ceaf-m	Blanc
None	33.67	57.93	34.43	42.72	60.60
Pre	35.40	59.13	35.29	43.72	61.38
Post	43.92	63.61	41.76	49.74	63.26
All	44.02	63.66	41.29	49.46	63.34

Table 4: F_1 scores for coreference resolution on the dev set.

Metric	R	P	F_1
MUC	46.39	39.56	42.70
B^3	63.60	57.30	60.29
Ceaf-m	45.35	45.35	45.35
Ceaf-e	35.05	42.26	38.32
Blanc	58.74	61.58	59.91

Table 5: Complete results on the test set

slightly improved by the use of these parses instead of the provided parses.

5 Results

Since our focus when extending our system for this task was on mention detection, we present results with variations in the sets of mention filters used. In particular, we have included results for our baseline system (None), when only the filters before coreference resolution are used (Pre), when only the filters after coreference resolution are used (Post), and when all filters are used (All).

The main approach behind the pre-coreference filters was to consider the parse to catch cases that are almost never mentions. In particular, these filters target cases that are explicitly excluded by the annotation scheme. As Table 1 shows, this led to a 1.90% increase in mention detection precision and 0.13% decrease in recall, which is probably a result of parse errors.

For the post-coreference filters, the approach was quite different. Each filter was introduced based on analysis of the errors in the mention sets produced by our system on the development set. Most of the filters constructed in this way catch some true mentions as well as spurious mentions, leading to significant improvements in precision at the cost of recall. Specifically an increase of 21.46% in precision and decrease of 8.85% in recall, but an overall increase of 12.74% in F_1-score.

As Tables 2 and 3 show, these changes in mention detection performance generally lead to improvements in precision at the expense of recall, with the exception of Ceaf-e where the trends are reversed. However, as shown in Table 4, there is an overall improvement in F_1 in all cases.

In general the change from only post-coreference filters to all filters is slightly negative. The final system used all of the filters because the process used to create the post-coreference filters was more susceptible to over-fitting, and the pre-coreference filters provided such an unambiguously positive contribution to mention detection.

6 Conclusion

We modified the coreference system of Haghighi and Klein (2010) to improve mention detection performance. We focused on tuning using the MUC and B^3 metrics, but found considerable improvements across all metrics.

One important difference between the system described here and previous work was the data available. Unlike Haghighi and Klein (2010), no extra data from Wikipedia or Bllip was used, a restriction that was necessary to be eligible for the closed part of the task.

By implementing heuristics based on the annotation scheme for the OntoNotes data set and our own analysis of system behavior on the development set we were able to achieve the results shown in Table 5, giving a final task score of 47.10.

7 Acknowledgments

We would like to thank the anonymous reviewers for their helpful suggestions. This research is supported by the Office of Naval Research under MURI Grant No. N000140911081, and a General Sir John Monash Fellowship.

References

Michael John Collins. 1999. *Head-driven statistical models for natural language parsing*. Ph.D. thesis, Philadelphia, PA, USA. AAI9926110.

Aria Haghighi and Dan Klein. 2010. Coreference resolution in a modular, entity-centered model. In *Proceed-*

ings of NAACL, pages 385–393, Los Angeles, California, June. Association for Computational Linguistics.

Slav Petrov, Leon Barrett, Romain Thibaux, and Dan Klein. 2006. Learning accurate, compact, and interpretable tree annotation. In *Proceedings of COLING-ACL*, pages 433–440, Sydney, Australia, July. Association for Computational Linguistics.

Sameer S. Pradhan, Lance Ramshaw, Ralph Weischedel, Jessica MacBride, and Linnea Micciulla. 2007. Unrestricted coreference: Identifying entities and events in ontonotes. In *Proceedings of the International Conference on Semantic Computing*, pages 446–453, Washington, DC, USA. IEEE Computer Society.

Sameer Pradhan, Lance Ramshaw, Mitchell Marcus, Martha Palmer, Ralph Weischedel, and Nianwen Xue. 2011. Conll-2011 shared task: Modeling unrestricted coreference in ontonotes. In *Proceedings of the Fifteenth Conference on Computational Natural Language Learning (CoNLL 2011)*, Portland, Oregon, June.

Coreference Resolution with Loose Transitivity Constraints

Xinxin Li, Xuan Wang, Shuhan Qi
Shenzhen Graduate School
Harbin Institute of Technology, ShenZhen, China
lixxin2@gmail.com, wangxuan@insun.hit.edu.cn
shuhan_qi@qq.com

Abstract

Our system treats coreference resolution as an integer linear programming (ILP) problem. Extending Denis and Baldridge (2007) and Finkel and Manning (2008)'s work, we exploit loose transitivity constraints on coreference pairs. Instead of enforcing transitivity closure constraints, which brings $O(n^3)$ complexity, we employ a strategy to reduce the number of constraints without large performance decrease, i.e., eliminating coreference pairs with probability below a threshold θ. Experimental results show that it achieves a better performance than pairwise classifiers.

1 Introduction

This paper describes our coreference resolution system participating in the close track of CoNLL 2011 shared task (Pradhan et al., 2011). The task aims to identify all mentions of entities and events and cluster them into equivalence classes in OntoNotes Corpus (Pradhan et al., 2007a). During the last decade, several machine learning methods for coreference resolution have been developed, from local pairwise classifiers (Soon et al., 2001) to global learning methods (Luo et al., 2004; Ng, 2005; Denis and Baldridge, 2007), from simple morphological, grammatical features to more liguistically rich features on syntactic structures and semantic relations (Pradhan et al., 2007b; Haghighi and Klein, 2009).

Our system supports both local classifiers and global learning. Maximum entropy model is used for anaphoricity and coreference, because it assigns probability mass to mentions and coreference pairs directly. In global phase, instead of determining each coreference pair independently in a greedy fashion, we employ an integer linear programming (ILP) formulation for this problem. Extending (Denis and Baldridge, 2007) and (Finkel and Manning, 2008)'s work, we introduce a loose selection strategy for transitivity constraints, attempting to overcome huge computation complexity brought by transitivity closure constraints. Details are described in section 2.3.

2 System Description

2.1 Mention Detection

Mention detection is a method that identifies the anaphoricity and non-anaphoricity mentions before coreference resolution. The non-anaphoric mentions usually influence the performance of coreference resolution as noises. Coreference resolution can benefit from accurate mention detection since it might eliminate the non-anaphoric mentions. We take mention detection as the first step, and then combine coreference classifier into one system.

Total 70 candidate features are used for mention detection, including lexical, syntactic, semantic features (Ng and Cardie, 2002). Features are selected according to the information gain ratio (Han and Kamber, 2006)

$$GainRation(A) = \frac{Gain(A)}{SplitInfo(A)}$$

The top 10 features with highest gain ratio are: string match, head word match, all uppercase, pronoun, starting with article, number, following preposition, nesting in verb phrase, nesting in preposition,

Proceedings of the 15th Conference on Computational Natural Language Learning: Shared Task, pages 107–111,
Portland, Oregon, 23-24 June 2011. ©2011 Association for Computational Linguistics

and starting with definite article. Many string features that cannot be calculated by gain ratio method are also added.

2.2 Coreference Determination

For coreference determination, we first build several baseline systems with different training instance generation methods and clustering algorithms. These strategies are shown below. Detailed description can be found in Ng (2005).

- training instance generation methods: McCarthy and Lehnerts method, Soon et al.'s method, Ng and Cardie's method.
- clustering algorithms: closest-first clustering, best-first clustering, and aggressive merge clustering.

Overall 65 features are considered in our system. Features are extracted from various linguistic information, including:

- distance: sentence distance, minimum edit distance (Strube et al., 2002)
- lexical: string match, partial match, head word match (Daumé III and Marcu, 2005)
- grammar: gender agreement, number agreement(Soon et al., 2001)
- syntactic: same head, path (Yang et al., 2006)
- semantic: semantic class agreement, predicate (Ponzetto and Strube, 2006; Ng, 2007)

Combining different training instance generation methods and clustering algorithms, we get total 9 baseline systems. For each system, we use a greedy forward approach to select features. Starting from a base feature set (Soon et al., 2001), each feature out of the base set is added one by one according to the performance change on development data. Finally, the procedure is ended until the performance is not improved. The baseline system with best performance is selected for further improvement.

2.3 ILP with Loose Transitivity Constraints

Previous systems usually take coreference resolution as binary classification problem, and build the coreference chain by determining each coreference pair indepedently. The binary classifier is easily implemented, but may cause inconsistency between coreference pairs. Several work have been developed to overcome the problem, e.g., Bell trees (Luo et al., 2004), conditional random fields (McCallum and Wellner, 2004) and reranker (Ng, 2005).

Denis and Baldridge (2007) proposed an ILP formulation to find the optimal solution for the problem. It utilizes the output of other local classifiers and performs global learning. The objective function for their conference-only model takes the form:

$$min \sum_{\langle i,j \rangle \in M^2} c_{\langle i,j \rangle} * x_{\langle i,j \rangle} + \bar{c}_{\langle i,j \rangle} * (1 - x_{\langle i,j \rangle})$$

where $c_{\langle i,j \rangle} = -\log(P_C)$, $\bar{c}_{\langle i,j \rangle} = -\log(1 - P_C)$. M is the candidate mention set for each document. P_C refers to the probability of coreference link between two mentions produced by our maximum entropy model, and $x_{\langle i,j \rangle}$ is a binary variable that is set to 1 if two mentions are coreferent, 0 otherwise.

However, as Finkel and Manning showed, D&B's coreference-only model without transitivity constraints is not really necessary, because they only select the coreference links with probability $P_C > 0.5$. Klenner (2007) and Finkel and Manning (2008)'s work extended the ILP framework to support transitivity constraints. The transitivity constraints are formulated as

$$\forall i,j,k \in M (i < j < k)$$
$$x_{\langle i,j \rangle} \geq x_{\langle j,k \rangle} + x_{\langle i,k \rangle} - 1$$
$$x_{\langle j,k \rangle} \geq x_{\langle i,j \rangle} + x_{\langle i,k \rangle} - 1$$
$$x_{\langle i,k \rangle} \geq x_{\langle i,j \rangle} + x_{\langle j,k \rangle} - 1$$

These constraints ensure that when any two corefrent links (e.g., $x_{\langle i,j \rangle}$, $x_{\langle i,k \rangle}$) among three mentions exist, the third one $x_{\langle j,k \rangle}$ must also be a link. However, these constraints also bring huge time and space complexity with n^3 constraints (n is number of candidate mention set M, which is larger than 700 in some documents), and cannot be solved in a restricted time and memory environment. We introduce a loose method to eliminate conference links

Ratio	Recall	Precision	F-value
0.4	**84.03**	43.75	57.54
0.6	70.6	70.85	**70.72**
0.8	64.24	74.35	68.93
1.0	58.63	**76.13**	66.25

Table 1: Results of mention dection

below a probability threshold θ. The constraints are transformed as

$$x_{\langle i,k \rangle} + x_{\langle j,k \rangle} \leq 1 \quad (1)$$

$$x_{\langle i,j \rangle} = 0 \quad (2)$$

when $P_C(i,j) < \theta$. The threshold θ is tuned on development data for faster computation without large performance decrease.

3 Experiments and Analysis

In the paper we mainly take noun phrases (NPs) and pronouns as candidate mentions, and ignore other phrases since more than 91% of the mentions are NPs and pronouns.

3.1 Mention Detection

We observe that the ratio of positive examples and negative examples is about 1:3 in training data. To balance the bias, we propose a ratio control method which sets a ratio to limit the number of negative examples. Our system will select all positive examples, and part of negative examples according to the ratio. By tuning the ratio, we can control the proportion of positive and negative examples. With different ratios for negative feature selection, the results on development data are shown in table 1.

From table 1, we can see that as the ratio increases, recall becomes smaller and precision becomes larger. Small threshold means less negative examples are generated in training procedure, and the classifier tends to determine a mention as positive. Finally, we choose the ratio 0.6 for our model because it gets the best F-value on the development data.

3.2 Coreference Resolution

Our system participates in the close track with auto mention and gold boundary annotation. The

TIGM	Soon	Soon	Soon	Ng
CA	A	B	C	B
MUC	44.29	**46.18**	**46.18**	45.33
B^3	59.76	**61.39**	60.03	60.93
CEAF(M)	42.77	**44.43**	43.01	44.41
CEAF(E)	35.77	36.37	36.08	**36.54**
BLANC	60.22	63.94	59.9	**63.96**
Official	46.6	**47.98**	46.76	47.6

Table 2: Results of baseline systems

the performance is evaluated on MUC, B-CUBED, CEAF(M), CEAF(E), BLANC metrics. The official metric is calculated as $^{(MUC+B^3+CEAF)}/_3$.

Table 2 summarizes the performance of top 4 of 9 baseline systems with different training instance generation methods and clustering algorithms on development data. In the table, TIGM means training instance generation method, and CA denotes clustering algorithm, which includes C as closest-first, B as best-first, and A as aggressive-merge clustering algorithm. The results in Table 2 show that the system with Soon's training instance generation method and best-first clustering algorithm achieves the best performance. We take it as baseline for further improvement.

In ILP model, we perform experiments on documents with less than 150 candidate mentions to find the suitable probability threshold θ for loose transitivity constraints. There are totol 181 documents meeting the condition in development data. We take two strategies to loose transitivity constraints: (I) formula 1 and 2, and (II) formula 2 only. Glpk package is used to solve our ILP optimization problems.[1]

Table 3 shows that as threshold θ increases, the running time reduces dramatically with a small performance decrease from 49.06 to 48.88. Strategy I has no benefit for the performance. Finally strategy II and $\theta = 0.06$ are used in our system.

We also combine mentions identified in first phase into coreference resolution. Two strategies are used: feature model and cascaded model. For feature model, we add two features which indicate whether the two candidate mentions of a coreference pair are mentions identified in first phase or not. For cascaded model, we take mentions identified in first phase as inputs for coreference resolution. For ILP

[1] http://www.gnu.org/software/glpk/

θ	0	0.02	0.02	0.04	0.04	0.06	0.06	0.08	0.08	0.1	0.1
Strategy		I	II	I	II	I	II	I	II	I	II
MUC	40.95	40.64	40.92	40.64	40.83	40.64	40.8	40.64	40.75	40.64	40.68
B^3	65.6	65.47	65.59	65.47	65.58	65.47	65.57	65.47	65.5	65.47	65.49
CEAF(M)	48.62	48.39	48.59	48.39	48.56	48.39	48.54	48.39	48.42	48.39	48.39
CEAF(E)	40.62	40.47	40.62	40.47	40.63	40.47	40.61	40.47	40.5	40.47	40.47
BLANC	61.87	61.76	61.85	61.76	61.84	61.76	61.83	61.76	61.79	61.76	61.78
Official	49.06	48.88	49.04	48.88	49.01	48.88	48.99	48.88	48.92	48.88	48.88
Time(s)	1726	1047	913	571	451	361	264	253	166	153	109

Table 3: Results on different probability thresholds and strategies

Model	Feature	Cascade	ILP
MUC	41.08	47.41	45.89
B^3	59.74	57.67	61.85
CEAF(M)	41.9	42.04	44.52
CEAF(E)	34.72	32.33	36.85
BLANC	61.1	62.99	63.92
Official	45.18	45.81	**48.19**

Table 4: Results of coreference resolution systems.

Data	Dev	Dev	Test	Test
Mention	Auto	Gold	Auto	Gold
MUC	45.89	46.75	46.62	44.00
B^3	61.85	61.48	61.93	57.42
CEAF(M)	44.52	45.17	44.75	42.36
CEAF(E)	36.85	37.19	36.83	34.22
BLANC	63.92	63.83	64.27	62.96
Official	48.19	**48.47**	**48.46**	45.21

Table 5: Results for development and test data

model, we perform experiments on coreference-only system with our loose transitivity constraints. The results on development data are shown in Table 4.

In Core Quad 2.40G CPU and 2G memory machine, our ILP model can optimize one document per minute on average. From table 4, we can see that the ILP model achieves the best F-value, implying the benefit of our algorithm. It also shows that traditional coreference resolution methods combining mention detection decrease the performance. For restricted time deadline, other constraints strategies (Klenner, 2007) and joint anaphoricity-coreference ILP model are not used in our system. It would be in our future work.

3.3 Test

Table 5 shows the performance of our system for both development and test data, with auto mention and gold boundary annotation.

The results in table 5 show that in auto mention annotation, the performance on test data is a little bit better than development data. The reason might be that the system on test data uses more data to train, including development data. A phenomenon surprises us is that the performance on test data with gold annotation is less than on development data, even than auto annotation. It turns out that the mistake is made because we confuse the the definition of gold bourdaries as gold mentions, which are "all" and "only" mentions in coreference chains.

4 Conclusion

In this paper, we present a coreference resolution system which employs an ILP formulation for global optimization. To reduce computation complexity, our system employs loose transitivity constraints to the ILP model. Experimental results show that it achieves a better performance than pairwise classifiers.

References

Hal Daumé III and Daniel Marcu. 2005. A large-scale exploration of effective global features for a joint entity detection and tracking model. In *Proceedings of Human Language Technology Conference and Conference on Empirical Methods in Natural Language Processing*, pages 97–104, Vancouver, British Columbia, Canada, October. Association for Computational Linguistics.

Pascal Denis and Jason Baldridge. 2007. Joint determination of anaphoricity and coreference resolution using integer programming. In *Human Language Technologies 2007: The Conference of the North American Chapter of the Association for Computational Linguistics; Proceedings of the Main Conference*, pages 236–243, Rochester, New York, April. Association for Computational Linguistics.

Jenny Rose Finkel and Christopher D. Manning. 2008. Enforcing transitivity in coreference resolution. In *Proceedings of ACL-08: HLT, Short Papers*, pages 45–48, Columbus, Ohio, June. Association for Computational Linguistics.

Aria Haghighi and Dan Klein. 2009. Simple coreference resolution with rich syntactic and semantic features. In *Proceedings of the 2009 Conference on Empirical Methods in Natural Language Processing*, pages 1152–1161, Singapore, August. Association for Computational Linguistics.

J. Han and M. Kamber. 2006. *Data mining: concepts and techniques*. Morgan Kaufmann.

Manfred Klenner. 2007. Enforcing consistency on coreference sets. In *Recent Advances in Natural Language Processing (RANLP)*, pages 323–328.

Xiaoqiang Luo, Abe Ittycheriah, Hongyan Jing, Nanda Kambhatla, and Salim Roukos. 2004. A mention-synchronous coreference resolution algorithm based on the bell tree. In *Proceedings of the 42nd Meeting of the Association for Computational Linguistics (ACL'04), Main Volume*, pages 135–142, Barcelona, Spain, July.

Andrew McCallum and Ben Wellner. 2004. Conditional models of identity uncertainty with application to noun coreference. In *NIPS 2004*.

Vincent Ng and Claire Cardie. 2002. Identifying anaphoric and non-anaphoric noun phrases to improve coreference resolution. In *Proceedings of the 19th international conference on Computational linguistics - Volume 1*, COLING '02, pages 1–7, Stroudsburg, PA, USA. Association for Computational Linguistics.

Vincent Ng. 2005. Machine learning for coreference resolution: From local classification to global ranking. In *Proceedings of the 43rd Annual Meeting of the Association for Computational Linguistics (ACL'05)*, pages 157–164, Ann Arbor, Michigan, June. Association for Computational Linguistics.

Vincent Ng. 2007. Shallow semantics for coreference resolution. In *Proceedings of IJCAI*, pages 1689–1694.

Simone Paolo Ponzetto and Michael Strube. 2006. Exploiting semantic role labeling, wordnet and wikipedia for coreference resolution. In *Proceedings of the Human Language Technology Conference of the NAACL, Main Conference*, pages 192–199, New York City, USA, June. Association for Computational Linguistics.

Sameer Pradhan, Eduard Hovy, Mitch Marcus, Martha Palmer, Lance Ramshaw, and Ralph Weischedel. 2007a. Ontonotes: A unified relational semantic representation. *International Journal of Semantic Computing (IJSC)*, 1(4):405–419.

Sameer Pradhan, Lance Ramshaw, Ralph Weischedel, Jessica MacBride, and Linnea Micciulla. 2007b. Unrestricted coreference: Identifying entities and events in ontonotes. In *in Proceedings of the IEEE International Conference on Semantic Computing (ICSC)*, September 17-19.

Sameer Pradhan, Lance Ramshaw, Mitchell Marcus, Martha Palmer, Ralph Weischedel, and Nianwen Xue. 2011. Conll-2011 shared task: Modeling unrestricted coreference in ontonotes. In *Proceedings of the Fifteenth Conference on Computational Natural Language Learning (CoNLL 2011)*, Portland, Oregon, June.

Wee Meng Soon, Hwee Tou Ng, and Daniel Chung Yong Lim. 2001. A machine learning approach to coreference resolution of noun phrases. *Comput. Linguist.*, 27:521–544, December.

Michael Strube, Stefan Rapp, and Christoph Müller. 2002. The influence of minimum edit distance on reference resolution. In *Proceedings of the ACL-02 conference on Empirical methods in natural language processing - Volume 10*, EMNLP '02, pages 312–319, Stroudsburg, PA, USA. Association for Computational Linguistics.

Xiaofeng Yang, Jian Su, and Chew Lim Tan. 2006. Kernel-based pronoun resolution with structured syntactic knowledge. In *Proceedings of the 21st International Conference on Computational Linguistics and 44th Annual Meeting of the Association for Computational Linguistics*, pages 41–48, Sydney, Australia, July. Association for Computational Linguistics.

UBIU: A Robust System for Resolving Unrestricted Coreference

Desislava Zhekova
University of Bremen
zhekova@uni-bremen.de

Sandra Kübler
Indiana University
skuebler@indiana.edu

Abstract

In this paper, we discuss the application of UBIU to the CoNLL-2011 shared task on "Modeling Unrestricted Coreference" in OntoNotes. The shared task concentrates on the detection of coreference not only in noun phrases but also involving verbs. The information provided for the closed track included WordNet as well as corpus generated number and gender information. Our system shows no improvement when using WordNet information, and the number information proved less reliable than the information in the part of speech tags.

1 Introduction

Coreference Resolution is the process of identifying the linguistic expressions in a discourse that refer to the same real world entity and to divide those expressions into equivalence classes that represent each discourse entity. For this task, a deeper knowledge of the discourse is often required. However, such knowledge is difficult to acquire. For this reason, many systems use superficial information such as string match. The CoNLL shared task on "Modeling Unrestricted Coreference in OntoNotes" (Pradhan et al., 2011) presents challenges that go beyond previous definitions of the task. On the one hand, mention extraction is part of the task while many previous approaches assumed gold standard mentions. On the other hand, coreference is not restricted to noun phrases, verbs are also included. Thus, in *Sales of passenger cars grew 22%. The strong growth followed year-to-year increases.*, the verb *grew* has an identity relation with the noun phrase *The strong growth.*

The system that we used for the shared task is the memory-based machine learning system UBIU (Zhekova and Kübler, 2010). We describe the most important components of the system in section 2. The system was originally developed for robust, multilingual coreference resolution, and thus had to be adapted to this shared task. We investigate the quality of our mention extraction in section 2.1 and the quality of the features used in the classifier in section 2.2. In section 3, we present UBIU's results on the development set, and in section 4, UBIU's final results in the shared task.

2 UBIU

UBIU (Zhekova and Kübler, 2010) was developed as a multilingual coreference resolution system. A robust approach is necessary to make the system applicable for a variety of languages. For this reason, we use a machine learning approach to classify mention pairs. We use TiMBL (Daelemans et al., 2007), a memory-based learner (MBL) that labels the feature vectors from the test set based on the k nearest neighbors in the training instances. We chose TiMBL since MBL has been shown to work well with small training sets. A non-exhaustive parameter optimization on the development set led us to use the *IB1* algorithm, similarity is computed based on weighted overlap, the relevance weights are computed using gain ratio and the number of nearest neighbors is set to $k = 3$ (for a description of the algorithm and parameters cf. (Daelemans et al., 2007)). The classifier is preceded by a mention extractor, which identifies possible mentions, and a feature extractor. The latter creates a feature vector for each possible pair of a potentially coreferring

Proceedings of the 15th Conference on Computational Natural Language Learning: Shared Task, pages 112–116,
Portland, Oregon, 23-24 June 2011.

mention and all possible antecedents in a context of 3 sentences. Another important step is to separate singleton mentions from coreferent ones since only the latter are annotated in OntoNotes. Our markable extractor overgenerates in that it extracts all possible mentions, and only after classification, the system can decide which mentions are singletons. We investigate the performance of the mention and feature extraction modules in more detail below.

2.1 Mention Extraction

UBIU's mention extractor uses part-of-speech (POS), syntactic, and lemma information provided in the OntoNotes data set to detect mentions. The module defines a mention for each noun phrase, based on syntactic information, as well as for all possessive pronouns and all proper nouns, based on their POS tags. Since for the shared task, verbs are also potentially coreferent, we included a mention for each of the verbs with a predicate lemma. An example of the output of the mention extraction module is shown in table 1. Each mention is numbered with an individual number and thus still represents a distinct entity. Since singleton mentions are not annotated in the OntoNotes data set, mentions without coreference relations after classification need to be removed from the answer set, which can only be performed after coreference resolution when all coreferent pairs are identified. For this reason, the markable extractor is bound to overgenerate. The latter can clearly be seen when the mention extraction output is compared to the provided gold mentions (cf. the last column in table 1).

We conducted a simple experiment on the development data in order to gain insight into the performance of the mention extraction module. Using the scorer provided by the shared task, we evaluated the output of the module, without performing coreference resolution and without removing singleton mentions. This led to a recall of 96.55 % and a precision of 18.55%, resulting in an F-score of 31.12. The high recall shows that the system is very reliable in finding mentions with the correct boundaries. However, since we do not remove any singletons, UBIU overgenerates and thus the system identified a considerable number of singletons, too. Nevertheless, the fact that UBIU identified 96.55% of all mentions shows that the performance of the mention extraction module is close to optimal.

#	Word	POS	Parse bit	ME output	Gold
0	Devastating	VBG	(TOP(NP(NP*	(1)|(2|(3	-
1	Critique	NN	*)	3)	-
2	of	IN	(PP*	-	-
3	the	DT	(NP*	(4	(32
4	Arab	JJ	*	-	-
5	World	NN	*))	4)	32)
6	by	IN	(PP*	-	-
7	One	CD	(NP(NP*)	(5|(6)	-
8	of	IN	(PP*	-	-
9	Its	PRP$	(NP*	(7)|(8	(32)
10	Own	JJ	*))))))	8)|5)|2)	-

Table 1: The output of the mention extractor for a sample sentence.

2.2 Feature Extraction

Feature extraction is the second important subtask for the UBIU pipeline. Since mentions are represented by their syntactic head, the feature extractor uses a heuristic that selects the rightmost noun in a noun phrase. However, since postmodifying prepositional phrases may be present in the mention, the noun may not be followed by a preposition. For each mention, a feature vector is created for all of its preceding mentions in a window of 3 sentences. After classification, a filter can optionally be applied to filter out mention pairs that disagree in number, and another filter deletes all mentions that were not assigned an antecedent in classification. Note that the number information was derived from the POS tags and not from the number/gender data provided by the shared task since the POS information proved more reliable in our system.

Initially, UBIU was developed to use a wide set of features (Zhekova and Kübler, 2010), which constitutes a subset of the features described by Rahman and Ng (2009). For the CoNLL-2011 shared task, we investigated the importance of various additional features that can be included in the feature set used by the memory-based classifier. Thus, we conducted experiments with a base set and an extended feature set, which makes use of lexical semantic features.

Base Feature Set Since the original feature set in Zhekova and Kübler (2010) contained information that is not easily accessible in the OntoNotes data set (such as grammatical functions), we had to restrict the feature set to information that can be derived solely from POS annotations. Further infor-

#	Feature Description
1	m_j - the antecedent
2	m_k - the mention to be resolved
3	Y if m_j is a pronoun; else N
4	number - S(ingular) or P(lural)
5	Y if m_k is a pronoun; else N
6	C if the mentions are the same string; else I
7	C if one mention is a substring of the other; else I
8	C if both mentions are pronominal and are the same string; else I
9	C if the two mentions are both non-pronominal and are the same string; else I
10	C if both mentions are pronominal and are either the same pronoun or different only w.r.t. case; NA if at least one of them is not pronominal; else I
11	C if the mentions agree in number; I if they disagree; NA if the number for one or both mentions cannot be determined
12	C if both mentions are pronouns; I if neither are pronouns; else NA
13	C if both mentions are proper nouns; I if neither are proper nouns; else NA
14	sentence distance between the mentions

Table 2: The pool of features used in the base feature set.

mation as sentence distance, word overlap etc. was included as well. The list of used features is shown in table 2.

Extended Feature Set Since WordNet information was provided for the closed setting of the CoNLL-2011 shared task, we also used an extended feature set, including all features from the base set along with additional features derived from WordNet. The latter features are shown in table 3.

2.3 Singletons

In section 2.1, we explained that singletons need to be removed after classification. However, this leads to a drastic decrease in system performance for two reasons. First, if a system does not identify a coreference link, the singleton mentions will be removed from the coreference chains, and consequently, the system is penalized for the missing link as well as for the missing mentions. If singletons are included, the system will still receive partial credit for them from all metrics but MUC. For this reason, we investigated filtered and non-filtered results in combination with the base and the extended feature sets.

3 Results on the Development Set

The results of our experiment on the development set are shown in table 4. Since the official scores of the shared task are based on an average of MUC, B^3, and CEAFE, we report these measures and their average. All the results in this section are based on automatically annotated linguistic information. The first part of the table shows the results for the base feature set (UBIU$_B$), the second part for the extended feature set (UBIU$_E$). We also report results if we keep all singletons (& Sing.) and if we filter out coreferent pairs that do not agree in number (& Filt.). The results show that keeping the singletons results in lower accuracies on the mention and the coreference level. Only recall on the mention level profits from the presence of singletons. Filtering for number agreement with the base set has a detrimental effect on mention recall but increases mention precision so that there is an increase in F-score of 1%. However, on the coreference level, the effect is negligible. For the extended feature set, filtering results in a decrease of approximately 2.0% in mention precision, which also translates into lower coreference scores. We also conducted an experiment in which we filter before classification (& Filt. BC), following a more standard approach. The reasoning

#	Feature Description
15	C if both are nouns and m_k is hyponym of m_j; I if both are nouns but m_k is not a hyponym of m_j; NA otherwise
16	C if both are nouns and m_j is hyponym of m_k; I if both are nouns but m_j is not a hyponym of m_k; NA otherwise
17	C if both are nouns and m_k is a partial holonym of m_j; I if both are nouns but m_k is not a partial holonym of m_j; NA otherwise
18	C if both are nouns and m_j is a partial holonym of m_k; I if both are nouns but m_j is not a partial holonym of m_k; NA otherwise
19	C if both are nouns and m_k is a partial meronym of m_j; I if both are nouns but m_k is not a partial meronym of m_j; NA otherwise
20	C if both are nouns and m_j is a partial meronym of m_k; I if both are nouns but m_j is not a partial meronym of m_k; NA otherwise
21	C if both are verbs and m_k entails m_j; I if both are verbs but m_k does not entail m_j; NA otherwise
22	C if both are verbs and m_j entails m_k; I if both are verbs but m_j does not entail m_k; NA otherwise
23	C if both are verbs and m_k is a hypernym of m_j; I if both are verbs but m_k is not a hypernym of m_j; NA otherwise
24	C if both are verbs and m_j is a hypernym of m_k; I if both are verbs but m_j is not a hypernym of m_k; NA otherwise
25	C if both are verbs and m_k is a troponym of m_j; I if both are verbs but m_k is not a troponym of m_j; NA otherwise
26	C if both are verbs and m_j is a troponym of m_k; I if both are verbs but m_j is not a troponym of m_k; NA otherwise

Table 3: The features extracted from WordNet.

	IM			MUC			B^3			CEAFE			Average
	R	P	F_1	R	P	F_1	R	P	F_1	R	P	F_1	F_1
$UBIU_B$	62.71	38.66	47.83	30.59	24.65	27.30	67.06	62.65	64.78	34.19	40.16	36.94	43.01
$UBIU_B$ & Sing.	95.11	18.27	30.66	30.59	24.58	27.26	67.10	62.56	64.75	34.14	40.18	36.92	42.97
$UBIU_B$ & Filt.	61.30	40.58	48.83	29.10	25.77	27.33	64.88	64.63	64.76	35.38	38.74	36.98	43.02
$UBIU_B$ & Filt. BC	61.33	40.49	48.77	28.96	25.54	27.14	64.95	64.48	64.71	35.23	38.71	36.89	42.91
$UBIU_E$	62.72	39.09	48.16	30.63	24.94	27.49	66.72	62.76	64.68	34.19	39.90	36.82	43.00
$UBIU_E$ & Sing.	95.11	18.27	30.66	29.87	20.96	24.64	69.13	57.71	62.91	32.28	42.24	36.59	41.38
$UBIU_E$ & Filt.	63.01	36.62	46.32	28.65	21.05	24.27	68.10	58.72	63.06	32.91	41.53	36.72	41.35
Gold ME	100	100	100	38.83	82.97	52.90	39.99	92.33	55.81	66.73	26.75	38.19	48.97

Table 4: UBIU system results on the development set.

is that the training set for the classifier is biased towards not assuming coreference since the majority of mention pairs does not have a coreference relation. Thus filtering out non-agreeing mention pairs before classification reduces not only the number of test mention pairs to be classified but also the number of training pairs. However, in our system, this approach leads to minimally lower results, which is why we decided not to pursue this route. We also experimented with instance sampling in order to reduce the bias towards non-coreference in the training set. This also did not improve results.

Contrary to our expectation, using ontological information does not improve results. Only on the mention level, we see a minimal gain in precision. But this does not translate into any improvement on the coreference level. Using filtering in combination with the extended feature set results in a more pronounced deterioration than with the base set.

The last row of table 4 (Gold ME) shows results when the system has access to the gold standard mentions. The MUC and B^3 results show that the classifier reaches an extremely high precision (82.97% and 92.33%), from which we conclude that the coreference links that our system finds are reliable, but it is also too conservative in assuming coreference relations. For the future, we need to investigate undersampling the negative examples in the training set and more efficient methods for filtering out singletons.

4 Final Results

In the following, we present the UBIU system results in two separate settings: using the test set with automatically extracted mentions (section 4.1) and using a test set with gold standard mentions, including singletons (section 4.2). An overview of all systems participating in the CoNLL-2011 shared task and their results is provided by Pradhan et al. (2011).

4.1 Automatic Mention Identification

The final results of UBIU for the test set without gold standard mentions are shown in the first part of table 5. They are separated into results for the coreference resolution module based on automatically annotated linguistic information and the gold annotations. Again, we report results for both the base feature set ($UBIU_B$) and the extended feature set using WordNet features ($UBIU_E$). A comparison of the system results on the test and the development set in the $UBIU_B$ setting shows that the average F-score is considerably lower for the test set, 40.46 vs. 43.01 although the quality of the mentions remains constant with an F-score of 48.14 on the test set and 47.83 on the development set.

The results based on the two data sets show that UBIU's performance improves when the system has access to gold standard linguistic annotations. However, the difference between the results is in the area of 2%. The improvement is due to gains of 3-5% in precision for MUC and B^3, which are counteracted by smaller losses in recall. In contrast, CEAFE shows a loss in precision and a similar gain in recall, resulting in a minimal increase in F-score.

A comparison of the results for the experiments with the base set as opposed to the extended set in 5 shows that the extended feature set using WordNet information is detrimental to the final results averaged over all metrics while it led to a slight improvement on the mention level. Our assumption is that while in general, the ontological information is useful, the additional information may be a mixture of relevant and irrelevant information. Mihalcea (2002) showed for word sense disambiguation that

		IM			MUC			B^3			CEAFE			Average
		R	P	F_1	R	P	F_1	R	P	F_1	R	P	F_1	F_1
Automatic Mention Identification														
auto	$UBIU_B$	67.27	37.48	48.14	28.75	20.61	24.01	67.17	56.81	61.55	31.67	41.22	35.82	40.46
	$UBIU_E$	67.49	37.60	48.29	28.87	20.66	24.08	67.14	56.67	61.46	31.57	41.21	35.75	40.43
gold	$UBIU_B$	65.92	40.56	50.22	31.05	25.57	28.04	64.94	62.23	63.56	33.53	39.08	36.09	42.56
	$UBIU_E$	66.11	40.37	50.13	30.84	25.14	27.70	65.07	61.83	63.41	33.23	39.05	35.91	42.34
Gold Mention Boundaries														
auto	$UBIU_B$	67.57	58.66	62.80	34.14	40.43	37.02	54.24	71.09	61.53	39.65	33.73	36.45	45.00
	$UBIU_E$	69.19	57.27	62.67	33.48	37.15	35.22	55.47	68.23	61.20	38.29	34.65	36.38	44.27
gold	$UBIU_B$	67.64	58.75	62.88	34.37	40.68	37.26	54.28	71.18	61.59	39.69	33.76	36.49	45.11
	$UBIU_E$	67.72	58.66	62.87	34.18	40.40	37.03	54.30	71.04	61.55	39.64	33.78	36.47	45.02

Table 5: Final system results for the coreference resolution module on automatically extracted mentions on the gold standard mentions for the base and extended feature sets.

memory-based learning is extremely sensitive to irrelevant features. For the future, we are planning to investigate this problem by applying forward-backward feature selection, as proposed by Mihalcea (2002) and Dinu and Kübler (2007).

4.2 Gold Mention Boundaries

UBIU was also evaluated in the experimental setting in which gold mention boundaries were provided in the test set, including for singletons. The results of the setting using both feature sets are reported in the second part of table 5. The results show that overall the use of gold standard mentions results in an increase of the average F-score of approx. 4.5%. Where mention quality and MUC are concerned, gold standard mentions have a significant positive influence on the average F-score. For B^3 and CEAFE, however, there is no significant change in scores. The increase in performance is most noticeable in mention identification, for which the F-score increases from 48.14 to 62.80. But this improvement has a smaller effect on the overall coreference system performance leading to a 5% increase of results. In contrast to the gold mention results in the development set, we see lower precision values in the test set. This is due to the fact that the test set contains singletons. Detecting singletons reliably is a difficult problem that needs further investigation.

5 Conclusion and Future Work

In the current paper, we presented the results of UBIU in the CoNLL-2011 shared task. We showed that for a robust system for coreference resolution such as UBIU, automatically annotated linguistic data is sufficient for mention-pair based coreference resolution. We also showed that ontological information as well as filtering non-agreeing mention pairs leads to an insignificant improvement of the overall coreference system performance. The treatment of singletons in the data remains a topic that requires further investigation.

References

Walter Daelemans, Jakub Zavrel, Ko van der Sloot, and Antal van den Bosch. 2007. TiMBL: Tilburg memory based learner – version 6.1 – reference guide. Technical Report ILK 07-07, Induction of Linguistic Knowledge, Computational Linguistics, Tilburg University.

Georgiana Dinu and Sandra Kübler. 2007. Sometimes less is more: Romanian word sense disambiguation revisited. In *Proceedings of the International Conference on Recent Advances in Natural Language Processing, RANLP 2007*, Borovets, Bulgaria.

Rada Mihalcea. 2002. Instance based learning with automatic feature selection applied to word sense disambiguation. In *Proceedings of the 19th International Conference on Computational Linguistics, COLING'02*, Taipeh, Taiwan.

Sameer Pradhan, Lance Ramshaw, Mitchell Marcus, Martha Palmer, Ralph Weischedel, and Nianwen Xue. 2011. CoNLL-2011 Shared Task: Modeling unrestricted coreference in OntoNotes. In *Proceedings of the Fifteenth Conference on Computational Natural Language Learning (CoNLL)*, Portland, Oregon.

Altaf Rahman and Vincent Ng. 2009. Supervised models for coreference resolution. In *Proceedings of EMNLP 2009*, Singapore.

Desislava Zhekova and Sandra Kübler. 2010. UBIU: A language-independent system for coreference resolution. In *Proceedings of the 5th International Workshop on Semantic Evaluation (SemEval)*, pages 96–99, Uppsala, Sweden.

A Machine Learning-Based Coreference Detection System For OntoNotes

Yaqin Yang
Computer Science Department
Brandeis University
Waltham, Massachusetts, USA
yaqin@brandeis.edu

Nianwen Xue
Computer Science Department
Brandeis University
Waltham, Massachusetts, USA
xuen@brandeis.edu

Peter Anick
Computer Science Department
Brandeis University
Waltham, Massachusetts, USA
peter_anick@yahoo.com

Abstract

In this paper, we describe the algorithms and experimental results of Brandeis University in the participation of the CoNLL Task 2011 closed track. We report the features used in our system, and describe a novel cluster-based chaining algorithm to improve performance of coreference identification. We evaluate the system using the OntoNotes data set and describe our results.

1 Introduction

This paper describes the algorithms designed and experiments finished in the participation of the CoNLL Task 2011. The goal of the Task is to design efficient algorithms for detecting entity candidates and identifying coreferences. Coreference identification is an important technical problem. Its importance in NLP applications has been observed in previous work, such as that of Raghunathan et al., Pradhan et al., Bergsma et al., Haghighi et al., and Ng et al.. While most of the existing work has evaluated their systems using the ACE data set, in this work we present our experimental results based on the OntoNotes data set used in the CoNLL 2011 Shared Task. We detail a number of linguistic features that are used during the experiments, and highlight their contribution in improving coreference identification performance over the OntoNotes data set. We also describe a cluster-based approach to multi-entity chaining. Finally, we report experimental results and summarize our work.

2 Data Preparation

We divide the CoNLL Task into three steps. First, we detect entities from both the training data and the development data. Second, we group related entities into entity-pairs. Finally, we use the generated entity-pairs in the machine learning-based classifier to identify coreferences. In this section, we describe how we extract the entities and group them into pairs.

2.1 Generating Entity Candidates

We use the syntactic parse tree to extract four types of entities, including noun phrase, pronoun, premodifier and verb (Pradhan et al., 2007). This method achieves 94.0% (Recall) of detection accuracy for gold standard trees in the development data. When using the automatic parses, not surprisingly, the detection accuracy becomes lower, with a performance drop of 5.3% (Recall) compared with that of using the gold standard trees. Nevertheless, this method can still cover 88.7% of all entities existing in the development data, thus we used it in our algorithm.

2.2 Generating Entity-Pairs From Individual Entities

In the annotated training documents, an entity has been marked in a coreference chain that includes all coreferential entities. In our algorithm, we only detect the closest antecedent for each entity, instead of all coreferences, of each entity. Specifically, we define each training and testing instance as a pair of entities. During the training process, for each entity encountered by the system, we create a *positive* instance by pairing an entity with its closest antecedent (Soon et al., 2001). In addition, a set of *negative* instances are also created by pairing the entity with any preceding entities that exist between its closest antecedent and the entity itself (note that the antecedent must be a coreference of the current entity, whereas preceding entities may not be coreferential). For example, in the entity sequence "A, B, C, D, E", let us assume that "A" is the closest antecedent of "D". Then, for entity "D", "A-D" is considered a positive instance, whereas "B-D" and "C-D" are two negative instances.

To generate testing data, every entity-pair within the same sentence is considered to form positive or negative instances, which are then used to form testing data. Since occasionally the distance between an entity and its closest antecedent can be far apart, we handle considerably distant coreferences by consid-

Proceedings of the 15th Conference on Computational Natural Language Learning: Shared Task, pages 117–121,
Portland, Oregon, 23-24 June 2011. ©2011 Association for Computational Linguistics

ering each entity-pair that exists within the adjacent N sentences. During our experiments, we observed that the distance between an entity and its closest antecedent could be as far as 23 sentences. Therefore, in the classification process, we empirically set N as 23.

3 Machine Learning-Based Classification

After labeling entity pairs, we formalize the coreference identification problem as a binary classification problem. We derive a number of linguistic features based on each entity-pair, i and j, where i is the potential antecedent and j the anaphor in the pair (Soon et al., 2001). Generally, we select a set of features that have been proved to be useful for the coreference classification tasks in previous work, including gender, number, distance between the antecedent and the anaphor, and WordNet (WordNet, 2010). In addition, we design additional features that could be obtained from the OntoNotes data, such as the speaker or author information that is mainly available in Broadcast Conversation and Web Log data (Pradhan et al., 2007). Moreover, we extract apposition and copular structures and used them as features. The features we used in the system are detailed below.

- **Independent feature:** 1) if a noun phrase is definite; 2) if a noun phrase is demonstrative; 3) gender information of each entity; 4) number information of each entity; 5) the entity type of a noun phrase; 6) if an entity is a subject; 7) if an entity is an object; 8) if an noun phrase is a coordination, the number of entities it has; 9) if a pronoun is preceded by a preposition; 10) if a pronoun is "you" or "me"; 11) if a pronoun is "you" and it is followed by the word "know".
- **Name entity feature:** 1) i-j-same-entity-type-etype=True, if i and j have the same entity type; 2) i-j-same-etype-subphrase=True, if i and j have the same entity type and one is the subphrase of the other.
- **Syntactic feature:** 1) i-j-both-subject=True, if i and j are both subjects; 2) if i and j are in the same sentence, record the syntactic path between i and j, e.g. i-j-syn-path=PRP∧NP!PRP; 3) i-j-same-sent-diff-clause=True, if i and j are in the same sentence but in different clauses.
- **Gender and number feature:** 1) i-j-same-gender=True/False, by comparing if i and j have the same gender; 2) i-j-same-num=True/False, by comparing if i and j have the same number; 3) i-j-same-num-modifier=True/False, by comparing if i and j have the same number modifier, e.g. "two countries" and "they both" have the same number modifier; 4) i-j-same-family=True/False, we designed seven different families for pronouns, e.g. "it", "its" and "itself" are in one family while "he", "him", "his" and "himself" are in another one.
- **Distance feature:** 1) i-j-sent-dist, if the sentence distance between i and j is smaller than three, use their sentence distance as a feature; 2) i-j-sent-dist=medium/far: if the sentence distance is larger than or equal to three, set the value of i-j-sent-dist to "medium", otherwise set it to "far" combined with the part-of-speech of the head word in j.
- **String and head word match feature:** 1) i-j-same-string=True, if i and j have the same string; 2) i-j-same-string-prp=True, if i and j are the same string and they are both pronouns; 3) i-j-sub-string=True, if one is the sub string of the other, and neither is a pronoun; 4) i-j-same-head=True, if i and j have the same head word; 5) i-j-prefix-head=True, if the head word of i or j is the prefix of the head word of the other; 6) i-j-loose-head, the same as i-j-prefix-head, but comparing only the first four letters of the head word.
- **Apposition and copular feature:** for each noun phrase, if it has an apposition or is followed by a copular verb, then the apposition or the subject complement is used as an attribute of that noun phrase. We also built up a dictionary where the key is the noun phrase and the value is its apposition or the subject's complement to define features. 1) i-appo-j-same-head=True, if i's apposition and j have the same head word; 2) i-j-appo-same-head=True, if j's apposition has the same head word as i; we define the similar head match features for the noun phrase and its complement; Also, if an i or j is a key in the defined dictionary, we get the head word of the corresponding value for that key and compare it to the head word of the other entity.
- **Alias feature:** i-j-alias=True, if one entity is a proper noun, then we extract the first letter of each word in the other entity. (The extraction process skips the first word if it's a determiner and also skips the last one if it is a possessive case). If the proper noun is the same as the first-letter string, it is the alias of the other entity.
- **Wordnet feature:** for each entity, we used Wordnet to generate all synsets for its head word, and for each synset, we get all hypernyms and hyponyms. 1) if i is a hypernym of j, then i-hyper-j=True; 2) if i is a hyponym of j, then i-hypo-j=True.
- **Speaker information features:** In a conversation, a speaker usually uses "I" to refer to himself/herself, and most likely uses "you" to refer to the next speaker. Since speaker or author name information is given in Broadcast Conversation and Web Log data, we use such information to design features that represent relations between pronouns and

speakers. 1) i-PRP1-j-PRP2-same-speaker=True, if both i and j are pronouns, and they have the same speaker; 2) i-I-j-I-same-speaker=True, if both i and j are "I", and they have the same speaker; 3) i-I-j-you-same-speaker=True, if i is "I" and j is "you", and they have the same speaker; 4) if i is "I", j is "you" and the speaker of j is right after that of i, then we have feature i-I-j-you&itarget=jspeaker; 5) if i is "you", j is "I" and the speaker of j is right after that of i, then we have feature i-you-j-I-itarget=jspeaker; 6) if both i and j are "you", and they followed by the same speaker, we consider "you" as a general term, and this information is used as a negative feature.

- **Other feature:** i-j-both-prp=True, if both i and j are pronouns.

4 Chaining by Using Clusters

After the classifier detects coreferential entities, coreference detection systems usually need to chain multiple coreferential entity-pairs together, forming a coreference chain. A conventional approach is to chain all entities in multiple coreferential entity-pairs if they share the same entities. For example, if "A-B", "B-C", and "C-D" are coreferential entity-pairs, then A, B, C, and D would be chained together, forming a coreference chain "A-B-C-D".

One significant disadvantage of this approach is that it is likely to put different coreference chains together in the case of erroneous classifications. For example, suppose in the previous case, "B-C" is actually a wrong coreference detection, then the coreference chain created above will cause A and D to be mistakenly linked together. This error can propagate as coreference chains become larger.

To mitigate this issue, we design a cluster-based chaining approach. This approach is based on the observation that some linguistic rules are capable of detecting coreferential entities with high detection precision. This allows us to leverage these rules to *double-check* the coreference identifications, and reject chaining entities that are incompatible with rule-based results.

To be specific, we design two lightweight yet efficient rules to cluster entities.

- **Rule One**. For the first noun phrase (NP) encountered by the system, if 1) this NP has a name entity on its head word position or 2) it has a name entity inside and the span of this entity includes the head word position, a cluster is created for this NP. The name entity of this NP is also recorded. For each following NP with a name entity on its head word position, if there is a cluster that has the same name entity, this NP is considered as a coreference to other NPs in that cluster, and is put into that cluster. If the system cannot find such a cluster, a new cluster is created for the current NP.
- **Rule Two**. In Broadcast Conversation or Web Log data, a speaker or author would most likely use "I" to refer to himself/herself. Therefore, we used it as the other rule to cluster all "I" pronouns and the same speaker information together.

Given the labeled entity pairs, we then link them in different coreference chains by using the cluster information. As the Maximum Entropy classifier not only labels each entity-pair but also returns a confidence score of that label, we sort all positive pairs using their possibilities. For each positive entity-pair in the sorted list, if the two entities are in different clusters, we consider this to be a conflict, and withdraw this positive entity-pair; if one entity belongs to one cluster whereas the other does not belong to any cluster, the two entities will be both included in that cluster. This process is repeated until no more entities can be included in a cluster. Finally, we chain the rest of entity pairs together.

5 Results and Discussion

To evaluate the features and the chaining approach described in this paper, we design experiments described as follows. Since there are five different data types in the provided OntoNotes coreference data set, we create five different classifiers to process each of the data types. We used the features described in Section 3 to train the classifiers, and did the experiments using a Maximum Entropy classifier trained with the Mallet package (McCallum, 2002). We use the gold-standard data in the training set to train the five classifiers and test the classifiers on both gold and automatically-parsed data in the development data set. The MUC metric provided by the Task is used to evaluate the results.

5.1 Performance without Clustering

First, we evaluate the system by turning the clustering technique off during the process of creating coreference chains. For entity detection, we observe that for all five data types, i.e. Broadcast (BC), Broad news (BN), Newswire (NW), Magazine (MZ), and Web blog (WB), the NW and WB data types achieve relatively lower F1-scores, whereas the BC, BN, and MZ data types achieve higher per-

	BC	BN	NW	MZ	WB
			Without Clustering		
Gold	57.40 (64.92/51.44)	59.45 (63.53/55.86)	52.01 (59.71/46.07)	55.59 (62.90/49.80)	49.53 (61.16/41.62)
Auto	54.00 (61.28/48.26)	55.40 (59.05/52.17)	48.44 (55.32/43.09)	52.21 (59.78/46.33)	47.02 (58.33/39.39)
			With Clustering		
Gold	57.44 (64.12/52.03)	56.56 (58.10/55.09)	51.37 (56.64/46.99)	54.26 (60.07/49.47)	49.00 (60.09/41.36)
Auto	54.19 (60.82/48.87)	52.69 (54.07/51.37)	48.01 (52.74/44.05)	50.82 (56.76/46.01)	46.86 (57.49/39.55)

Table 1: Performance comparison of coreference identification between using and without using the clustering technique in chaining. Note that the results are listed in sequence of F1-scores (Recalls/Precisions). The results shown are based on MUC.

formance. Due to limited space, the performance table of entity detection is not included in this paper.

For coreference identification, as shown in Table 1, we observe pretty similar performance gaps among different data types. The NW and WB data types achieve the lowest F1-scores (i.e. 52.01% and 49.53% for gold standard data, and 48.44% and 47.02% for automatically-parsed data) among all the five data types. This can be explained by seeing that the entity detection performance of these two data types are also relatively low. The other three types achieves more than 55% and 52% F1-scores for gold and auto data, respectively.

These experiments that are done without using clustering techniques tend to indicate that the performance of entity detection has a positive correlation with that of coreference identification. Therefore, in the other set of experiments, we enable the clustering technique to improve coreference identification performance by increasing entity detection accuracy.

Metric	Recall	Precision	F1
MUC	59.94	45.38	51.65
BCUBED	72.07	53.65	61.51
CEAF (M)	45.67	45.67	45.67
CEAF (E)	29.43	42.54	34.79
BLANC	70.86	60.55	63.37

Table 2: Official results of our system in the CoNLL Task 2011. Official score is 49.32. ((MUC + BCUBED + CEAF (E))/3)

5.2 Performance with Clustering

After enabling the clustering technique, we observe an improvement in entity detection performance. This improvement occurs mainly in the cases of the NW and WB data types, which show low entity detection performance when not using the clustering technique. To be specific, the performance of the NW type on both the gold standard and automatic data improves by about 0.5%, and the performance of the WB type on the automatic data improves about 0.1%. In addition, the performance of the BC type on both the gold standard and automatic data also increases about 0.2% to 0.6%.

Although the clustering technique succeeds in improving entity detection performance for multiple data types, there is no obvious improvement gained with respect to coreference identification. This is quite incompatible with our observation in the experiments that do not utilize the clustering technique. Currently, we attribute this issue to the low accuracy rates of the clustering operation. For example, "H. D. Ye." and "Ye" can be estimated correctly to be coreferential by the Maxtent classifier, but the clustering algorithm puts them into different clusters since "H. D. Ye." is a PERSON type name entity while "Ye" is a ORG type name entity. Therefore, the system erroneously considers them to be a conflict and rejects them. We plan to investigate this issue further in our future work.

The official results of our system in the CoNLL Task 2011 are summarized in Table 2.

6 Conclusion

In this paper, we described the algorithm design and experimental results of Brandeis University in the CoNLL Task 2011. We show that several linguistic features perform well in the OntoNotes data set.

References

Andrew Kachites McCallum. 2002. Mallet: A machine learning for language toolkit. http://mallet.cs.umass.edu.

Sameer S. Pradhan, Lance Ramshaw, Ralph Weischedel, Jessica MacBride, and Linnea Micciulla. 2007. Unrestricted Coreference: Identifying Entities and Events in OntoNotes. *International Conference on Semantic Computing (ICSC 2007)*, pages 446–453, September.

W.M. Soon, H.T. Ng, and D.C.Y. Lim. 2001. A machine learning approach to coreference resolution of noun phrases. *Computational Linguistics*, 27(4):521–544.

WordNet. 2010. Princeton University "About WordNet." WordNet. Princeton University. 2010. http://wordnet.princeton.edu.

Reconciling OntoNotes: Unrestricted Coreference Resolution in OntoNotes with Reconcile

Veselin Stoyanov
CLSP
Johns Hopkins University
Baltimore, MD

Uday Babbar and **Pracheer Gupta** and **Claire Cardie**
Department of Computer Science
Cornell University
Ithaca, NY

Abstract

This paper describes our entry to the 2011 CoNLL closed task (Pradhan et al., 2011) on modeling unrestricted coreference in OntoNotes. Our system is based on the Reconcile coreference resolution research platform. Reconcile is a general software infrastructure for the development of learning-based noun phrase (NP) coreference resolution systems. Our entry for the CoNLL closed task is a configuration of Reconcile intended to do well on OntoNotes data. This paper describes our configuration of Reconcile as well as the changes that we had to implement to integrate with the OntoNotes task definition and data formats. We also present and discuss the performance of our system under different testing conditions on a withheld validation set.

1 Introduction

Noun phrase (NP) coreference resolution is one of the fundamental tasks of the field of Natural Language Processing (NLP). Recently, the creation of the OntoNotes corpus (Pradhan et al., 2007) has provided researchers with a large standard data collection with which to create and empirically compare coreference resolution systems.

Reconcile (Stoyanov et al., 2010b) is a general coreference resolution research platform that aims to abstract the architecture of different learning-based coreference systems and to provide infrastructure for their quick implementation. Reconcile is distributed with several state-of-the art NLP components and a set of optimized feature implementations. We decided to adapt Reconcile for the OntoNotes corpus and enter it in the 2011 CoNLL shared task with three goals in mind: (i) to compare the architecture and components of Reconcile with other state-of-the-art coreference systems, (ii) to implement and provide the capability of running Reconcile on the OntoNotes corpus, and, (iii) to provide a baseline for future algorithm implementations in Reconcile that evaluate on the OntoNotes corpus.

Although Reconcile can be easily adapted to new corpora, doing so requires introducing new components. More precisely, the system has to be modified to be consistent with the specific definition of the coreference task embodied in the OntoNotes annotation instructions. Additionally, different corpora use different data formats, so the system needs to implement capabilities for dealing with these new formats. Finally, Reconcile can be configured with different features and components to create an instantiation that models well the particular data.

In this paper we describe, $Reconcile_{CoNLL}$, our entry to the 2011 CoNLL shared task based on the Reconcile research platform. We begin by describing the general Reconcile architecture (Section 2), then describe the changes that we incorporated in order to enable Reconcile to work on OntoNotes data (Sections 3 and 4). Finally, we describe our experimental set up and results from running $Reconcile_{CoNLL}$ under different conditions (Section 5).

2 Overview of Reconcile

In this section we give a high-level overview of the Reconcile platform. We refer the reader for more details to Stoyanov et al. (2010a) and Stoyanov et al. (2010b). Results from running a Reconcile-based coreference resolution system on different corpora can be found in Stoyanov et al. (2009).

Reconcile was developed to be a coreference resolution research platform that allows for quick implementation of coreference resolution systems. The platform abstracts the major processing steps (components) of current state-of-the-art learning-based coreference resolution systems. A description of the steps and the available components can be found in the referenced papers.

3 The $Reconcile_{CoNLL}$ System

To participate in the 2011 CoNLL shared task, we configured Reconcile to conform to the OntoNotes general coreference resolution task. We will use the name $Reconcile_{CoNLL}$, to refer to this particular instantiation of the general Reconcile platform. The remainder of this section describe the changes required to enable $Reconcile_{CoNLL}$ to run (accurately) on OntoNotes data.

Proceedings of the 15th Conference on Computational Natural Language Learning: Shared Task, pages 122–126,
Portland, Oregon, 23-24 June 2011. ©2011 Association for Computational Linguistics

$Reconcile_{CoNLL}$ employs the same basic pipelined architecture as Reconcile. We describe the specific components used in each step.

1. Preprocessing. Documents in the OntoNotes corpus are manually (or semi-automatically) annotated with many types of linguistic information. This information includes tokens, part-of-speech tags, and named entity information as well as a constituent syntactic parse of the text. For the purpose of participating in the shared task, we rely on these manual annotations, when available. Thus, we do not run most of the standard Reconcile preprocessing components. One type of information not provided in the OntoNotes corpus is a dependency parse. Several of Reconcile's features rely on a dependency parse of the text. Thus, we ran the Stanford dependency parser (Klein and Manning, 2003), which performs a constituent parse and uses rules to convert to a dependency format.[1]

Two additional changes to the preprocessing step were necessary for running on the OntoNotes data. The first is the implementation of components that can convert data from the OntoNotes format to the Reconcile internal format. The second is adaptation of the Coreference Element (CE) extractor to conform to the OntoNotes definition of what can constitute a CE. Our implementations for these two tasks are briefly described in Sections 4.1 and 4.2, respectively.

2. Feature generation. $Reconcile_{CoNLL}$ was configured with 61 features that have proven successful for coreference resolution on other data sets. Due to the lack of time we performed no feature engineering or selection specific to OntoNotes. We used a new component for generating the pairwise CEs that comprise training and test instances, which we dub SMARTPG (for smart pair generator). This is described in Section 4.3.

3. Classification. We train a linear classifier using the averaged perceptron algorithm (Freund and Schapire, 1999). We use a subset of 750 randomly selected documents for training, since training on the entire set required too much memory.[2] As a result, we had ample validation data for tuning thresholds, etc.

4. Clustering. We use Reconcile's single-link clustering algorithm. In other words, we compute the transitive closure of the positive pairwise predictions. Note that what constitutes a positive prediction depends on a threshold set for the classifier from the previous step. This clustering threshold is optimized using validation data. More details about the influence of the validation process can be found in Section 5.

5. Scoring. The 2011 CoNLL shared task provides a scorer that computes a set of commonly used coreference resolution evaluation metrics. We report results using this scorer in Section 5. However, we used the Reconcile-internal versions of scorers to optimize the threshold. This was done for pragmatic reasons – time pressure prevented us from incorporating the CoNLL scorer in the system. We also report the Reconcile-internal scores in the experiment section.

This concludes the high-level description of the $Reconcile_{CoNLL}$ system. Next, we describe in more detail the main changes implemented to adapt to the OntoNotes data.

4 Adapting to OntoNotes

The first two subsection below describe the two main tasks that need to be addressed when running Reconcile on a new data set: annotation conversion and CE extraction. The third subsection describes the new Smart CE Pairwise instance generator — a general component that can be used for any coreference data set.

4.1 Annotation Conversion

There are fundamental differences between the annotation format used by OntoNotes and that used internally by Reconcile. While OntoNotes relies on token-based representations, Reconcile uses a stand-off bytespan annotation. A significant part of the development of $Reconcile_{CoNLL}$ was devoted to conversion of the OntoNotes manual token, parse, named-entity and coreference annotations. In general, we prefer the stand-off bytespan format because it allows the reference text of the document to remain unchanged while annotation layers are added as needed.

4.2 Coreference Element Extraction

The definition of what can constitute an element participating in the coreference relation (i.e., a Coreference Element or CE) depends on the particular dataset. Optimizing the CE extraction com-

[1] A better approach would be to use the rules to create the dependency parse from the manual constituent parse. We decided against this approach due to implementation overhead.

[2] It is easy to address the memory issue in the on-line perceptron setting, but in the interest of time we chose to reduce the size of the training data. Training on the set of 750 documents is done efficiently in memory by allocating 4GB to the Java virtual machine.

Optimized Metric	Thres-hold	B-Cubed	CEAF	MUC
BCubed	0.4470	**0.7112**	0.1622	0.6094
CEAF	0.4542	0.7054	**0.1650**	0.6141
MUC	0.4578	0.7031	0.1638	**0.6148**

Table 1: Reconcile-internal scores for different thresholds. The table lists the best threshold for the validation data and results using that threshold.

Pair Gen.	BCubed	CEAFe	MUC
SMARTPG	0.6993	0.1634	0.6126
All Pairs	0.6990	0.1603	0.6095

Table 3: Influence of different pair generators.

ponent for the particular task definition can result in dramatic improvements in performance. An accurate implementation limits the number of elements that the coreference system needs to consider while keeping the recall high.

The CE extractor that we implemented for OntoNotes extends the existing Reconcile ACE05 CE extractor (ACE05, 2005) via the following modifications:

Named Entities: We exclude named entities of type CARDINAL NUMBER, MONEY and NORP, the latter of which captures nationality, religion, political and other entities.

Possessives: In the OntoNotes corpus, possessives are included as coreference elements, while in ACE they are not.

$Reconcile_{CoNLL}$ ignores the fact that verbs can also be CEs for the OntoNotes coreference task as this change would have constituted a significant implementation effort.

Overall, our CE extractor achieves recall of over 96%, extracting roughly twice the number of CEs in the answer key (precision is about 50%). High recall is desirable for the CE extractor at the cost of precision since the job of the coreference system is to further narrow down the set of anaphoric CEs.

4.3 Smart Pair Generator

Like most current coreference resolution systems, at the heart of Reconcile lies a pairwise classifier. The job of the classifier is to decide whether or not two CEs are coreferent or not. We use the term *pair generation* to refer to the process of creating the CE pairs that the classifier considers. The most straightforward way of generating pairs is by enumerating all possible unique combinations. This approach has two undesirable properties – it requires time in the order of $O(n^2)$ for a given document (where n is the number of CEs in the document) and it produces highly imbalanced data sets with the number of positive instances (i.e., coreferent CEs) being a small fraction of the number of negative instances. The latter issue has been addressed by a technique named instance generation (Soon et al., 2001): during training, each CE is matched with the first preceding CE with which it corefers and all other CEs that reside in between the two. During testing, a CE is compared to all preceding CEs until a coreferent CE is found or the beginning of the document is reached. This technique reduces class imbalance, but it has the same worst-case runtime complexity of $O(n^2)$.

We employ a new type of pair generation that aims to address both the class imbalance and improves the worst-case runtime. We will use SMARTPG to refer to this component. Our pair generator relies on linguistic intuitions and is based on the type of each CE. For a given CE, we use a rule-based algorithm to guess its type. Based on the type, we restrict the scope of possible antecedents to which the CE can refer in the following way:

Proper Name (Named Entity): A proper name is compared against all proper names in the 20 preceding sentences. In addition, it is compared to all other CEs in the two preceding sentences.

Definite noun phrase: Compared to all CEs in the six preceding sentences.

Common noun phrase: Compared to all CEs in the two preceding sentences.

Pronoun: Compared to all CEs in the two preceding sentences unless it is a first person pronoun. First person pronouns are additionally compared to first person pronouns in the preceding 20 sentences.

During development, we used SMARTPG on coreference resolution corpora other than OntoNotes and determined that the pair generator tends to lead to more accurate results. It also has runtime linear in the number of CEs in a document, which leads to a sizable reduction in running time for large documents. Training files generated by SMARTPG also tend to be more balanced. Finally, by omitting pairs that are unlikely to be coreferent, SMARTPG produces much smaller training sets. This leads to faster learning and allows us to train on more documents.

Optimized Metric	Threshold	BCubed	CEAFe	MUC	BLANC	CEAFm	**Combined**
BCubed	0.4470	0.6651	0.4134	0.6156	0.6581	0.5249	0.5647
CEAF	0.4542	0.6886	0.4336	0.6206	0.7012	0.5512	0.5809
MUC	0.4578	**0.6938**	**0.4353**	**0.6215**	**0.7108**	**0.5552**	**0.5835**

Table 2: CoNLL scores for different thresholds on **validation data**.

CoNLL Official Test Scores	BCubed	CEAFe	MUC	BLANC	CEAFm	**Combined**
Closed Task	0.6144	0.3588	0.5843	0.6088	0.4608	**0.5192**
Gold Mentions	0.6248	0.3664	0.6154	0.6296	0.4808	**0.5355**

Table 4: Official CoNLL 2011 test scores. Combined score is the average of MUC, BCubed and CEAFe.

5 Experiments

In this section we present and discuss the results for $Reconcile_{CoNLL}$ when trained and evaluated on OntoNotes data. For all experiments, we train on a set of 750 randomly selected documents from the OntoNotes corpus. We use another 674 randomly selected documents for validation. We report scores using the scorers implemented internally in Reconcile as well as the scorers supplied by the CoNLL shared task.

In the rest of the section, we describe our results when controlling two aspects of the system – the threshold of the pairwise CE classifier, which is tuned on training data, and the method used for pair generation. We conclude by presenting the official results for the CoNLL shared task.

Influence of Classifier Threshold As previously mentioned, the threshold above which the decision of the classifier is considered positive provides us with a knob that controls the precision/recall trade-off. Reconcile includes a module that can automatically search for a threshold value that optimizes a particular evaluation metric. Results using three Reconcile-internal scorers (BCubed, CEAF, MUC) are shown in Table 1. First, we see that the threshold that optimizes performance on the validation data also exhibits the best results on the test data. The same does not hold when using the CoNLL scorer for testing, however: as Table 2 shows, the best results for almost all of the CoNLL scores are achieved at the threshold that optimizes the Reconcile-internal MUC score. Note that we did not optimize thresholds for the external scorer in the name of saving implementation effort. Unfortunately, the results that we submitted for the official evaluations were for the suboptimal threshold that optimizes Reconcile-internal BCubed score.

Influence of Pair Generation Strategies Next, we evaluate the performance of SMARTPG pair generators. We run the same system set-up as above substituting the pair generation module. Results (using the internal scorer), displayed in Table 3, show our SMARTPG performs identically to the generator producing all pairs, while it runs in time linear in the number of CEs.

Official Scores for the CoNLL 2011 Shared Task Table 4 summarizes the official scores of $Reconcile_{CoNLL}$ on the CoNLL shared task. Surprisingly, the scores are substationally lower than the scores on our held-out training set. So far, we have no explanation for these differences in performance. We also observe that using gold-standard instead of system-extracted CEs leads to improvement in score of about point and a half.

The official score places us 8th out of 21 systems on the closed task. We note that because of the threshold optimization mix-up we suffered about 2 points in combined score performance. Realistically our system should score around 0.54 placing us 5th or 6th on the task.

6 Conclusions

In this paper, we presented $Reconcile_{CoNLL}$, our system for the 2011 CoNLL shared task based on the Reconcile research platform. We described the overall Reconcile platform, our configuration for the CoNLL task and the changes that we implemented specific to the task. We presented the results of an empirical evaluation performed on held-out training data. We discovered that results for our system on this data are quite different from the official score that our system achieved.

Acknowledgments

This material is based upon work supported by the National Science Foundation under Grant # 0937060 to the Computing Research Association for the CIFellows Project.

References

ACE05. 2005. NIST ACE evaluation website. In *http://www.nist.gov/speech/tests/ace/2005.*

Yoav Freund and Robert E. Schapire. 1999. Large margin classification using the perceptron algorithm. In *Machine Learning*, pages 277–296.

D. Klein and C. Manning. 2003. Fast Exact Inference with a Factored Model for Natural Language Parsing. In *Advances in Neural Information Processing (NIPS 2003).*

Sameer S. Pradhan, Lance Ramshaw, Ralph Weischedel, Jessica MacBride, and Linnea Micciulla. 2007. Unrestricted coreference: Identifying entities and events in ontonotes. In *Proceedings of the International Conference on Semantic Computing.*

Sameer Pradhan, Lance Ramshaw, Mitchell Marcus, Martha Palmer, Ralph Weischedel, and Nianwen Xue. 2011. Conll-2011 shared task: Modeling unrestricted coreference in ontonotes. In *Proceedings of the Fifteenth Conference on Computational Natural Language Learning (CoNLL 2011)*, Portland, Oregon, June.

W. Soon, H. Ng, and D. Lim. 2001. A Machine Learning Approach to Coreference of Noun Phrases. *Computational Linguistics*, 27(4):521–541.

V. Stoyanov, N. Gilbert, C. Cardie, and E. Riloff. 2009. Conundrums in noun phrase coreference resolution: Making sense of the state-of-the-art. In *Proceedings of ACL/IJCNLP.*

V. Stoyanov, C. Cardie, N. Gilbert, E. Riloff, D. Buttler, and D. Hysom. 2010a. Reconcile: A coreference resolution research platform. Technical report, Cornell University.

Veselin Stoyanov, Claire Cardie, Nathan Gilbert, Ellen Riloff, David Buttler, and David Hysom. 2010b. Coreference resolution with reconcile. In *Proceedings of the ACL 2010.*

Coreference Resolution System using Maximum Entropy Classifier

Weipeng Chen,Muyu Zhang,Bing Qin
Center for Information Retrieval
Harbin Institute of Technology
{wpchen,myzhang,bing.qin}@ir.hit.edu.cn

Abstract

In this paper, we present our supervised learning approach to coreference resolution in ConLL corpus. The system relies on a maximum entropy-based classifier for pairs of mentions, and adopts a rich linguisitically motivated feature set, which mostly has been introduced by Soon et al (2001), and experiment with alternaive resolution process, preprocessing tools,and classifiers. We optimize the system's performance for MUC (Vilain et al, 1995), BCUB (Bagga and Baldwin, 1998) and CEAF (Luo, 2005) .

1. Introduction

The coreference resolution is the task in which all expressions refer to the same entity in a discourse will be identified. As the core of natural language processing, coreference resolution is significant to message understanding, information extraction, text summarization, information retrieval, information filtration, and machine translation.

A considerable engineering efforts is needed for the full coreference resolution task, and a significant part of this effort concerns feature engineering. The backbone of our system can be split into two subproblems: mention detection and creation of entitly. We train a mention detector on the training texts. Once the mentions are identified, coreference resolution involves partitioning them into subsets corresponding to the same entity. This problem is cast into the binary classification problem of deciding whether two given mentions are coreferent. Our system relies on maximum entropy-based classifier for pairs of mentions. Our system relies on a rich linguistically motivated feature set. Our system architecture makes it possible to define other kinds of features: atmoic word and markable features. This approach to feature engineering is suitable not only for knowledge-rich but also for knowledge-poor datasets. Finally, we use the best-first clustering to create the coreference chains.

2. System Description

This section briefly describes our system. First the mention detection is presented. Next, the features which we import are described. Finally, we describled the learning and encoding methods.

2.1 Mention Detector

The first stage of the coreference resolution process try to identify the occurrence of mentions in document. To detect system mention from a test text, we train a mention detector on the training data. We formulate the mention problem as a classification, by assigning to each token in the text a label, indicating whether it is a mention or not. Hence, to learn the detector, we create one training text and derive its class value (one of **b**, **i**, **o**) from the annotated data. Each instance represents the w_i, the token under consideration, and consists of 19 linguistic features, many of which are modeled after the systems of Bikel et al. (1999) and Florian et al. (2004) , as describled below.

(1) **Lexical:** Tokens in the windows of three words before and after the target word: $\{w_{i-3}, \ldots, w_{i+3}\}$.
(2) **Capitalization:** Determine whether w_i is IsAllCaP (all the characters of word are capitalized, such as "BBN"), IsInitCap (the word starts with a capitalized character,

Proceedings of the 15th Conference on Computational Natural Language Learning: Shared Task, pages 127–130,
Portland, Oregon, 23-24 June 2011. ©2011 Association for Computational Linguistics

such as "Sally"), IsCapPeriod (more than one characters of word are capitalized but not all, and the first character is not capitalized too, such "M."), and IsAllLower (all the character of word aren't capitalized, such as "can") (see Bikel et al. (1999)).

(3) **Grammatical:** The single POS tags of the tokens in the window of three words before and after the target word$\{t_{i-3},\ldots,t_{i+3}\}$.

(4) **Semantic:** The named entity (NE) tag and the Noun Phrase tag of w_i.

We employ maximum entropy-based classifier, for training the mention detector. These detected mentions are to be used as system mentions in our coreference experiment.

2.2 Features

To determine which mentions belong to same entitly, we need to devise a set of features that is useful in determining whether two mentions corefer or not. All the feature value are computed automatically, without any manual intervention.

(1) **Distance Feature:** A non-negative integer feature capture the distance between anaphor and antecedent. If anaphor and antecedent are in the same sentence, the value is 0; If their sentence distance is 1, the value is 1, and so on.

(2) **Antecedent-pronoun Feature:** A Boolean feature capture whether the antecedent is pronoun or not. True if the antecedent is a pronoun. Pronouns include reflexive pronouns, personal pronouns, and possessive pronouns.

(3) **Anaphor-pronoun Feature:** A Boolean feature capture whether the anaphor is pronoun or not. True if the anaphor is a pronoun.

(4) **String Match Feature:** A non-negative integer feature. If one candidate is a substring of another, its value is 0, else the value is 0 plus the edit distance.

(5) **Anaphor Definite Noun Phrase Feature:** A Boolean feature capture whether the anaphor is a definite noun phrase or not. True if the anaphor is a pronoun. In our definition, a definite noun phrase is someone that start with the word "the".

(6) **Anaphor Demonstrative Noun Phrase Feature:** A Boolean feature capture whether the anaphor is a demonstractive noun or not. True if the anaphor is a demonstractive noun. In our definition, a demonstractive noun is someone that start with the word, such as this, that, those, these.

(7) **ProperName Feature:** A Boolean feature. True if anphor and antecedent both are proper name.

(8) **Gender Feature:** Its value are true, false or unknow. If gender of pair of instance matches, its value is true,else if the value is umatches, the value is false; If one of the pair instance's gender is unknown, the value is uknown.

(9) **Number Feature:** A Boolean feature. True if the number of pair of instance is matches;

(10) **Alias Feature:** A Boolean feature. True if two markables refer to the same entity using different notation(acronyms, shorthands, etc), its value is true.

(11) **Semantic Feature:** Its value are true, false, or unknown. If semantic class relateness of a pair instance is the same, or one is the parent of other, its value is true; Else if they are unmatch,the value is false; If one of the the pair instance's semantic class is unknown, the value is unknown.

2.3 Learning

We did not make any effort to optimize the number of training instances for the pair-wise learner: a positive instance for each adjacent coreferent markable pair and negative training instances for a markable *m* and all markables disreferent with *m* that occur before *m* (Soon et al.,2001). For decoding it generates all the possible links inside a window of 100 markables.

Our system integrate many machine learning methods, such as maximum entropy (Tsuruoka, 2006) , Descision Tree,Support Vector Machine (Joachims, 2002) . We compare the result using different method in our system, and decide to rely on maximum entropy-based classifier, and it led to the best results.

2.4 Decoding

In the decoding step, the coreference chains are created by the best-first clustering. Each mention is compared with all of its previous mentions with probability greater than a fixed threshold, and is clustered with the one hightest probability. If none has probability greater than the threshold, the mention becomes a new cluster.

3. Setting and data

3.1 Setting

Our system has participated in the closed settings for English. Which means all the knowledge required by the mention detector and feature detector is obtained from the annotation of the corpus(see Pradhan et al. (2007)), with the exception of WordNet.

3.2 Data

We selecte all ConLL training data and development data, contain "gold" files and "auto" file, to train our final system. The "gold" indicates that the annotation is that file is hand-annotated and adjudicated quality, whereas the second means it was produced using a combination of automatic tools. The training data distribution is shown in Table 1.

Category	bc	bn	mz	nw	wb
Quantity	40	1708	142	1666	190

Table 1: Final system's training data distribution

In this paper, we report the results from our development system, which were trained on the training data and tested on the development set. The detail is shown in Table 2,3.

Category	bc	bn	mz	nw	wb
Quantity	32	1526	128	1490	166

Table 2: Experiment system's training data distribution

Category	bc	bn	mz	nw	wb
Quantity	8	182	14	176	24

Table 3: Experiment system's test set distribution

4. Evaluation

First, we have evaluated our mention detector module, which is train by the ConLL training data. It regards all the token as the candidate, and cast it into the mention detector, and the detector decides it is mention or not. The mention detector's result is shown in Table4.

Metric	R	P	F
Value	63.6	55.26	59.14

Table 4: Performance of mention detector on the development set

Second, we have evaluated our system with the system mention, and we use the previous mention detector to determine the mention boundary. As follow, we list the system perfomance of using MUC, B-CUB,CEAF (E) , CEAF (M) , BLANC (Recasens and Hovy, in prep) in Table 5 .

Metric	R	P	F
MUC	45.53	47.00	46.25
BCUB	61.29	68.07	64.50
CEAF(M)	47.47	47.47	47.47
CEAF(E)	39.23	37.91	38.55
BLANC	64.00	68.31	65.81

Table 5 :Result using system mentions

Finally, we have evaluated our system with the gold mentions, which mention's boundary is corect. The system performance is shown in Table 6:

Metric	R	P	F
MUC	50.15	80.49	61.78
BCUB	48.87	85.75	62.62
CEAF(M)	54.50	54.50	54.50
CEAF(E)	67.38	32.72	44.05
BLANC	66.03	78.41	70.02

Table6:Result using gold mentions

Result of system shows a big difference between using gold mentions and using system mentions. In comparison to the system using system mentions, we see that the F-score rises significantly by 4.21- 15.53 for the system using gold mentions. It is worth noting that the F-scorer when using the B-CUB metric, the system using system mention rises 2.12 for system using gold mention. Although t-his is surprising, in my opinion this correlation is because the mention detection recall more candid-ate mention, and the BCUB metric is benefit for t-he mention which is merge into the erroneous chain.

5. Conclusion

In this paper, we have presented a new modular system for coreference in English. We train a mention detector to find the mention's boundary based on maximum entropy classifier to decide pairs of mention refer to or not.

Due to the flexible architecture, it allows us extend the system to multi-language. And if it is necessary, we can obtain other modules to support the system. The results obtained confirm the feasibility of our system.

References

Wee Meng Soon,Hwee You Ng,and Daniel Chung Yong Lim.2001.A machine learing approach to coreference resolution of noun phrases.*Computational Linguistic(special Issue on Computational Anaphora Resolution),*27(4):521-544

Marc Vilain,John Burger,John Aberdeen,Dennis Connolly,and Lynette Hirschman.1995.A modeltheoretic coreference scoring scheme.In *Proceedings of the 6th Message Understanding Conference,pages 45-52.*

Amit Bagga and Breck baldwin.1998.Algorithms for scoring coreference chains.In *Proceedings of the linguistic Coreference Workshoop at the International Conference on Language Resources and Evaluation(LREC-1998),*pages 563-566.

Xiaoqiang Luo.2005.On coreference resoluton performance metrics.In *Proceeddings of the Annual Meeting of the North American Chapter of the Association for Computational Linguistics-Human Language Technology Conference(NAACL/HLY-2005),*pages 25-32

Josef Steinberger,Massimo Poesio,Mijail A.kabadjov-b,and Karel jezek.2007.Two uses of anaphora resolution in summarization.In *Information Processing and management,Special issue on Summarization,*pages 1663-1680

Bikel,R.Schwartz,and R.Weischedel.1999.An algorithm that learns what's in a name.Machine Learning,34(1-3):pages211-231

Florian,H.Hassan,A.Ittycheriah,H.Jing,N.Kambhatla, X. Luo,N.Nicolov,and I.Zitouni.2004.A statistical model for multilingual entity detection and tracking.In *Proc.of* HLA/NAACL.

Sameer Pradhan and Lance Ramshaw and Ralph Weischedel and Jessica MacBride and Linnea Micciulla. 2007.Unrestricted Coreference: Identifying Entities and Events in OntoNotes. In *Proceedings of the IEEE International Conference on Semantic Computing (ICSC),* Irvine, CA

Marta Recasens and Eduard Hovy.in prep.BLAN-C:Implementing the rand index for coreference evaluation.

Yoshimasa Tsuruoka.2006.A simple c++ library for maxium entropy classifiction.Ysujii laboratory,Department of Computer Science,University of Tokyo.

Throsten Joachims.1999.Making large-scale SVM learning practical.In B.Scholkopf,C.Burges,and A.S-mola,editors,*Advances in Kernel Methods-Support Vector Learning*.MIT-Press.

Link Type Based Pre-Cluster Pair Model for Coreference Resolution

Yang Song†, Houfeng Wang† and Jing Jiang‡
†Key Laboratory of Computational Linguistics (Peking University) Ministry of Education,China
‡School of Information Systems, Singapore Management University, Singapore
{ysong, wanghf}@pku.edu.cn, jingjiang@smu.edu.sg

Abstract

This paper presents our participation in the CoNLL-2011 shared task, Modeling Unrestricted Coreference in OntoNotes. Coreference resolution, as a difficult and challenging problem in NLP, has attracted a lot of attention in the research community for a long time. Its objective is to determine whether two mentions in a piece of text refer to the same entity. In our system, we implement mention detection and coreference resolution seperately. For mention detection, a simple classification based method combined with several effective features is developed. For coreference resolution, we propose a link type based pre-cluster pair model. In this model, pre-clustering of all the mentions in a single document is first performed. Then for different link types, different classification models are trained to determine wheter two pre-clusters refer to the same entity. The final clustering results are generated by closest-first clustering method. Official test results for closed track reveal that our method gives a MUC F-score of 59.95%, a B-cubed F-score of 63.23%, and a CEAF F-score of 35.96% on development dataset. When using gold standard mention boundaries, we achieve MUC F-score of 55.48%, B-cubed F-score of 61.29%, and CEAF F-score of 32.53%.

1 Introduction

The task of coreference resolution is to recognize all the mentions (also known as noun phrases, including names, nominal mentions and pronouns) in a text and cluster them into equivalence classes where each quivalence class refers to a real-world entity or abstract concept. The CoNLL-2011 shared task[1] uses OntoNotes[2] as the evaluation corpus. The coreference layer in OntoNotes constitutes one part of a multi-layer, integrated annotation of the shallow semantic structures in the text with high inter-annotator agreement. In addition to coreference, this data set is also tagged with syntactic trees, high coverage verb and some noun propositions, partial verb and noun word senses, and 18 named entity types. The main difference between OntoNotes and another wellknown coreference dataset ACE is that the former does not label any singleton entity cluster, which has only one reference in the text. We can delete all the singleton clusters as a postprocessing step for the final results. Alternatively, we can also first train a classifier to separate singleton mentions from the rest and apply this mention detection step before coreference resolution. In this work we adopt the second strategy.

In our paper, we use a traditional learning based pair-wise model for this task. For mention detection, we first extract all the noun phrases in the text and then use a classification model combined with some effective features to determine whether each noun phrase is actually a mention. The features include word features, POS features in the given noun phrase and its context, string matching feature in its context, SRL features, and named entity features among others. More details will be given in Section 3. From our in-house experiments, the final F-scores for coreference resolution can be improved by this mention detection part. For coreference res-

[1] http://conll.bbn.com
[2] http://www.bbn.com/ontonotes/

Proceedings of the 15th Conference on Computational Natural Language Learning: Shared Task, pages 131–135,
Portland, Oregon, 23-24 June 2011. ©2011 Association for Computational Linguistics

Features describing c_i or c_j	
Words	The first and last words of the given NP in c_i (or c_j) , also including the words in the context with a window size 2
POS Tags	The part of speech tags corresponding to the words
Pronoun	Y if mentions in c_i(or c_j) are pronouns; else N
Definite	Y if mentions in c_i(or c_j) are definite NP; else N
Demonstrative	Y if mentions in c_i(or c_j) are demonstrative NP; else N
Number	Singular or Plural, determined using a data file published by Bergsma and Lin (2006)
Gender	Male, Female, Neuter, or Unknown, determined using a data file published by Bergsma and Lin (2006)
Semantic Class	Semantic Classes are given by OntoNotes for named entities
Mentino Type	Common Noun Phrases or Pronouns

Table 1: The feature set describing c_i or c_j.

olution, a traditinal pair-wise model is applied, in which we first use exact string matching to generate some pre-clusters. It should be noted that each pronoun must be treated as a singleton pre-cluster, because they are not like names or nominal mentions, which can be resolved effectively with exact string matching. We then implement a classification based pre-cluster pair model combined with several effective coreference resolution features to determine whether two pre-clusters refer to the same entity. Finally, we use closest-first clustering method to link all the coreferential pre-clusters and generate the final cluster results. As mentioned before, mentions have three types: names, nominal mentions and pronouns. Among them pronouns are very different from names and nominal mentions, because they can only supply limited information literally. So we define three kinds of link types for pre-cluster pairs: NP-NP link, NP-PRP link and PRP-PRP link. (Here NP means Noun Phrases and PRP means Pronominal Phrases.) One link represents one pre-cluster pair. Intuitively, different link types tend to use different features to determine whether this kind of link is coreferential or not. We implement three kinds of pre-cluster pair model based on three link types. Experimental results show that combined with outputs from different link type based pre-cluster pair model can give better results than using an unified classification model for three different kinds of link types. For all the classification models, we use opennlp.maxent[3] package.

The rest of this paper is organized as follows. Section 2 describes our mention detection method. We discuss our link type based pre-cluster pair model for coreference resolution in Section 3, evaluate it in Section 4, and conclude in Section 5.

2 Mention Detection

We select all the noun phrases tagged by the OntoNotes corpus as mention candidates and implement a classification-based model combined with several commonly used features to determine whether a given noun phrase is a mention. The features are given below:

- Word Features - They include the first word and the last word in each given noun phrase. We also use words in the context of the noun phrase within a window size of 2.
- POS Features - We use the part of speech tags of each word in the word features.
- Position Features - These features indicate where the given noun phrase appears in its sentence: begining, middle, or end.
- SRL Features - The Semantic Role of the given noun phrase in its sentence.
- Verb Features - The verb related to the Semantic Role of the given noun phrase.

[3]http://incubator.apache.org/opennlp/

Features describing the relationship between c_i and c_j	
Distance	The minimum distance between mentions in c_i and c_j
String Match	Y if mentions are the same string; else N
Substring Match	Y if one mention is a substring of another; else N
Levenshtein Distance	Levenshtein Distance between the mentions
Number Agreement	Y if the mentions agree in number; else N
Gender Agreement	Y if the mentions agree in gender; else N
N & G Agreement	Y if mentions agree in both number and gender; else N
Both Pronouns	Y if the mentions are both pronouns; else N
Verb Agreement	Y if the mentions have the same verb.
SRL Agreement	Y if the mentions have the same semantic role
Position Agreement	Y if the mentions have the same position (Beginning, Middle or End) in sentences

Table 2: The feature set describing the relationship between c_i and c_j.

- Entity Type Features - The named entity type for the given noun phrase.
- String Matching Features - True if there is another noun phrase wich has the same string as the given noun phrase in the context.
- Definite NP Features - True if the given noun phrase is a definite noun phrase.
- Demonstrative NP Features - True if the given noun phrase is a demonstrative noun phrase.
- Pronoun Features - True if the given noun phrase is a pronoun.

Intutively, common noun phrases and pronouns might have different feature preferences. So we train classification models for them respectively and use the respective model to predicate for common noun phrases or pronouns. Our mention detection model can give 52.9% recall, 80.77% precision and 63.93% F-score without gold standard mention boundaries on the development dataset. When gold standard mention boundaries are used, the results are 53.41% recall, 80.8% precision and 64.31% F-score. (By using the gold standard mention boundaries, we mean we use the gold standard noun phrase boundaries.)

3 Coreference Resolution

After getting the predicated mentions, we use some heuristic rules to cluster them with the purpose of generating highly precise pre-clusters. For this task

Metric	**Recall**	**Precision**	**F-score**
MUC	49.64%	67.18%	57.09%
BCUBED	59.42%	70.99%	64.69%
CEAF	45.68%	30.56%	36.63%
AVERAGE	51.58%	56.24%	52.80%

Table 3: Evaluation results on development dataset without gold mention boundaries

Metric	**Recall**	**Precision**	**F-score**
MUC	48.94%	67.72%	56.82%
BCUBED	58.52%	72.61%	64.81%
CEAF	46.49%	30.45%	36.8%
AVERAGE	51.32%	56.93%	52.81%

Table 4: Evaluation results on development dataset with gold mention boundaries

only identity coreference is considered while attributive NP and appositive construction are excluded. That means we cannot use these two important heuristic rules to generate pre-clusters. In our system, we just put all the mentions (names and nominal mentions, except pronouns) which have the same string into the identical pre-clusters. With these pre-clusters and their coreferential results, we implement a classification based pre-cluster pair model to determine whether a given pair of pre-clusters refer to the same entity. We follow Rahman and Ng (2009) to generate most of our features. We also include some other features which intuitively seem effective for coreference resolution. These features

Metric	Recall	Precision	F-score
MUC	42.66%	53.7%	47.54%
BCUBED	61.05%	74.32%	67.04%
CEAF	40.54%	32.35%	35.99%
AVERAGE	48.08%	53.46%	50.19%

Table 5: Evaluation results on development dataset with gold mention boundaries using unified classification model

Metric	Recall	Precision	F-score
MUC	53.73%	67.79%	59.95%
BCUBED	60.65%	66.05%	63.23%
CEAF	43.37%	30.71%	35.96%
AVERAGE	52.58%	54.85%	53.05%

Table 6: Evaluation results on test dataset without gold mention boundaries

are shown in Table 1 and Table 2. For simplicity, we use c_i and c_j to represent pre-clusters i and j. Each pre-cluster pair can be seen as a link. We have three kinds of link types: NP-NP link, NP-PRP link and PRP-PRP link. Different link types may have different feature preferences. So we train the classification based pre-cluster pair model for each link type separately and use different models to predicate the results. With the predicating results for pre-cluster pairs, we use closest-first clustering to link them and form the final cluster results.

4 Experimental Results

We present our evaluation results on development dataset for CoNLL-2011 shared Task in Table 3, Table 4 and Table 5. Official test results are given in Table 6 and Table 7. Three different evaluation metrics were used: MUC (Vilain et al., 1995), B^3 (Bagga and Baldwin, 1998) and CEAF (Luo, 2005). Finally, the average scores of these three metrics are used to rank the participating systems. The difference between Table 3 and Table 4 is whether gold standard mention boundaries are given. Here "mention boundaries" means a more broad concept than the mention definition we gave earlier. We should also detect real mentions from them. From the tables, we can see that the scores can be improved little by using gold standard mention boundaries. Also the results from Table 5 tell us that combining different link-type based classification models performed

Metric	Recall	Precision	F-score
MUC	46.66%	68.40%	55.48%
BCUBED	54.40%	70.19%	61.29%
CEAF	43.77%	25.88%	32.53%
AVERAGE	48.28%	54.82%	49.77%

Table 7: Evaluation results on test dataset with gold mention boundaries

better than using an unified classification model. For official test results, our system did not perform as well as we had expected. Some possible reasons are as follows. First, verbs that are coreferential with a noun phrase are also tagged in OntoNotes. For example, "grew " and "the strong growth" should be linked in the following case: "Sales of passenger cars grew 22%. The strong growth followed year-to-year increases." But we cannot solve this kind of problem in our system. Second, we should perform feature selection to avoid some useless features harming the scores. Meanwhile, we did not make full use of the WordNet, PropBank and other background knowledge sources as features to represent pre-cluster pairs.

5 Conclusion

In this paper, we present our system for CoNLL-2011 shared Task, Modeling Unrestricted Coreference in OntoNotes. First some heuristic rules are performed to pre-cluster all the mentions. And then we use a classification based pre-cluster pair model combined with several cluster level features. We hypothesize that the main reason why we did not achieve good results is that we did not carefully examine the features and dropped the feature selection procedure. Specially, we did not make full use of background knowledge like WordNet, PropBank, etc. In our future work, we will make up for the weakness and design a more reasonable model to effectively combine all kinds of features.

Acknowledgments

This research is supported by National Natural Science Foundation of Chinese (No.60973053, No.91024009) and Research Fund for the Doctoral Program of Higher Education of China (No.20090001110047).

References

Sameer Pradhan, Lance Ramshaw, Mitchell Marcus, Martha Palmer, Ralph Weischedel and Nianwen Xue. 2011. *CoNLL-2011 Shared Task: Modeling Unrestricted Coreference in OntoNotes.* In Proceedings of the Fifteenth Conference on Computational Natural Language Learning (CoNLL 2011), Portland, Oregon.

M. Vilain, J. Burger, J. Aberdeen, D. Connolly, and L. Hirschman. 1995. *A Model-Theoretic Coreference Scoring Scheme.* In Proceedings of the Sixth Message Understanding Conference (MUC-6), pages 4552, San Francisco, CA. Morgan Kaufmann.

Amit Bagga and Breck Baldwin. 1998. *Algorithms for Scoring Coreference Chains.* In Proceedings of the 1st International Conference on Language Resources and Evaluation, Granada, Spain, pp. 563566.

Xiaoqiang Luo. 2005. *On Coreference Resolution Performance Metrics.* In Proceedings of the Human Language Technology Conference and the 2005 Conference on Empirical Methods in Natural Language Processing, Vancouver, B.C., Canada, pp. 2532.

Vincent Ng. 2008. *Unsupervised Models for Coreference Resolution.* In Proceedings of the 2008 Conference on Empirical Methods in Natural Language Processing, pp. 640–649.

Altaf Rahman and Vincent Ng. 2009. *Supervised Models for Coreference Resolution.* In Proceedings of the 2009 Conference on Empirical Methods in Natural Language Processing.

Vincent Ng. 2010. *Supervised Noun Phrase Coreference Research: The First Fifteen Years.* In Proceedings of the 48th Meeting of the Association for Computational Linguistics (ACL 2010), Uppsala, pages 1396-1411.

Shane Bergsma and Dekang Lin. 2006. *Bootstrapping Path-Based Pronoun Resolution.* In COLING–ACL 2006, pages 33–40.

Author Index